Deregulating Freight
Transportation

AEI STUDIES IN REGULATION AND FEDERALISM
Christopher C. DeMuth and Jonathan R. Macey, series editors

COSTLY POLICIES: STATE REGULATION AND ANTITRUST EXEMPTION
IN INSURANCE MARKETS
Jonathan R. Macey and Geoffrey P. Miller

DEREGULATING FREIGHT TRANSPORTATION:
DELIVERING THE GOODS
Paul Teske, Samuel Best, and Michael Mintrom

FEDERALISM IN TAXATION: THE CASE FOR GREATER UNIFORMITY
Daniel Shaviro

THE GENIUS OF AMERICAN CORPORATE LAW
Roberta Romano

PRODUCT-RISK LABELING: A FEDERAL RESPONSIBILITY
W. Kip Viscusi

STATE AND FEDERAL REGULATION OF NATIONAL ADVERTISING
J. Howard Beales and Timothy J. Muris

Deregulating Freight
Transportation
Delivering the Goods

Paul Teske, Samuel Best,
and Michael Mintrom

The AEI Press

Publisher for the American Enterprise Institute
WASHINGTON, D.C.

1995

Library of Congress Cataloging-in-Publication Data

Teske, Paul Eric.
    Deregulating freight transportation : delivering the goods / Paul
Teske, Samuel Best, and Michael Mintrom.
        p.   cm.
    Includes bibliographical references.
    ISBN 978-0-8447-3897-0 (pbk)   —ISBN 0-8447-3897-2 (pbk. :
alk. paper)
    1. Trucking—Deregulation—United States.   2. Freight and
freightage—Deregulation—United States.   3. Transportation—
Deregulation—United States.   I. Best, Samuel.   II. Mintrom,
Michael, 1963–   .   III. Title.
HE5623.T475   1995
388.3'24'0973—dc20   95-42120
                                                              CIP

1   3   5   7   9   10   8   6   4   2

THE AEI PRESS
Publisher for the American Enterprise Institute
1150 17th Street, N.W., Washington, D.C. 20036

Contents

LIST OF FIGURES

Acknowledgments

First, we would like to thank Christopher DeMuth, president of AEI, for the opportunity to write this book as part of the series of AEI Studies in Regulation and Federalism. We would also like to thank Diana Furchtgott-Roth, resident fellow and assistant to the AEI president, for her assistance and continuing support for all phases of this project. We also appreciate the administrative support provided by Audrey Williams of AEI and editorial support from Cheryl Weissman and Dana Lane of the AEI Press.

We wish to thank our academic colleagues Peter VanDoren, Rick Waterman, and Larry Rothenberg for their helpful comments based on readings of the manuscript. We would also like to thank the state and Washington, D.C., area policy makers and transportation analysts, who were uniformly generous in providing us with their time, considerably useful information, and different perspectives. In particular, we want to acknowledge the assistance of James Burnley, Robert Voltman, Earl Eisenhart, Edward Rastatter, Frank Kruesi, John Collins, Marie Gilliland Wheat, Karen Borlaug Phillips, Gregory Walden, James Rogers, Thom Rubel, Tom McNamara, and Michael Redisch.

We would also like to acknowledge the efforts of Clark Hubbard, who was involved in the early aspects of our research into state trucking regulation, and who read the entire manuscript. We thank Robert L. Boucher, Jr., for his implementation of our survey of 1994 state trucking regulations. We also appreciate the support of the Political Science Department at SUNY Stony Brook.

Paul Teske thanks his wife Kimberly Hartman and Sam Best thanks his wife Niki for their support and patience during the most intense periods of our efforts on this book. Additional special thanks are due to Catherine Hartman, who provided us with the most charming (and free) bed and breakfast hospitality in Alexandria while we had interviews in Washington, D.C. Thanks also to Oscar, Chelsea, Kate, and Nicky, faithful canine companions, who provided unconditional support and an escape from the arcane details of transportation regulation.

Acronyms

AAMVA	American Association of Motor Vehicle Administrators
AASHTO	American Association of State Highway Officials
ADA	Airline Deregulation Act
AIP	Airport Improvement Program
ASCT	Association for Safe and Competitive Transportation
ATA	American Trucking Associations
AUHTP	Alliance for Uniform Hazmat Transportation Procedures
BSWG	Base State Working Group on Motor Carrier Programs
CAA	Civil Aeronautics Authority
CAA	Clean Air Act
CAAA	Clean Air Act Amendments
CAB	Civil Aeronautics Board
CDL	Commercial driver's license
COD	Collect-on-delivery
CPUC	California Public Utility Commission
CVSA	Commercial Vehicle Safety Alliance
DOT	Department of Transportation
EAS	Essential air service
EPA	Environmental Protection Agency
FAA	Federal Aviation Administration
FedEx	Federal Express
FHWA	Federal Highway Administration
FIP	Federal Implementation Plan
FMC	Federal Maritime Commission
4R Act	Railroad Revitalization and Regulatory Reform Act
FTC	Federal Trade Commission
GNP	Gross national product
GRC	General Rate Committee
GVW	Gross vehicle weight
HMTA	Hazardous Materials Transportation Act

HMTUSA	Hazardous Materials Transportation Uniform Safety Act of 1990
ICA	Interstate Commerce Act
ICC	Interstate Commerce Commission
IFTA	International Fuel Tax Agreement
IRC	Independent Regulatory Commission
IRP	International registration plan
ISTEA	Intermodal Surface Transportation Efficiency Act
LCV	Longer combination vehicle
LTL	Less-than-truckload carrier
MCA	Motor Carrier Act
MCARTS	Michigan Citizens Allied for Responsible Transportation Safety
MCSAP	Motor Carrier Safety Assistance Program
MTA	Motor Truck Association
NAFTA	North American Free Trade Agreement
NARUC	National Association of Regulatory Utility Commissioners
NCSL	National Conference of State Legislatures
NMFTA	National Motor Freight Traffic Association
NRA	Negotiated Rates Act
PAC	Political action committee
PJAX	Pittsburgh-Johnstown-Altoona Express, Incorporated
PSC	Public Service Commission
PUC	Public Utility Commission
RFTA	New England Regional Fuel Tax Agreement
SRC	Standing Rate Committee
SSRS	Single State Registration System
STAA	Surface Transportation Assistance Act
TEX-AID	Texas Association to Improve Distribution
3R Act	Regional Rail Reorganization Act
TL	Truckload carrier
TLA	Transportation Lawyers Association
TMTA	Texas Motor Transport Association
TRC	Texas Railroad Commission
UPS	United Parcel Service

1
Introduction

If you bought it, a truck brought it.
—FORMER MOTTO OF THE AMERICAN TRUCKING ASSOCIATIONS

Transportation performs a critical linking function in the American economy. Virtually every product consumed by the public originates away from its final marketplace and requires shipment by some form of carriage. Today, freight moves by rail, road, air, and water and increasingly involves some combination of these modes. As markets keep expanding geographically, freight transportation will only continue to grow in importance for both direct users of these services and consumers at large.

For most of this century, the federal and state governments heavily regulated freight transportation. Recognizing the considerable public benefits of this function, as well as the potentially disastrous consequences from disruptions of the industry, all levels of government engaged in varying degrees of economic or safety regulation. Regulatory federalism in the transportation sector, though, produced problems that ultimately proved costly to the American economy. In response, governments substantially reduced their involvement in the industry over the past several decades, eliminating virtually all economic regulation. The nature and timing of deregulation, however, like those of regulation, varied considerably in different governmental settings and within different transportation modes. While most forms of economic regulation now no longer exist, governments continue to rely on other regulations that affect the performance of these industries.

In this book, we examine the effects of government intervention on the operations of the transportation industry, detailing the consequences of federal and state regulation and deregulation on participants, as well as on the national economy. More important, we analyze the causes of various government approaches to regulation in an effort to understand how political processes shape economic outcomes. By focusing on regulatory federalism rather than simply on either federal or state involvement, we not only offer a more comprehensive picture of the transportation industry but also demonstrate how existing interpretations of regulatory decision making are sometimes incomplete and misleading. We begin by providing an overview of the transportation industry and describing the evolution of government responses over time.

The American Transportation Market

Transportation of people and goods constitutes a sizable portion of the American economy. In the United States, the whole transport sector now represents approximately 17 percent of gross national product (GNP).[1] Passenger transportation, or the movement of people from one location to another, is the largest segment of the industry, representing roughly 11 percent of GNP. The freight transportation sector, or the shipment of goods, is smaller, at 6.3 percent of GNP, but it still generates $400 billion in revenues annually.

While the economic effects of the passenger sector of the transportation industry exceed those of the freight sector, important differences exist. The passenger transportation sector is overwhelmingly private, with nearly 80 percent of revenues related to privately owned automobiles, with, in order, cars, gasoline, repairs, and other vehicles as the largest expenditures. Conversely, only 20 percent of revenues are generated from for-hire passenger carriers, including airlines, buses, taxicabs, and mass transit. Thus, transactions in the passenger transportation sector tend to have private and immediate

---

1. Although the transportation sector represents an enormous share of the nation's economy, the relative size of the industry has actually shrunk in the past quarter-century. Since 1960, transportation as a share of GNP has shrunk from nearly 21 percent to under 17 percent. Most of this drop can be attributed to the decline in freight transport that occurred after federal deregulation in the 1970s and 1980s, partly a result of efficiencies and greater productivity. From 1980 to 1992, while GNP increased 117 percent, passenger transport revenues grew 90 percent, and freight revenues grew only 78 percent. See *Transportation in America* (Washington, D.C.: Eno Transportation Foundation, Inc., 1993).

2

effects, while transactions in the freight sector reverberate throughout the whole economy.

In the past 100 years, freight transportation has evolved into an integral part of the infrastructure for the national industrial economy. In fact, most goods purchased by American consumers require several movements by freight transporters. Bulk raw materials, such as coal and agricultural products, must be moved from their point of excavation or growth to places where they are transformed into a higher-value-added product. Intermediate goods, such as steel for automobiles, must be moved from one chain of the production process to a later chain in the process. Final goods, such as television sets, must be brought to stores that will sell them to consumers. Hence, the speed and economic efficiency of freight transportation are critical to making a modern economy operate at an optimal level. This is especially true in the United States where manufacturing and retail inventories are now kept at record low levels and new techniques like "just-in-time inventory" are growing in use.

Freight transportation is a vital component of the American economy. Its effect will only grow as American businesses continue to expand into international markets. Without coordinated freight carriage, international agreements such as the North American Free Trade Agreement (NAFTA) and the European Union would operate far less efficiently than expected. Considering the importance of freight transportation to the economic well-being of the nation, it is not surprising that governments have felt compelled, at times, to intervene in the operations of freight transporters to ensure their successful performance.[2]

---

2. For the most part, governments have not directly regulated the economic performance of most of the passenger transportation sector. This is not meant to suggest that governments do not intervene in this sector. Simple rules (public goods) like driving on the right-hand side of the road, "green lights mean go, red lights mean stop," or rules about drivers' licenses and insurance are all examples of regulations that affect private passenger transportation. The vehicles themselves also confront numerous regulations in terms of safety, fuel efficiency, and pollution emissions as do the production, distribution, and sale of the fuel that makes these automobiles operate. Thus, governments are involved in passenger transportation. But rate structures and entry restrictions, which often determine the economic performance of industry participants, have not been directly regulated in the American passenger transportation sector.

TABLE 1–1
SHARE BY MODE OF U.S. FREIGHT MARKET, 1960–1990

Year	Total (billions of $)	Truck (%)	Rail (%)	Water (%)	Oil Pipe (%)	Air (%)
1960	47.8	68	19	7	2	1
1970	84.0	74	14	6	2	1
1980	213.7	73	13	7	4	2
1990	351.9	77	9	6	2	4

SOURCE: *Transportation in America* (Washington, D.C.: Eno Transportation Foundation, Inc., 1993).

Freight Transportation Modes and Trends. The American freight transportation industry is composed primarily of five modes of carriage: truck, rail, water, air, and oil pipe. Table 1–1 presents the past thirty years of trends in freight transportation market share. Trucking is by far the most important sector of the industry, generating more than three-quarters of the revenues of the freight transport industry. In 1994 alone, this amounted to more than $300 billion in revenues, or about 5 percent of GNP.[3] Railroads generate the second-largest share of revenue in the industry, approximately 9 percent, with waterborne freight next at 6 percent, airline cargo moving up with 4 percent, and oil pipelines with 2 percent.

If other measures of market share by sector are employed, the relative output transported by each mode differs. For instance, if tons of freight carried are considered, trucking's share falls to about 42 percent and railroad's share rises. If ton-miles (one ton of freight carried one mile in distance) are compared, trucking falls to about 26 percent. This comparison illustrates the point that different modes carry different types of freight. Trucks charge more than other modes to carry higher-valued freight a shorter distance, which is consistent with trucking's comparative advantage—flexibility to reach any destination easily. Railroads and barges carry lower-valued cargo longer distances, on more fixed routes with fewer stops. Airlines can carry

---

3. By comparison, this amount is greater than most estimates of the current size of the information technology sector, including local and long-distance telecommunications, cable television, and computer networks.

4

freight to its destination most quickly but are most efficient for light-weight items. Thus, the American freight transportation industry is multimodal, with competition across modes, as well as considerable specialization within modes.

The relative importance of each mode depends on how output is measured and also the time frame. Market shares have all changed dramatically over the past few decades. As the entire industry has grown, the trucking sector has steadily gained freight market share, largely at the expense of railroads, with the other modes remaining as minor players. Over a longer period, the taking of market share by trucking from railroads is remarkable, almost completely reversing the percentages carried by each mode just over fifty years ago. Recently, airlines have grown in importance, posing increasing challenges to these traditional modes. The airlines' market share has more than doubled in the past decade, with the air cargo industry now generating more than $7 billion in revenue.[4]

Perhaps the most important recent trend in freight transportation, though, is the use of intermodal carriers. Intermodal carriers often combine movements by air, water, rail, and truck carriers. By using multiple modes, shippers can enhance the speed and flexibility of delivery without substantially increasing costs, especially important in a time of shrinking inventories and expanding markets. A 1993 survey by the National Industrial Transportation League found that 72 percent of U.S. shippers used intermodal services in 1993, up from 64 percent just three years earlier.

Over time, government regulatory policies had large effects on the performance of each of these sectors of the American freight transportation industry. The policies were formulated by both state and federal governments.

Overview of Federal and State Regulation

Historically, American governments engaged in three overlapping policies related to freight transportation. The first was promotion, in which the federal government, and some states, subsidized the

---

4. For comparative reference, the domestic airline *passenger* market was about $60 billion in 1991. Thus the air cargo market is over 10 percent of the total domestic airline industry. See *Transportation in America*.

development of these nascent infrastructural industries. Second, as the industries grew and became more complex, the federal and state governments regulated them, both directly and indirectly. Third, recognizing that these industries had changed and that the regulation was no longer productive, the federal government, and some states, deregulated.

Governments first promoted railroads in the nineteenth century, trucking in the early part of the twentieth century, and airlines in the 1930s to develop these infant industries and to connect national markets. Government policies included providing free land and protection (for example, for the westward expansion of railroads), subsidized capital costs (for instance, highway construction for trucks), and institutionalized labor (the Air Traffic Controllers Agency, for example). Most of these activities proved quite successful, accelerating the growth of each of these modes.

Not long after these industries became competitive, governments intervened to oversee their activities, typically applying common-law notions of common carriage. Such intervention could often be justified in normative terms based on the market failure model. There were and are some economies of scale, in railroads, airlines, and waterborne freight at least, if not in the trucking sector. Safety concerns could be considered an information asymmetry problem that required government intervention, especially for shippers who did not ship freight very often. Finally, potential negative externalities existed for land and communities near transportation facilities and for other vehicle operators interacting with industry participants. It is not clear, though, whether any of these market failures actually required the intensive government intervention that eventually developed.

More likely, the choice of regulatory solutions was the result of political processes. The objectives of policy makers were complex but usually included both public and private interest rationales. On the one hand, governments sought to protect consumers (who were often themselves businesses) from high rates or poor services.[5] On the other hand, some of this regulation was demanded by industry

---

5. Competition normally achieves this goal better than regulation, but many parties were concerned that these markets were not fully competitive or that the competition would become "destructive," leading to price wars and unsafe transport.

participants, such as the transportation firms themselves, which sought to protect their markets and cartelize the industry,[6] and shippers, who desired favorable cross-subsidization.[7]

Over time, government policies evolved to include direct regulation of prices, entry, and mergers of each mode. Moreover, some of these sectors also faced considerable, and in some cases still growing, indirect regulation of vehicle safety, vehicle weight, licensing, taxes, hazardous materials, and environmental pollution. In fact, by the start of the 1970s, virtually every significant issue in the transportation industry was resolved by government intervention, not by market forces.

Gradually, it became clear that regulation was not working effectively or efficiently in most sectors of the industry. First, regulators had often been manipulated politically by those they were supposed to be regulating. Market failures were soon replaced by government failures, such as the implementation of policies favorable to concentrated regulated firms at the expense of more dispersed consumers. Second, rather than promoting technological and economic changes, regulation stymied growth and innovation in most transportation sectors. Finally, regulation of transportation appeared to affect the American economy adversely, leading many members of the academic community to advocate the elimination of regulatory policies.[8]

Beginning in the late 1970s, the regulatory apparatus began to be dismantled. Governments removed rate controls, entry barriers, and numerous other economic regulations from the airline, railroad, and trucking industries. Today most economic aspects of American freight transportation are no longer regulated. For intercity freight movement of any kind, for example, fully 69 percent of the total

---

6. See, for example, Gordon Tullock, "Welfare Costs of Tariffs, Monopoly and Theft," *Western Economic Journal*, vol. 5 (1967), pp. 224–32; George Stigler, "The Theory of Economic Regulation," *Bell Journal of Economics and Management Science*, vol. 2 (1971), pp. 3–21; Sam Peltzman, "Toward a More General Theory of Regulation," *Journal of Law and Economics*, vol. 19 (1976), pp. 211–40.

7. See Richard Posner, "Taxation by Regulation," *Bell Journal of Economics and Management Science*, vol. 2 (1971), pp. 548–63.

8. See Martha Derthick and Paul Quirk, *The Politics of Deregulation* (Washington, D.C.: Brookings Institution, 1985); and Dorothy Robyn, *Braking the Special Interests* (Chicago: University of Chicago Press, 1987).

TABLE 1–2
PERCENTAGE SHARE OF INTERCITY FREIGHT TON-MILES REGULATED BY
THE FEDERAL GOVERNMENT, 1950–1990

Year	Total	Rail	Truck	Air	Oil Pipe	Water
1950	62	100	38	100	81	20
1960	58	100	37	100	79	20
1970	59	100	41	100	85	13
1980	55	100	44	0	84	8
1990	31	26	28	0	84	8

SOURCE: *Transportation in America* (Washington, D.C.: Eno Transportation Foundation, Inc., 1993).

freight ton-miles is not regulated by the federal government (see table 1–2).

Even with economic deregulation, governments continue to intervene in the transportation industry. Governments oversee numerous "noneconomic" activities in each mode, such as setting safety standards, assessing taxes, and registering vehicles. At times, this involvement affects the financial performance of the industry nearly as much as traditional forms of economic regulation.

Transportation Regulatory Federalism. While numerous rationales exist for government intervention, determining which level of government will supervise particular activities has been considerably more problematic. The question appears simple, with the Constitution itself bearing directly on it: the federal government is to regulate interstate commerce, while the states are to regulate commerce within their borders. In reality, though, the separation between these two kinds of commerce is quite complex. Since the formation of the United States, the relationship has been shaped by complicated legal questions of where the boundaries between *inter*state and *intra*state commerce should be drawn, which activities fall under these classifications, and when the federal government can preempt the states to achieve pressing national goals.

Theoretically, using a dual system of government regulation has considerable advantages. Granting states the autonomy to regulate intrastate commerce has the benefit of allowing the government juris-

8

dictions closest to the industry the authority to regulate it. State officials' proximity to transportation firms permits them to understand industry operations more fully and the relationship of the industry to the local economy. As a result, regulators can shape policies that better match participants' needs. This might mean, for example, tailoring regulations to the concerns of specific types of shippers, such as coal miners or grain producers. Moreover, state governments can enact programs that more closely reflect the desires of their constituents. Individual states, as compared with the entire nation, are likely to contain more homogeneous populations, so that state policies can be matched more closely to citizens' preferences.

State regulation also allows experimentation, with particular states acting as quasi-laboratories for new policies. Since many forms of transportation regulation began at the state level, state experiments can serve as a guide for federal and other states' policy choices.

Finally, maintaining state regulatory autonomy provides states with economic incentives to regulate in productive ways, since states are in competition with one another to some degree for mobile, productive resources. If their regulation harms mobile resources, those resources are likely to shift to more favorable jurisdictions. Thus, states have the motivation to be innovative in shaping effective and efficient regulatory policies.

Balancing these advantages of a dual system are several advantages of a unitary system that implements regulations through the national government. First, a single national regulatory policy promotes consistency, which can provide stability to firms in an industry. Policy makers have used this argument to centralize transportation regulation, particularly in the railroad industry. Such consistency arguments are now being used in the European Community, in debates over transportation regulation and regulation of other industries.[9]

---

9. The European Union launched a single trucking market on January 1, 1993. As in the United States, trucks carry more than 75 percent of all intra-EU freight, with railroads and barges carrying most of the rest. A July 1994 report found the "single trucking market is being distorted by a lack of uniform standards, widespread flouting of operating rules, and lax enforcement of regulations across the 12-nation bloc." Thus, the United States is not the only jurisdiction with problems harmonizing transportation regulations, but in the United States it involves states, not sovereign nations. See Bruce Barnard, "European Union's Trucking Market Lacks Enforcement, Executives Say," *Journal of Commerce* (July 8, 1994), p. 3B.

A second rationale for national regulation arises when state regulations of the industry exhibit significant effects beyond the state. These effects are called jurisdictional externalities. Choices made in one state should not adversely affect firms, shippers, or citizens in another state. If they do, that indicates interstate commerce and suggests a need for national regulation to balance conflicting interests. Otherwise, state regulation could be used to impede interstate commerce.

A third advantage of national regulation is that one regulator may be better able to marshal adequate analytic and oversight resources than can fifty states of varying sizes and complexity. In other words, there may be economies of scale in the development and implementation of regulatory policy. Although none of the federal transportation regulatory staffs are very large today, at one time the Interstate Commerce Commission included over 2,000 staff members when it was regulating actively. Further, the extremely small size of some state transportation regulatory agencies (often two or fewer staff people in small states) can provide a rationale for this argument.

Finally, national regulation is generally perceived to be less susceptible to interest-group manipulation than state regulation. In general, more interest groups are active in Washington, D.C., than in state capitals. A larger number of groups are more likely to provide balanced policy input in a pluralistic manner. At the state level, certain interest groups may be too powerful and not counterbalanced effectively by other groups or coalitions, allowing them to manipulate state regulators more easily than they could federal regulators.[10] Thus, depending on the nature of government responsiveness, the "closeness" between state regulators and interest groups can be viewed either positively or negatively.

Determining whether a dual or a unitary system is the most suitable for regulating business activities is often difficult and controversial. Forty years ago, the U.S. Commission on Intergovernmental Relations noted the following justifications for federal preemption of state authority, which correspond with the aforementioned considerations. The federal government should preempt when: (1) conflicting

---

10. For a discussion of the relative strength of business interests at the state and at the federal level, see E. E. Schattschneider, *The Semi-Sovereign People* (New York: Holt, 1960).

state policies create a burden for interstate commerce; (2) one state's policies inflict (external) problems on other states; (3) there is a pressing need for one national policy, perhaps because of security or trade concerns; and (4) states lack the resources to carry out policy.[11] In practice, direct political influence by affected groups has influenced congressional and judicial decisions about the extent of federal preemption as much as or more than these conditions.

Regulatory Federalism in Practice. For most of this century, oversight of the transportation industry has been shared by the federal and state governments. Over this time span, however, the federal government showed an increasing reluctance to allow states to supervise segments of the transportation industry. Generally, as markets became more nationalized, the federal government limited the role of the state governments because of the increasing difficulty in distinguishing between interstate and intrastate commerce. When the federal government eventually decided to end regulation of modes within the industry, this retreat typically foreshadowed the end of state intervention altogether.

State governments typically initiated their involvement as each transportation mode developed. States were the first to promote and regulate water barges, railroads, and trucks. The approaches of the states often reflected the particular needs of their jurisdiction, with regulations designed to serve the demands of local economies. This framework proved quite conducive to the needs of various modes during their infancy, when relatively primitive technologies limited the scope of the markets they could serve.

As transportation modes grew, the geographic area they could serve efficiently and effectively expanded. In time, a truly national market emerged, with more goods being shipped between states than within states. This shift toward interstate movements, and away from intrastate movements, is reflected in table 1–3, which illustrates how the average length of haul has grown in all the major transportation sectors over the past several decades.

With the development of national consumer markets, the federal

---

11. U.S. Advisory Commission on Intergovernmental Relations, *A Report to the President for Transmittal to Congress* (Washington, D.C.: U.S. Government Printing Office, 1955).

TABLE 1–3

AVERAGE NUMBER OF MILES OF DOMESTIC FREIGHT HAUL, 1960–1990

Year	Rail	Truck	Air	Water	Oil Pipe
1960	489	272	953	282	—
1970	546	263	1,014	330	500
1980	587	363	1,052	405	500
1990	646	391	1,389	449	600

SOURCE: *Transportation in America* (Washington, D.C.: Eno Transportation Foundation, Inc., 1993).

government sought increasing control over transportation regulation. Since the patchwork of regulations that evolved in most segments of the industry proved quite cumbersome to transporters operating in multiple states, the federal government often limited the oversight of state governments, even on issues that came up entirely within a single jurisdiction. States opposed this encroachment on their autonomy, frequently fighting preemption in Congress and in court. Generally, states lost these battles, but states had greater success in some areas than in others.

In railroad regulation, where a large share of the shipments were interstate by the time of federal government intervention, federal regulators reduced the role of the states to a minimum. Most state regulation of domestic waterborne transportation and air cargo carriage was preempted by Congress. Only in trucking were the states able to play a major role in the economic performance of the industry.

As deregulation emerged as the federal approach to transportation regulation, though, even this remaining influence was eventually removed from the states.[12] The little state regulation of railroads that remained in 1980 when Congress deregulated was effectively preempted. In trucking, where intrastate shipments were still much more important, representing about half the total market,[13] federal

---

12. Deregulation policy did not entail a complete withdrawal of governmental activity but rather a removal of many regulatory obstacles to more competitive market structures, such as entry barriers and rate controls.

13. As reported in W. Bruce Allen, Arayah Preechemetta, Gary Shao, and Scott Singer, "The Impact of State Economic Regulation of Motor Carriage on Intrastate and Interstate Commerce" (Washington, D.C.: U.S. Department of Transportation, 1990), intrastate trucking revenues made up 45 percent of the regulated national

preemption of the states took considerably longer to occur, reflecting the strong role that long-established and well-organized state-level interests played in maintaining regulations. Today, both state and federal governments apply minimal economic regulations in these industries.

Explaining Regulatory Outcomes

Ultimately, we are interested not only in documenting the evolution of the transportation regulatory apparatus but also in understanding what propelled regulatory decisions over time. Over the years, considerable academic attention has focused on the causes of regulatory outcomes. Scholars often developed theories in response to new regulatory initiatives that did not fit existing conceptualizations. Today, most research on regulatory decision making can be grouped into one of three theoretical approaches: economic theory, institutionalism, and the politics of ideas. Each of these theories highlights a different set of participants or factors as causing regulatory change.

The *economic theory* of regulation views regulatory policy as a result of supply and demand between government representatives and interest groups. Public officials, motivated by their desire to be reelected, need votes, money, and manpower to ensure their electoral security. Conversely, interest groups are primarily concerned with maximizing their economic welfare. One way for interest groups to obtain greater profits is to secure government regulations that limit competition and reduce costs, such as restrictions on entry, price controls, and subsidies. The success with which interest groups can acquire these privileges, though, depends on their ability to deliver electoral resources to public officials.

Initially, concentrated producer groups were believed to be the only interest groups capable of providing these resources to government officials because of their ability to overcome collective action problems that plagued more dispersed consumer groups.[14] This al-

---

market in the late 1970s. When private truck carrier movements were included, total intrastate revenues represented about two-thirds of the national market.

14. Smaller, more concentrated groups typically have lower organizational costs, higher per capita stakes, and less free riding than more dispersed groups. See Mancur Olson, *The Logic of Collective Action* (Cambridge, Mass.: Harvard University Press, 1965).

lowed them to "capture" regulatory agencies and manipulate policies to produce substantial economic benefits at the expense of consumers. Regulatory decision making did not reflect the interests of policy makers or voters but was merely a consequence of the mobilization and resource allocation efforts of producer groups.[15]

The emergence of environmental and social regulation, which significantly reduced producer groups' advantages, forced revisions in the economic theory of regulation in the past two decades. Departures from pure protection are now recognized by proponents of the economic theory as optimal political strategies when consumer groups or competing producer groups (that is, groups outside the regulatory apparatus) can offer sufficient votes or money to public officials.[16] In other words, political representatives are viewed as allocating benefits across consumer and producer groups so that total political utility is maximized. The magnitude of organization and information costs makes it extremely unlikely that producer groups will withdraw all their support from public officials who do not ensure the greatest possible profits. Since producer groups still possess lower organizational costs and greater resources, however, they normally obtain the lion's share of the profits, though limited by general economic efficiency.[17] In short, the economic theory argues that regulatory policies simply mirror the balance of interest-group demands.

Some political scientists were troubled by this portrayal of public officials as solely vote maximizers who execute interest-group demands without exercising any independent influence on regulatory

15. George Stigler, "The Theory of Economic Regulation," *Bell Journal of Economics and Management Science*, vol. 2 (1971), pp. 3–21.

16. Sam Peltzman, "Toward a More General Theory of Regulation," *Journal of Law and Economics*, vol. 19 (1976), pp. 211–40; Sam Peltzman, "The Economic Theory of Regulation after a Decade of Deregulation," in *Brookings Papers on Economic Activity: Microeconomics*, ed. Martin Neil Baily and Clifford Winston (Washington, D.C.: Brookings Institution, 1989); Thomas Romer and Howard Rosenthal, "Modern Political Economy and the Study of Regulation," in *Public Regulation: New Perspectives on Institutions and Policies*, ed. Elizabeth E. Bailey (Cambridge, Mass.: MIT Press, 1987).

17. Gary S. Becker, "A Theory of Competition among Pressure Groups for Political Influence," *Quarterly Journal of Economics*, vol. 98 (1983), pp. 371–400; Gary S. Becker, "Public Policies, Pressure Groups, and Dead Weight Costs," *Journal of Public Economics*, vol. 28 (1985), pp. 330–47.

outcomes. Instead, they put forward a state-centered approach often labeled *institutionalism*. Advocates of this perspective contend that political institutions often mediate the influence of organized interests, exerting a separate and distinguishable impact on regulatory decision makers.[18] Rather than merely intervening to secure votes, public officials are viewed as pursuing numerous interests, including promoting policy principles and enhancing power. Institutional impact can occur directly by mandating the actions of regulatory agencies or indirectly by establishing parameters that agencies must operate within, further reducing the likelihood of unobstructed interest-group domination.

Originally, Congress was perceived to be the primary institutional actor affecting regulatory decision making. Members, particularly those on committees responsible for overseeing a particular agency, possessed numerous mechanisms to influence agency decisions, including authorizing programs, appropriating budgets, and investigating activities of regulatory agencies.[19] The structure of this relationship did not even require Congress to supervise agency actions actively to ensure agency cooperation (that is, police patrol oversight) but permitted it to institute procedures that allowed affected interests and citizens to signal inappropriate agency behavior (that is, fire-alarm oversight).[20] Congress was viewed as possessing both the incentives and the ability to influence regulatory decisions independently.

Over time, proponents of the institutionalist approach expanded this perspective to include the president, the courts, and the agency itself as additional mediators in regulatory decision making. Each

---

18. Kenneth Shepsle, "Studying Institutions: Some Lessons from the Rational Choice Approach," *Journal of Theoretical Politics*, vol. 1 (1989), pp. 131–48; and Paul Teske, "Interests and Institutions in State Regulation," *American Journal of Political Science*, vol. 35 (1991), pp. 139–54.

19. Barry Weingast and Mark Moran, "Bureaucratic Discretion or Congressional Control: Regulatory Policymaking by the Federal Trade Commission," *Journal of Political Economy*, vol. 91 (1983), pp. 765–800; Mathew McCubbins, Roger Noll, and Barry Weingast, "Administrative Procedures as Instruments of Elite Control," *Journal of Law, Economics, and Organization*, vol. 3 (1987), pp. 243–77.

20. Matthew McCubbins and Thomas Schwartz, "Congressional Oversight Overlooked: Police Patrols versus Fire Alarms," *American Journal of Political Science*, vol. 28 (1984), pp. 165–79.

possesses different incentives and unique powers that allow it to exert independent roles. Presidents are believed to be responsive to a more diverse constituency and broader policy concerns than their political counterparts. They can articulate these priorities to regulatory agencies by their ability to appoint high-level agency members, veto congressional legislation, and alter budgets.[21]

The courts, in contrast, have far fewer opportunities to affect regulatory outcomes. Courts can intervene in agency behavior only when policies are appealed to them during the judicial process. Increasingly, many regulatory decisions do get taken to court. If they choose, judges can implement decisions that have broad, widespread effects on agencies, far beyond the specific action in question. Since judges do not possess a constituency to whom they are responsible, they can advance their own ideological philosophies.[22]

Finally, some institutionalists view the agencies themselves as exercising an influence on regulatory decisions. Agency members are characterized as possessing different motivations from other institutional actors, such as expanding their power and serving professional norms.[23] Since none of the institutions charged with supervising the behavior of agencies can ensure compliance with every decision, agencies may possess considerable discretion and opportunities for shirking their mandates and pursuing their own interests.[24]

In sum, advocates of institutional theories argue that political institutions mediate and redirect the influence of interest groups on regulatory agencies. Rather than simply succumbing to interest-

---

21. Terry Moe, "Regulatory Performance and Presidential Administration," *American Journal of Political Science*, vol. 26 (1982), pp. 197–224; Terry Moe, "An Assessment of the Positive Theory of 'Congressional Dominance,' " *Legislative Politics Quarterly*, vol. 12 (1987), pp. 475–520; and Dan Wood and Richard Waterman, "The Dynamics of Political Control of the Bureaucracy," *American Political Science Review*, vol. 85 (1991), pp. 801–28.

22. See, for example, Jeremy Rabkin, *Judicial Compulsions* (New York: Basic Books, 1989).

23. William Niskanen, *Bureaucracy and Representative Government* (Chicago: Aldine, 1971); James Q. Wilson, *The Politics of Regulation* (New York: Basic Books, 1980).

24. See, for example, James Q. Wilson, *Bureaucracy* (New York: Basic Books, 1989), and Kenneth Meier, *The Political Economy of Regulation: The Case of Insurance* (Albany, NY: State University of New York Press, 1988).

group demands, institutional actors frequently pursue their own separate interests. Regulatory outcomes result from the interaction of these various actors. On some issues (those with low visibility or low stakes, for example), many actors will be uninterested, allowing a particular institution, often the agency itself, to shape decisions. On other issues (those with high visibility or high stakes, for example), each institution will seek to exercise influence, resulting in policies that are an amalgamation of these efforts.

The final theoretical approach, the *politics of ideas*, arose in the aftermath of economic deregulation in several visible infrastructural industries.[25] Proponents of this perspective argue that deregulation, or for that matter regulation, requires coordination by influential political institutions. Each political institution is very protective of its interests, while possessing the capacity to block policy initiatives by competing institutions. Without simultaneous cooperation, gridlock will occur, and the status quo will remain intact. Thus, to understand the evolution of regulatory decisions, sources of institutional coordination must be identified.

Intellectual ideas are the coordinating forces most evident in regulatory decision making, particularly in recent deregulatory initiatives. Ideas, developed and tested within academic settings, are often disseminated into regulatory agencies. They are adopted and serve as a justification to institutional superiors for discretionary behavior. Once established within an agency, these ideas gradually convert actors in other political institutions who together begin promoting policy changes grounded in these new theories. The process provides incentives to institutional actors by permitting them to gravitate to these ideas on their own, without coercion, thereby allowing them to claim credit from their relevant constituencies. Rather than identifying particular participants, the politics of ideas endorses academic theories as the source of regulatory decision making. These ideas can become powerful enough to overcome strong interest groups that oppose policies shaped by these ideas.

Evidence for each of these theoretical approaches—economic theory, institutionalism, and the politics of ideas—exists in various regulatory settings at different times. In fact, these perspectives have

---

25. Martha Derthick and Paul Quirk, *The Politics of Deregulation* (Washington, D.C.: Brookings Institution, 1985).

been shaped considerably by analyses of the transportation industry. This makes a fundamental drawback of such research that much more surprising: none of these theories considers governmental decision making in the context of American federalism, instead treating regulatory outcomes as if they were entirely derived from a unitary national system. They ignore the differences in decision making that often occur on the state level and how these state-level decisions affect federal behavior. This oversight is especially troubling considering the increasing nationalization that has occurred in most industries and the number of federal regulatory decisions that have come in response to state activities. These theories may operate differently, if at all, on the state level. Until greater attention is given to the entire structure of the regulatory environment, conclusions about the sources, timing, and impact of regulatory decisions remain partially untested.

Structure of the Book

In this book, we examine both the causes and the effects of government intervention in the operations of the freight transportation industry. While we provide overviews of all major segments of the industry, we focus on the trucking mode in particular. Trucking is the largest and most important component of freight transportation and arguably has the most varied regulatory history. For most of this century, trucking has been governed by a prototypical dual system that granted considerable autonomy to both levels of government. Hence, it is a good case from which to analyze the consequences of multilevel government policy and demonstrate how even seemingly minor state operating restrictions can have sizable effects on the performance of the industry and the economy at large. More important, the trucking industry's regulatory structure provides a fair test of whether contemporary theories of regulatory decision making are valid within a federal system. We advance the thesis that none of these theories is entirely appropriate on the state level and that a new synthesis needs to be developed that recognizes the entire governmental framework. All these arguments are developed at length in the chapters that follow.

Chapter 2 explores the evolution of the federal system of government regulation in the freight transportation industry, detailing the regulatory structures that emerged at the state and federal levels for each mode. We demonstrate how economic and political factors have influenced the degree of regulation, as well as the level of government used to supervise these activities. In the process, we analyze why deregulation and preemption eventually developed as successful regulatory strategies in the airline and railroad sectors.

In chapter 3, we present the structure of the trucking industry in greater detail. This chapter examines *interstate* trucking regulation in particular. We summarize the reasons for the emergence of federal deregulation and the results of this approach. We conclude the chapter by showing that federal deregulatory efforts did not entirely end economic regulation, although political activity in 1995 draws us closer to that outcome.

Chapter 4 focuses on *state* economic regulation of trucking. We illustrate various regulatory approaches states have undertaken, demonstrating the consequences they have had on interstate as well as intrastate regulation. Moreover, we consider why the federal government did not intervene and preempt state regulatory authority at the time they were doing so in other industries (1980) and waited for nearly fifteen years to preempt the states.

Chapter 5 examines other state restrictions on trucking operating authority. While these are normally considered "noneconomic" regulations, as we will show, state differences in these restrictions can have a sizable influence on the performance of the trucking industry. Recently, the federal government has attempted to coordinate state efforts, but problems persist. In addition, we highlight two areas, state hazardous materials transportation and state environmental regulations, which are creating new challenges for the trucking industry.

Chapter 6 summarizes our main observations on the effects of government intervention on the freight transportation industry, especially the trucking segment. We advance some further initiatives that could be undertaken to improve the performance of the industry. Finally, we evaluate the success of various theoretical approaches in explaining regulatory decision making, noting some discrepancies and highlighting certain questions that will need to be explained by future research.

2

The Development of
Transportation Regulatory
Federalism

Once you establish a commission . . . you have the devil's own time passing any act abolishing it.
—REPRESENTATIVE JAMES J. WADSWORTH (D, N.Y.)[1]

In this chapter, we analyze the historical development of regulatory federalism in American transportation. We then discuss the factors that led to varying amounts of deregulation in the airlines, railroads, and trucking sectors in the late 1970s and early 1980s. We follow this discussion with a brief examination of the effects of deregulation as they have been experienced in the airline and railroad industries. The effects of interstate trucking deregulation are given detailed treatment in chapter 3. To conclude the present chapter, we draw out the major themes in transportation regulatory federalism as they have developed in this country.

Early History

The earliest important mode of freight carriage regulated and shaped by American government involved water transportation. Compared with horse-drawn carriages, barges could carry much larger amounts of freight over longer distances. New York State recognized this po-

---

1. Cited in Bernard Schwartz, *The Economic Regulation of Business and Industry: A Legislative History of U.S. Regulatory Agencies*, vol. IV (New York: Chelsea House, 1973), p. 2984. The comment was made in a debate over the Civil Aeronautics Act and whether a new agency or the Interstate Commerce Commission should be empowered to regulate the airlines.

tential and in 1817 established commissions to finance and supervise the construction of the Erie Canal.[2] Because government was involved at the outset, rates were set by these governmental commissions. After its completion in 1825, the canal successfully aided New York–based businesses partly because it employed discriminatory tariffs against out-of-state producers and generated revenues to extend the system and to aid New York State producers. Seeing this success, several other states, including Ohio, Pennsylvania, Indiana, and Illinois, imitated New York and began to build their own canals for water-borne freight.[3]

As a result of the need for transportation by both intrastate and interstate producers and transporters, controversy over where to draw the boundaries between regulation of interstate and intrastate commerce began in this era of water transport. The U.S. Supreme Court decided the first important case about the interstate commerce clause in 1824, *Gibbons v. Ogden*, in which the Court voided New York's authorization of a steamboat monopoly.[4] While this interpretation seemingly gave the federal government expansive powers, a subsequent case, *Cooley v. Board of Wardens of the Port of Philadelphia*,[5] balanced that power by upholding a Pennsylvania statute regulating pilotage of vessels also engaged in interstate and foreign commerce, using the interpretation that state statutes are not excluded by the Constitution. These early court decisions focused on the conflicts between the police power of the state to regulate and the interstate commerce clause.[6]

The Development of the Railroads

The history of transportation is partly a history of technological development. The invention of steam engines for railroads after 1830 led

---

2. Carter Goodrich, *Government Promotion of American Canals and Railroads, 1800–1890* (New York: Columbia University Press, 1960).

3. Harry Scheiber, "State Law and Industrial Policy in American Development, 1790–1985," New York Economic Development Working Paper, Rockefeller Institute of Government, 1987.

4. Gibbons v. Ogden, 9 Wheaton 1 (1824).

5. Cooley v. Board of Wardens of the Port of Philadelphia, 53 U.S. (12 Howard) 299 (1851).

6. William Childs, *Trucking and the Public Interest: The Emergence of Federal Regulation 1914–1940* (Knoxville: University of Tennessee Press, 1985), p. 69.

to the eventual overtaking of much water-borne freight by the rail-roads. In fact, in only ten years, by 1840, U.S. railroad mileage equaled that of canals.[7] Railroads, which helped fuel the develop-ment of national markets that allowed the Industrial Revolution to expand, were themselves among the first giant firms of that era.[8] Railroads frequently carried bulk items such as iron ore, coal, and agricultural goods.

As the railroad industry developed and expanded, particularly after the Civil War, disputes arose about how to regulate this growing industry and, in particular, over where to draw the interstate versus intrastate regulatory boundaries.[9] While neither state nor federal gov-ernments actively regulated railroads before 1870,[10] they did assist railroad development, first with state subsidies, tax advantages, and bond underwriting, followed by federal land grants and loans. As early as 1835, for example, Congress had allowed individual rail-roads free rights of way on public land, a policy that it made more general in 1852. In 1838, Congress had made every railway into a postal route, which provided a source of guaranteed revenues for this infant industry. As westward expansion became a clearer goal, Congress increased the government role in railroad construction start-ing in 1850 and building toward the Pacific Railroad Bill of 1862.[11]

To the extent that railroads were under a form of regulation at this time, at either the state or the federal level, it was under well-established common law, applied to common carriers. Under this concept, courts expected railroads that were offering their services to the public to serve all groups that sought service, to charge reason-able rates, and to deliver goods and persons safely.[12] Some of these

---

7. Richard Vietor, *Strategic Management in the Regulatory Environment: Cases and Industry Notes* (Englewood Cliffs, N.J.: Prentice Hall, 1989), p. 210.

8. See, for example, Albert Fishlow, *American Railroads and the Transformation of the Ante Bellum Economy* (Cambridge: Harvard University Press, 1965).

9. Thomas McCraw, *Prophets of Regulation* (Cambridge: Harvard University Press, 1984).

10. Rhode Island had established a commission to regulate railroads as early as 1839, but it had no effective powers (see ibid).

11. Thamar Emilia Dufwa, *Transcontinental Railroad Legislation, 1835–1862* (New York: Arno Press, 1981).

12. Theodore Keeler, *Railroads, Freight and Public Policy* (Washington, D.C.: Brookings Institution, 1983), p. 20.

common-carrier requirements had been established as early as 1518 in England, where carriers were held to a "duty to serve" and held liable for damage to shipments. The common-carrier concept was extended in American courts to include equal rates for different shippers requiring the same service.[13]

As railroads expanded to become a critical national infrastructure, regulation and control only through common-carrier law proved insufficient. Courts, for example, were not able to establish what constituted "reasonable" rates. As a result, advocates argued that the only solution was congressional railroad regulation under the Constitution's interstate commerce clause. Farmers and commercial interests in the western and southern states, who particularly objected to high freight rates, pressured Congress for such regulation. The railroads themselves were divided on this issue. Some railroad firms preferred federal regulation to escape varied state restrictions that were emerging in piecemeal fashion, while others preferred state regulation that they thought they could dominate. Most railroads opposed any regulation.[14]

Because of market and economic instability, leading to many bankruptcies, railroads did seek to ensure themselves of more stable profits. They established the first pooling associations, to attempt to set and stabilize prices through cartels, in 1875. These associations were particularly successful in setting and maintaining short-haul rates, because the short-haul markets in any given region were typically served by fewer firms. Thus, short-haul rates were set higher than long-haul rates, leaving shippers in the Midwest particularly disadvantaged, relative to those in the West and Northeast. Large shippers with bargaining power, such as Standard Oil, were able to use their purchasing power to obtain "rebates," which gave them lower effective rates than other shippers, despite common-carrier principles of nondiscriminatory rates for the same service. Independent oil producers seeking to limit these rebates had an interstate commerce bill introduced in Congress in 1877 and for each of the next ten years. At the same time, more railroads began to favor regulation to stabilize their markets.[15]

---

13. Childs, *Trucking and the Public Interest*, p. 67.

14. Morton Keller, *Affairs of State: Public Life in Late Nineteenth Century America* (Cambridge, Mass.: Belknap/Harvard University Press, 1977), p. 177.

15. Vietor, *Strategic Management in the Regulatory Environment*, p. 210.

As is true with most of the freight transportation modes we analyze, effective railroad regulation developed first in the states. The earliest state efforts to oversee railroad operations started in New England, as Rhode Island in 1839, New Hampshire in 1844, Connecticut in 1853, Vermont in 1855, and Maine in 1858 established forms of railroad oversight.[16] These were not highly successful. The first potent oversight agency, the Massachusetts Board of Railroad Commissioners, was originally headed in 1869 by Charles Francis Adams, who aimed to employ experts in railroad activity.[17] This represented the independent regulatory commission (IRC) concept that would later characterize most American transportation regulation. Even though the initial board had few explicit powers, Adams skillfully used it and media attention to provide "sunshine" into railroad rate and safety practices. The Massachusetts example was adopted by fourteen other states.[18]

In contrast, in the Midwestern states, the Granger farming interests developed a more direct and populist approach to railroad regulation, in which state legislators would provide the actual regulations. With pressure from the Grangers, Illinois even placed transportation regulation into its constitution in 1870. Minnesota, Wisconsin, and Iowa soon adopted Granger legislation.[19] The major railroads challenged these Granger laws in the courts, however, and lobbied the legislatures for change. Resulting modified regulatory laws, some prorailroad court decisions, and "captured" state railroad commissions made state supervision only a limited success.[20] In the late 1880s, the states did attempt to coordinate and learn from one another through the establishment of the National Association of Railroad and Utility Commissions (NARUC), an organization that would come to play an important role in regulatory battles between the states and the federal government in several transportation industries.

---

16. Donald Harper, *Economic Regulation of the Motor Trucking Industry* (Urbana, Ill.: University of Illinois Press, 1959).

17. For an excellent history of Adams's efforts, see McCraw, *Prophets of Regulation*, chap. 2.

18. Vietor, *Strategic Management in the Regulatory Environment*, p. 211.

19. Keller, *Affairs of State*, p. 179.

20. Ibid., p. 423.

In this context of largely ineffective state regulation, Congress actively debated some form of federal regulation of interstate railroad activities but was severely divided based on differing regional concerns and railroad versus shipper interest group battles.[21] Finally, as states were attempting to fill in the interstate regulatory vacuum, the U.S. Supreme Court ruled in 1886 that the states were not empowered to regulate interstate commerce, even in the absence of federal regulation.[22] This decision, as well as the growing number of groups affected by the railroads, the limited character of state regulation, and the increasing assumption of regulatory oversight by the federal courts, forced Congress to adopt the Interstate Commerce Act (ICA) in 1887.[23]

The Start of Federal Regulation

The ICA made explicit several legal principles already embedded in common law. It required that rates be just and reasonable, prohibited discrimination against persons or shippers and undue preferences among regional areas, and forbade the practice of charging more for a short haul than for a longer one. Perhaps as important, the ICA took up the concept of an independent regulatory commission and established a new institution, the Interstate Commerce Commission (ICC), the first federal regulatory agency, to enforce and implement the law on a continuing basis. In terms of federalism, section 1 of the ICA explicitly reserved powers of intrastate rate regulation to the states.

The act also went substantively beyond the common law in some ways. It made collusion to control the amount of service provided illegal, for example, as some firms had colluded through an elaborate set of procedures to ensure that no railroad "cheated" and expanded service beyond the agreed-upon levels.[24]

---

21. See, for example, Thomas Gilligan, William Marshall, and Barry Weingast, "Regulation and the Theory of Legislative Choice: The Interstate Commerce Act of 1887," *Journal of Law and Economics*, vol. 32 (1989), pp. 35–61.

22. The case was Wabash, St. Louis, and Pacific Railway Co. v. Illinois, 118 U.S. 557 (1886).

23. Interstate Commerce Act, 24 Stat. 379 (1887); (formerly codified at former 49 U.S.C. 1).

24. Keeler, *Railroads, Freight and Public Policy*, pp. 22–23.

The ICA did not, however, clear up all railroad regulation problems. The Supreme Court did not allow the ICC much power, nullifying its ability to set maximum rates and allowing court review of its decisions. From 1887 to 1905, the Supreme Court decided fifteen of the sixteen railroad cases it heard in favor of the industry and not the ICC.[25] One important case for federalism was *Smyth v. Ames*, in 1898, in which the Supreme Court ruled that federal courts had the authority to review *state* rate-setting decisions to ensure that they were just and reasonable.

The continued use of rebates to provide rate discrimination for different shippers was the major problem the ICC faced in the 1890s. The act left several other loopholes and ambiguities that the courts did not help clarify. As a result, regulation advocates successfully sought better legislation. The Elkins Act of 1903 prohibited rebates. The Hepburn Act of 1906 explicitly gave the ICC the power to set maximum rates. The Mann-Elkins Act of 1910 addressed long-haul versus short-haul rate differentials. These acts, along with court cases in subsequent years, also reduced the role of the states in railroad regulation, as illustrated below.

By 1910, ICC regulation finally satisfied most of the shippers who had first wanted railroad regulation thirty years earlier. Railroad rates were largely reduced in the next few years. Some railroad managers were relatively pleased that the maximum rates the ICC imposed on various routes served as a better stabilizer of profitable rates than had any previous cartel arrangements. The ICA, however, still left open the possibility of intrastate rate discrimination that could adversely affect interstate railroad commerce. Thus, according to William Childs, "the ICC, despite objections from the railways and the state commissioners, began to set the intrastate levels. The Supreme Court sustained this broad use of federal authority in the Shreveport case of 1914."[26]

In 1914, the U.S. Supreme Court decided the first of these so-called *Shreveport* cases in railroad regulation, when the Texas Railroad Commission had tried to gain advantage for Texas ports by setting discriminatory rates against rival port Shreveport, Louisi-

---

25. Vietor, *Strategic Management in the Regulatory Environment*, p. 213.

26. Childs, *Trucking and the Public Interest*, p. 85.

ana.[27] The court upheld the ICC's preemption of Texas rates on the grounds that intrastate rates clearly affected interstate commerce. This series of decisions began to reduce the autonomy of state railroad rate regulation. The *Shreveport* cases established the important precedent that even in their intrastate regulation, states can be preempted from regulation that harms national policy goals.

The railroad industry faced many problems in 1916, and when the nation needed assistance for the war effort, federal officials were surprised at the inefficiency of rail operations. To provide coordination, during World War I the federal government temporarily took over the railroads. The Transportation Act of 1920 returned railroad firms to private ownership and broadened the ICC's powers significantly over the states, in part by incorporating the *Shreveport* doctrine into section 416 of the law.[28] The act also transferred control of entry into and exit from rail routes from the states to the ICC.[29] While the states maintained some regulatory powers over railroads until 1980, their role was reduced substantially by the federal regulators, who would grow to over 2,000 ICC employees by 1930. A major goal of federalization of regulation was to improve the financial health of the railroads.

Next came further technological changes—in this case, the rise of trucking as a viable form of freight transportation—leading to important changes in the administration of the American regulatory regime.

The Rise of Trucking as a Competitor for Railroads

According to William Childs, "By the early 1930s, the truck was no longer a simple, convenient substitute for the horse and wagon, but

---

27. See Shreveport Rate Cases, 234 U.S. 342 (1914), including Houston, E. & W. Texas Railway v. U.S., 234 U.S. 342 (1914). See also Minnesota Rate Cases, 230 U.S. 352 (1913).

28. See David Baker, "Section 214 of the Staggers Rail Act: Is It Working as Congress Intended," *Transportation Law Journal*, vol. 14 (1986), p. 207; see also Frank Dixon, *Railroads and Government: Their Relations in the United States, 1910–1921* (New York: Scribner, 1922), p. 201; and Keeler, *Railroads, Freight and Public Policy*, p. 24.

29. Transportation Act of 1920, 41 Stat. 484 (1920). To this day, state governments are fervently opposed to abandonments.

rather a direct competitor of the railroad."[30] This competition developed very rapidly. A Lake Michigan agricultural port shipped out 90 percent of its produce by railroad in 1925, for example, but only seven years later the same port was shipping 90 percent of its produce by truck.[31]

As is often the case in American industry, wartime advanced an infant industry—this time trucking, by the motorization of the U.S. cavalry in 1915 and the contribution trucking made to logistics during World War I. In 1916, the Federal Road Aid Act began, in a limited way that was greatly expanded later, to provide federal government funds for highways. The concept of paying for the use of these roads through gasoline taxes also emerged at this time, as Oregon, Colorado, and New Mexico began this policy in 1919 and by 1929 all states imposed gasoline taxes.[32]

With more roads, trucking began to emerge as a viable industry and a potential competitor for other modes of freight transport, although a competitor with many small firms rather than a national giant like the railroads. Much of the regulation of trucking has been related to railroad regulatory issues, at both the federal and the state levels.

As with railroads, the first significant trucking regulation developed within the states, starting with Pennsylvania in 1914. After Pennsylvania, state regulation was initiated in Illinois in 1914; Colorado, New York, Maryland, and Wisconsin in 1915; and California and Utah in 1917.[33] A U.S. Supreme Court case in 1915 upheld state trucking regulation in the absence of federal legislation.[34] E. V. Kuykendall, a prominent early regulator from Washington State, developed a model uniform state statute for trucking regulation in 1923. By 1925, trucking regulation was established in thirty-five states.[35]

---

30. Childs, *Trucking and the Public Interest*, p. 25.

31. The specific port was Benton Harbor, Michigan; ibid., p. 21.

32. Ibid., p. 15.

33. Harper, *Economic Regulation of the Motor Carrier Industry*, p. 39.

34. The case was Hendrick v. Maryland, 235 U.S. 610 (1915).

35. For a detailed early history of state trucking regulation see Childs, *Trucking and the Public Interest*.

This early state trucking regulation addressed safety, service quality, and inconsistent pricing created by the emergence of thousands of trucks in the freight-hauling market. From the start, though, state regulation lacked uniformity, despite some attempts at uniform statutes, imposing disparate weight restrictions, licensing fees, entry conditions, and rate controls.

This patchwork pattern of laws posed few problems when freight shipments were largely intrastate, as they were at first. By 1935, however, 10 percent of revenues from trucking traffic moved interstate, and this share was growing rapidly. Even more than with the railroads, "border wars" accompanied the growth of interstate trucking, in which enforcement of regulations in one state led to retaliation by neighboring states. Reciprocal agreements between states helped with some of these problems but did not eliminate contradictory rules. Varying indirect controls over truck size, fees, and taxes made it difficult for truckers to operate interstate. The economic aspects of trucking regulation, aimed at rates, service, and entry, were largely ineffective until the Supreme Court upheld the concept in 1932.[36]

Other regulatory problems were emerging at the state level. Private carriers that were using trucking as an adjunct to their main business made up 85 percent of all trucking activity, and these were left largely unregulated.[37] But regulators were not sure how to handle the 9 percent of firms that were contract carriers, serving only some shippers but not offering themselves as common carriers. Until 1932, they were not regulated by the states, although with several contracts, some of these firms were essentially similar to their regulated counterparts, the common carriers. Common carriers, which were the largest firms but represented only about 6 percent of all the trucking firms, were not pleased to be facing unregulated competitors. This disparity led to contentious political battles. As Childs notes: "In the early 1930s, state legislative sessions became miniature Roman senates in which lobbyists for the various transportation groups plotted against each other to enact legislation favorable to them and detrimental to their opponents."[38] Some of these battles had already moved into the courtrooms.

---

36. Ibid., p. 51.

37. Farmers owned 26 percent of all trucks at that time. Ibid., p. 34.

38. Ibid., p. 61.

In 1925, the Supreme Court ruled, in *Michigan Public Utilities Commission v. Duke*,[39] that a state law requiring permits for all carriers could not be applied to contract carriers and that a state could not impede interstate commerce through such regulations, unless "public safety and order" were threatened. In 1925, in *Buck v. Kuykendall*,[40] the Supreme Court also ruled that Washington State could not deny a permit to an interstate carrier from Oregon, and in *George W. Bush and Sons v. Maloy*,[41] the Court ruled that a Maryland law was too general in allowing its Public Utility Commission to deny permits harming interstate carriers. Together, these Supreme Court decisions curtailed clearly discriminatory state regulations that affected interstate commerce, ruling that states had disrupted interstate commerce and overstepped their legal jurisdictions. These were three of a series of Supreme Court cases on trucking that, over the next seven years, would clarify regulation of the three classes of trucking, delineate state powers over each, and indicate that Congress should address jurisdictional problems related to interstate commerce.

In its 1926 case *Frost et al. v. Railroad Commission of California*,[42] the Supreme Court invalidated regulation of contract carriers that was clearly oriented to protecting common carriers and not consumers. In the 1931 case, *Smith v. Cahoon*, the Court ruled that the states needed to define *contract* and *common carriers* appropriately and to regulate them separately.

State legislatures responded to these decisions by writing bills arguing that the public had a legitimate interest in contract carriers, that they were separate from common carriers and therefore required permits rather than certificates for operating, and that they had to file minimum rates that were not lower than the common carriers. The 1931 Texas Motor Vehicle Act, for example, argued that all this regulation was necessary as part of the state's police power over the highways (although it was really meant to protect Texas railroad interests). This act was upheld in the 1932 Supreme Court case

---

39. Michigan Public Utilities Commission et al. v. Duke, 266 U.S. 570 (1925).

40. Buck v. Kuykendall, 267 U.S. 307 (1925).

41. Bush, George W., and Sons v. Maloy, 267 U.S. 317 (1925).

42. Frost et al. v. Railroad Commission of State of California, 271 U.S. 583 (1926).

Sproles v. Binford.[43] Interested parties interpreted this ruling to mean that states could regulate trucking even if the purpose seemed to be the protection of railroad interests. The related case decision in *Stephenson v. Binford*[44] upheld Texas's regulation of contract carriers.

Some truckers sought to avoid onerous state regulation by developing interstate commerce. The first bills to develop federal regulation of the interstate trucking industry were introduced in 1925, followed by thirty-seven unsuccessful bills over the next decade.[45] The National Association of Railroad and Utility Commissions called for federal regulatory legislation every year from 1925 through 1935 to prevent truckers from using "interstate subterfuges" to serve intrastate markets.[46] Railroads, which were losing market share rapidly in the early years of the Great Depression and actually saw their revenues drop in 1930 for the first time ever, also called for federal regulation to try to slow down the gains of the emerging trucking industry. The Great Depression, rather than slowing the trucking industry as it did the railroads, aided truckers as flexibility and low rates became even more critical to shippers.[47]

To address all these concerns, different types of truckers began forming a variety of political action associations in the 1920s and 1930s, with the most restricted group, common carriers, organizing first. These groups led to the formation of the American Trucking Associations in 1933, as a consortium of state associations, to deal with federal regulatory issues. The associations would soon develop into the most powerful interest group in the transportation arena.

As with other problems of this era, federal officials employed an "associationalist" approach to transportation issues. President Franklin Roosevelt signed the Code of Fair Competition for the Trucking Industry in 1934. But this self-regulation approach did not work effectively. President Roosevelt then appointed Joseph Eastman, who

---

43. Sproles et al. v. Binford, 286 U.S. 374 (1932). For greater detail on these developments, see Childs, *Trucking and the Public Interest*, pp. 74–76.

44. Stephenson v. Binford, 287 U.S. 251 (1932).

45. Vietor, *Strategic Management in the Regulatory Environment*, p. 217.

46. Daniel Baker, "State Regulation and Federal Preemption," Transportation Lawyers Association, Report 1989, p. 56.

47. Childs, *Trucking and the Public Interest*, pp. 25–28.

had a long history of regulatory experience, as federal coordinator of transportation, to address these concerns.

Not everyone favored federal trucking regulation. The National Grange argued that regulation would lead to rising rates and monopolistic practices, while some trucking firms, organized labor, and some shipping groups complained that regulation would raise their operating costs and thus prices to shippers. Common carriers favored regulation to stabilize their markets, but they were concerned about lack of uniformity, and inefficient enforcement.[48]

With coalitions supporting and opposed to regulation, and a political battle with parallels to that of federal railroad regulation in the 1870s and 1880s, several draft bills that would incorporate interstate trucking regulation into the ICC were debated in Congress. As the Great Depression reduced profits from trucking, the American Trucking Associations and the Teamsters union reconsidered their opposition and supported federal regulation that would limit entry and eliminate price wars.

As a Congressional Research Service report notes: "By 1935, the motor carrier industry had grown to sufficient size to be a threat to the railroads and, because of fierce internal competition, a threat to its own stability. There was broad-based support in both industries to bring trucking companies under federal regulatory control."[49]

Related to *state* regulation, Childs notes about the debate: "NARUC opposed two features of the truck bill: final authority of the ICC and inclusion of the Shreveport doctrine, which allowed the ICC to set intrastate rates." As a result, "the final House version assured the rights of the states would be preserved and stated flatly that the commission [ICC] would have no authority over intrastate truck operations."[50] Lawrence Rothenberg adds about the final House bargaining: "The most important changes were exemptions of (1) all intrastate rates from federal regulations, to placate the state commissioners."[51]

48. Ibid., p. 61.

49. Kenneth DeJarnette, *Changing Regulation of Surface Transportation: Development and Implications of Current Policies*, Congressional Research Service Report No. 86-64E, Washington, D.C., April 1986, p. 4.

50. Childs, *Trucking and the Public Interest*, p. 137.

51. Lawrence Rothenberg, *Regulation, Organizations, and Politics: Motor Carrier Regulation at the ICC* (Ann Arbor: University of Michigan Press, 1994), p. 51.

With state regulation maintained intact, Congress passed the Motor Carrier Act in 1935.[52] This legislation gave the ICC broad powers over interstate trucking entry and rates by common and contract carriers. The ICC would grant trucking firms operating rights to carry specific commodities on certain routes. Rates were to be set by cartels that were euphemistically called "rate bureaus." These rate bureaus were later specifically exempted from antitrust action by Congress in the 1948 Reed-Bulwinkle Act.

As important as the Motor Carrier Act was, however, its economic controls applied to only 20 percent of all interstate trucking, not to private carriers and exempt shipments, and, because intrastate was still the predominant type of carriage, to only 2 percent of all trucking in the country.[53]

In addition to political pressure not to preempt, Congress did *not* preempt state regulation because the legislators thought that intrastate routes were clearly distinguishable from interstate routes. Most truck freight still moved intrastate; in 1940, even measured by ton miles, a method that favors long-distance movement, 94 percent of truck ton miles moved intrastate in California, 81 percent in Washington, 73 percent in Wisconsin, 71 percent in Pennsylvania, 57 percent in Illinois, and 55 percent in Ohio.[54] And states were regulating this activity with great enthusiasm; by 1946 all states except New Jersey regulated intrastate common-carriage trucking and forty-six states regulated contract carriers. Eleven states also chose to regulate private carriers.[55]

After 1935, the federal government pressured the states to conform somewhat to federal standards, and many states adopted such federal practices as distinguishing regulations according to the type of carrier, creating rate bureaus, and establishing entry standards of

---

52. For additional historical background on this act, see Robyn, *Braking the Special Interests*; and John Felton and Dale Anderson, *Regulation and Deregulation of the Motor Carrier Industry* (Ames: Iowa State University Press, 1987).

53. Childs, *Trucking and the Public Interest*, p. 139.

54. Harper, *Economic Regulation of the Motor Carrier Industry*, p. 46.

55. W. Bruce Allen, Arayah Preechemetta, Gary Shao, and Scott Singer, "The Impact of State Economic Regulation of Motor Carriage on Intrastate and Interstate Commerce" (Washington, D.C.: U.S. Department of Transportation Report, 1991), p. 14.

"public convenience and necessity." While the regulatory framework of most states resembled the ICC, the level of most requirements— the operating ratio, the weight restrictions, and the licensing fees— varied by state.[56]

The most prominent attempt to harmonize federal and state regulation was through the "joint board," which dealt with truckers operating in more than three states and involved state officials on the boards. The boards listened to evidence and made recommended decisions.[57] Joint board decisions were mostly sustained by the ICC (fewer than 5 percent were reversed), but the process of bringing the relevant state officials to Washington, D.C., was difficult; and the joint board practice was diluted substantially in the Transportation Act of 1940.[58]

This 1940 act was designed to establish a national transportation policy, and it added water-carrier regulation to the ICC.[59] One of its goals was to prevent one mode of transport from undercutting the rates of others to maintain the financial health of transportation firms.

---

56. Childs, *Trucking and the Public Interest*.

57. Ibid., p. 141; see also Paul Kauper, "Utilization of State Commissioners in the Administration of the Federal Motor Carrier Act," *Michigan Law Review* (November 1935).

58. Childs, *Trucking and the Public Interest*, p. 149.

59. Interestingly, the Transportation Act of 1940 placed water-barge transportation under the regulatory authority of the ICC, but it kept private carriage, most bulk carriage, and carriage of such materials as liquid cargo exempt from regulation. Effectively, much of the barge industry was thus not regulated. It has operated quite efficiently under this regime ever since. Today, less than 10 percent of the ton miles handled by barges is subject to ICC regulation. Bulk commodities, such as coal and grain, have low value-to-weight ratios and are often transported over long distances. Principal commodities carried by barges include petroleum and petroleum products (40 percent), coal (20 percent), grain (10 percent), and chemicals (7 percent). See, General Accounting Office, *The Impact of the Staggers Act on the Railroad Industry* (Washington, D.C.: U.S. Government Printing Office, 1990), pp. 20–21; and U.S. Department of Commerce, *U.S. Industrial Outlook 1993* (Lanham, Md.: Bernan Press, 1993), sec. 42, p. 14.

In addition, *intrastate* water-barge transportation is not an important issue, because there is so little of it. Robert Lieb notes: "Due to the limited importance of intrastate water carriage, it [the 1940 act] did not apply the Shreveport principle to such operations." Robert Lieb, *Transportation: The Domestic System* (Reston, Va.: Reston Publishing, 1978), p. 153.

Rate bureaus were upheld to set most rates in the railroad and trucking sectors. In 1945, however, the Supreme Court ruled that regulated industries were not exempt from antitrust laws, which led to rail and trucking lobbying for the 1948 Reed-Bulwinkle Act, which Congress passed easily over President Truman's veto. Rate bureaus approved by the ICC were allowed and exempted from antitrust action. With the Reed-Bulwinkle Act, the regulatory regime under which the trucking and railroad industries would operate for the next twenty-five years was set.

By the early 1970s, however, that regulatory regime was unraveling both from changing economic circumstances and from changing attitudes toward economic regulation of these industries, first on the part of academics and later on the part of politicians. We examine in detail these changes in trucking regulation in chapter 3.

In the next section, we explore the development of airlines—their evolution through government support and control to deregulation in 1978—and their current operation under minimal economic regulation. Even though airlines mainly carry passengers, the debate over airline regulation was critical for changing the attitude of regulators and politicians alike, not just those with a direct interest in the airline industry.[60] As we shall make clear, by 1980 the climate of ideas in Washington, D.C., fostered renewed respect for market forces and hence *deregulation* as the new orthodoxy.[61] This was a far

---

60. Interestingly, despite the success of the largely unregulated barge industry, it was not referred to much during the debates that helped fuel deregulation during the 1970s and early 1980s in the much larger airline, railroads, and trucking industries.

61. James Q. Wilson, *The Politics of Regulation* (New York: Basic Books, 1980), pp. 386–87, notes the differences in the arguments university students in the 1960s received about regulation compared with what students in the 1930s learned. He then says of the students of the 1960s: "These students would later enter government service carrying with them the political residue of these intellectual arguments: agencies should be reorganized to prevent their capture, regulation of entry and rates is of questionable value, and regulating the nature and quality of the product and the conditions of the workplace will produce substantial benefits." McCraw, *Prophets of Regulation,* chap. 7 discusses the same phenomenon while tracing the role that Alfred Kahn played in laying the intellectual foundations for, and then playing an important part in implementing, the deregulatory movement of the 1970s.

cry from the "destructive competition" and "faith-in-government" orthodoxy characteristic of the Great Depression of the 1930s.

The Airline Industry and the Case against Economic Regulation

The commercial airline industry began in the late 1920s with the hauling of mail for the U.S. Postal Service.[62] In the Kelly Airmail Act of 1925,[63] Congress, as it did with the railroads and overland mail, transferred responsibility for airmail from the army to private firms. Although markets developed for freight and passenger transportation in the late 1920s and early 1930s to supplement revenues from mail delivery, government mail contracts and other subsidies sustained the airline companies.

A fractured air transportation system developed; to coordinate it, in 1930 the postmaster general pushed for the merging of several smaller airlines into Trans World Airlines and American, which then received rigged government contracts. A Senate investigation discovered this system in 1934[64] and tried to improve it with the comprehensive Airmail Act of 1934,[65] which attempted to ensure competition by placing rates and contracts under ICC jurisdiction.[66] The ICC set up a competitive bidding system based on low prices. Airlines often submitted low bids to retain their routes, expecting to raise rates afterward. The ICC did not permit such rate increases, however, forcing many airlines close to bankruptcy. Ignoring the government role, regulatory advocates thus argued that an unregulated airline industry would be plagued by "destructive competi-

---

62. The following discussion relies particularly on these sources: Michael Levine, "Is Regulation Necessary? California Air Transportation and National Regulatory Policy," *Yale Law Journal*, vol. 74 (1965), pp. 1416–23; and W. Kip Viscusi, John Vernon, and Joseph Harrington, Jr., *Economics of Regulation and Antitrust* (Lexington, Mass.: D.C. Heath, 1992), pp. 526–28.

63. 43 Stat. 805 (1925).

64. Levine, "Is Regulation Necessary?" p. 1418.

65. 48 Stat. 933 (1934).

66. For a discussion of this episode, see H. L. Smith, *Airways: The History of Commercial Aviation in the United States* (1942), pp. 249–58.

tion."[67] The proregulation argument won out. At this time, fourteen states already had specific laws regulating intrastate activities of air carriers, and most other states treated them as common carriers subject to public utility laws.[68]

Under the Civil Aeronautics Act of 1938,[69] Congress created the Civil Aeronautics Authority (CAA). The CAA controlled maximum and minimum rates using the procedure for rate making from the Interstate Commerce Act of 1887.[70] In addition, the CAA controlled not only entry into and exit from the industry but also the route structures of airlines. It could prevent an existing airline from entering or abandoning a route. Besides control over price and market structure, Congress initially gave the CAA responsibility for airline safety, which was transferred to the Federal Aviation Administration (FAA) in 1958, when the CAA was renamed the Civil Aeronautics Board (CAB).[71]

This tight regulatory regime prevailed for almost forty years, during which time the "big four" airlines[72] and the CAB shared "an almost pathological fear of open competition."[73] In addition, the CAB believed that, unregulated, the industry would become monopolistic, either through mergers and collusion or through destructive competition that would leave only a single survivor.[74]

From the start, the CAB used its power to control air fares and the number of competitors, and in a strong display of this power it established a route moratorium in the early 1970s because of excess capacity among airlines and declining industry profits.[75] This move not only prevented new firms from entering the industry but also kept

67. Viscusi et al., *Economics of Regulation and Antitrust*, p. 527.

68. Baker, "State Regulation and Federal Preemption," p. 56.

69. 52 Stat. 977 (1938).

70. Interstate Commerce Act, 24 Stat. 379 (1887).

71. The role of the CAB was virtually unchanged from that of the CAA. See 72 Stat. 731 (1958), especially U.S.C. §§ 1301–1542.

72. The "big four" airlines were American Airlines, Eastern Airlines, Trans World Airlines, and United Airlines.

73. Levine, "Is Regulation Necessary?" p. 1423.

74. Ibid., pp. 1423–24.

75. Viscusi et al., *Economics of Regulation and Antitrust*, p. 527.

existing firms from expanding the number of routes they served, as the CAB feared that increased competition would decrease industry profits.

Government regulation of airlines generated a considerable literature, much of which supported regulation.[76] This academic support for airline regulation continued through the 1950s, focusing on destructive competition.[77] As early as 1949, however, economists viewed the applicability of this idea to the airline industry skeptically, with Lucile Keyes leading the argument that entry control was a mistake.[78] Although academic controversy over the nature of airline regulation continued into the 1960s, by the mid-1970s most academics believed that a deregulated airline business would be reasonably competitive. The argument against airline regulation advanced so rapidly among economists because of evidence about the operations of less regulated airlines.[79]

Michael Levine provided the most important empirical evidence in his study of the essentially unregulated Los Angeles to San Francisco market.[80] Unregulated price competition was possible on this route because, as a wholly *intrastate* route, it was free of CAB control, and the California Public Utilities Commission had no power to limit entry and practiced minimal rate regulation. Thus comparison of this route—the one major unregulated market—with other *regulated*

---

76. Michael Levine carefully traces the relevant academic literature in "Airline Competition in Deregulated Markets: Theory, Firm Strategy, and Public Policy," *Yale Journal on Regulation*, vol. 4 (1987), pp. 393–494.

77. See, for example, Frederick Gill and Gilbert Bates, *Airline Competition* (Boston: Harvard Business School Press, 1949), and Samuel Richmond, *Regulation and Competition in Air Transportation* (New York: Columbia University Press, 1961).

78. Lucile Keyes, "National Policy toward Commercial Aviation—Some Basic Problems," *Journal of Air Law and Commerce*, vol. 21 (1949), p. 50.

79. See, for example, Douglas Caves, *Air Transport and Its Regulators: An Industry Study* (Cambridge: Harvard University Press, 1962); George Douglas and James C. Miller, *Economic Regulation of Domestic Air Transport* (Washington, D.C.: Brookings Institution, 1974); William Jordan, *Airline Regulation in America: Effects and Imperfections* (Baltimore: Johns Hopkins University Press, 1970); and Levine, "Is Regulation Necessary?"

80. Levine, "Is Regulation Necessary?"

markets constituted "the closest thing to a 'controlled experiment' in public policy."[81] Levine concluded:

> Lack of regulation has not caused chaos in California. Unregulated entry and price competition have not resulted in a multitude of tiny firms scrambling for passengers to the confusion of the public. . . .
>
> [T]he California experience . . . indicates that the public has little to fear from unregulated entry. Participants in a market will be naturally limited to a number which ensures both competition and technical efficiency without chaos. The free-entry California market has and will have for the immediate future approximately the same structure—two or three major carriers—as most regulated routes. The important question is whether these carriers ought to be chosen administratively or by the competitive forces of the market. And the important difference is that transportation by air in the California unregulated market can be purchased for half to seven-tenths as much as it costs elsewhere.[82]

Evidence of competitive markets' operating without extensive regulation continued to emerge. By the mid-1970s, Southwest Airlines in Texas and Pacific Southwest in California had implemented successful business strategies that combined very low fares with high load factors. This evidence, combined with the growing academic consensus, provided justifications for deregulation. In the 1975 Senate hearings held by Senator Edward Kennedy, the idea of regulatory reform was given serious consideration.[83] McCraw notes that, in the

---

81. Alfred Kahn, *The Economics of Regulation: Principles and Institutions* (New York: John Wiley and Sons, 1971), p. 218. Kahn, who was appointed as chairman of the CAB in 1977, included extended quotations from Levine's 1965 article in his discussion of airline regulation in this 1971 textbook.

82. Levine, "Is Regulation Necessary?" pp. 1440–41.

83. Derthick and Quirk, *The Politics of Deregulation,* go so far as to claim that "if economists had not made the case for procompetitive deregulation, it would not have occurred—at least not on the scale the nation has witnessed." The documentation of the Senate deliberations is contained in: *Hearings on the Oversight of Civil Aeronautics Board Practices and Procedures before the Subcommittee on Administrative Practice and Procedure of the Senate Committee on the Judiciary,* 94th Congress., 1st

case against the CAB, the example of these two airlines' operating intrastate routes beyond CAB jurisdiction proved to be the clincher.[84] Although such evidence had been available to academic economists for some time, the Kennedy hearings revealed it more broadly in clear, current figures.

At this point, the consensus for regulatory reform had spread. High-level bureaucrats had already started using their administrative discretion to give airlines greater flexibility. The CAB, under the new chairman John Robson, with strong staff support, advocated not just regulatory reform but full deregulation. Robson took the first step in deregulating airlines by relaxing entry restrictions. For the first time since the 1960s, the CAB allowed entry into currently served markets. Alfred Kahn, the next CAB chairman, accelerated deregulation by further reducing entry restrictions and control over fares.[85]

As a result of these CAB reforms, fares fell and industry profits went up in 1978. With such positive results from increased competition, Congress passed the Airline Deregulation Act in 1978, which called for the phased deregulation of the airline industry and pre-empted all state-level regulation of airlines. Within one year, airlines were free to serve any route. By 1980, the CAB allowed unlimited downward flexibility in fares and substantial upward flexibility and encouraged independent pricing. By 1983, airlines were operating in an unregulated environment. Later, we review the consequences of airline deregulation.

This discussion of the evolution of the airline industry has emphasized the importance that changes in thinking about the costs and benefits of regulation, combined with strong evidence from unregulated *intrastate* airline markets, played in promoting deregulation. In contrast, as we address next, moves toward deregulation in the railroads were initiated almost entirely as a consequence of industry problems.

Sessions (1975). These hearings are frequently referred to as the Kennedy Hearings.

84. McCraw, *Prophets of Regulation*, p. 266.

85. For detailed discussions of these moves toward deregulation in the 1970s, see McCraw, *Prophets of Regulation*, chap. 7; and Derthick and Quirk, *The Politics of Deregulation*.

The Move to Deregulate Railroads

As noted, the Great Depression had hit the railroads hard, and emerging competition from trucking greatly reduced railroad profits.[86] As the economic theory suggests, the railroads' first defense was to bring the trucks under regulation in 1935.[87] This change did not improve railroad industry profitability, however, and was not enough to overcome other barriers to railroad success: "Local, state and federal agencies subsidized airline expansion, through mail contracts and airport construction, and more trucking expansion, through public highway construction. The federal government paid capital and maintenance costs for inland waterways and even subsidized barge operations (some nonprofit). The railways, meanwhile, appear to have suffered from government policies."[88]

Railroad problems continued. In the 1958 Transportation Act, Congress gave the ICC greater flexibility to encourage rates more competitive with trucks and water barges and also gave the ICC additional authority to investigate *state* railroad rates even if state regulatory commissions were analyzing the same issue. By the 1960s, large portions of the railroad industry faced serious problems: even though competition eroded many markets and demographic shifts made much rail track obsolete, the ICC limited route abandonment.[89]

Despite shedding unprofitable intercity rail passenger service by the congressional establishment of Amtrak in 1970, the railroads' financial problems continued, resulting in bankruptcies of several Northeastern and Midwestern freight railroads.[90] Regulation had prevented the railroads from competing effectively. Other factors, such as high labor costs, restrictive work rules, and questionable manage-

---

86. Keeler, *Railroads, Freight and Public Policy*, p. 24.

87. Peltzman, "The Economic Theory of Regulation after a Decade of Deregulation," p. 22.

88. Childs, *Trucking and the Public Interest*, p. 42.

89. Richard Levin, "Regulation, Barriers to Exit, and the Investment Behavior of Railroads," in *Studies in Public Regulation*, ed. Gary Fromm (Cambridge, Mass.: MIT Press, 1981), p. 181.

90. Clifford Winston, Thomas Corsi, Curtis Grimm, and Carol Evans, *The Economic Effects of Surface Freight Deregulation* (Washington, D.C.: Brookings Institution, 1990), p. 6.

ment choices, also contributed to railroads' financial problems. In 1973, Congress passed the 3R Act (Regional Rail Reorganization Act), which established the United States Railway Association to help reorganize the bankrupt railroads. However, 3Rs were not enough. In 1976, the 4R Act (Railroad Revitalization and Regulatory Reform Act) subsidized Conrail, the new Northeast rail system, and provided funds for Northeast corridor passenger service. While Congress recognized the importance of fundamental changes in railroad regulation, the actual reforms in the bill, especially as implemented by the ICC, did not adequately free up the railroads.[91]

Since these efforts did not solve all industry problems, in 1980 Congress deregulated the railroads, with both industry and labor support. The Staggers Rail Act of 1980 sought to restore railroads' profitability through the market.[92] The act reduced regulation by giving rail carriers freedom to set their rates, by authorizing private shipping contracts, and by putting the burden of proof of further regulation on the ICC. Significantly, the Staggers Act preempted state authority over railroad rates, rules, and practices and provided for state regulation in these areas only if state agencies were certified by the ICC. Preemption advocates argued successfully that inconsistent state and federal standards, restrictive state regulation over intrastate rail traffic, and state regulatory lag were partly responsible for the industry's poor performance.[93]

Section 214 of the Staggers Act preempted the independent authority of state regulatory agencies over interstate rail transportation by providing that a state may exercise jurisdiction only if it does so "exclusively in accordance with the provisions" of the Interstate Commerce Act. This preemption was less extreme than the original House of Representatives' version of the Staggers Act, which eliminated any state role. Prompted by NARUC and state public utility commission pressure, however, the House adopted an amendment

91. For a full discussion of 3R and 4R, see Frederick Stephenson, *Transportation USA* (New York: Addison-Wesley, 1987), pp. 115–16.

92. The Staggers Rail Act of 1980 was passed as Public Law 96-448 on October 14, 1980, and is codified in 49 U.S.C. 10101.

93. Samuel Sipe, "Section 214 of the Staggers Act and the Preemption of State Regulation of Intrastate Rail Transportation," *Transportation Practitioners Journal*, vol. 52 (Spring 1986), p. 281.

designed to "achieve a better balance between federal regulation and state regulation."[94] Samuel Sipe notes: "As construed to date, section 214 allows the states an essentially mechanical role in regulating intrastate rail rates and practices, but precludes virtually any exercise of discretionary state authority."[95] Thus, railroad regulatory preemption is not complete; but even though state regulators retained their jobs, they have no real power.

After 1980, four states—Alabama, Illinois, Montana, and Texas—unsuccessfully challenged the constitutionality of section 214 of the Staggers Act, arguing that it exceeded congressional power under the commerce clause and violated the Tenth Amendment. The U.S. District Court for the District of Columbia and the Fifth Circuit Court rejected their claims.[96] The Fifth Circuit Court in Texas ruled:

> Section 214 of the Staggers Act clearly passes constitutional muster under the "minimum scrutiny" test required by accepted commerce clause analysis. At least since 1914, the courts have recognized that the regulation of intrastate railroad rates has a direct and substantial effect on interstate commerce. . . . The information presented to Congress during its consideration of the Staggers Act furnished ample evidence that independent state regulation of the intrastate rates of interstate rail carriers was imposing substantial costs upon those carriers.[97]

The congressional goal of uniform regulation was not an end in itself but a means to achieve a less regulated and healthier railroad industry, which would have been difficult to achieve if the states retained significant power.[98] The Staggers Act did not completely deregulate the railroads, but it did remove most ICC authority over railroad activities in which competition was already constraining railroad rates.[99]

---

94. Ibid., p. 281.

95. Ibid., p. 280.

96. Ibid., p. 284.

97. Texas v. United States, 730 F.2d at 348–349 (5th Cir. 1984).

98. Sipe, "Section 214 of the Staggers Act and the Preemption of State Regulation of Intrastate Rail Transportation," p. 297.

99. U.S. Department of Commerce, U.S. Industrial Outlook 1990 (Lanham, Md.: Bernan Press, 1990), sec. 42, p. 14.

As we shall see, the implementation of both railroad and airline deregulation achieved many objectives, eliminating expensive restrictions and returning these industries to profitability.

The Results of Deregulation and Preemption

Airlines. Deregulation of the airline industry has been a major success story for air passengers, cargo carriers, and for many airlines. Here, we review evidence of the performance of the deregulated airline industry with respect to benefits to the public, airline organization and profitability, and safety. We also briefly assess continuing problems and suggest why any form of re-regulation would be inappropriate. Most of the information is from the passenger sector, which is more extensively documented, but air cargo deregulation shows similar successes.

Before regulation, most economists believed that regulation caused fares that were too high and that, because fares were regulated and airlines competed on service, the quality of service was also too high. Fares have fallen as a result of deregulation, but while some aspects of in-flight service have declined, perhaps the most important element of service, the frequency of flights, has improved considerably.[100]

Because of deregulation, between 1976 and 1990, average passenger fares declined by 30 percent in real (inflation-adjusted) terms. The introduction of jets had caused fares to decline before 1976, but the best estimates show that deregulated fares average 10 to 18 percent lower than without deregulation. Total savings to consumers have been from $5 billion to $10 billion per year.[101] The additional benefits from improved service frequency were estimated to be $4.3 billion, in 1977 dollars, by Steven Morrison and Clifford Winston.[102]

---

100. For predicted and assessed effects of regulatory reform on prices and service, see table 3 in Clifford Winston, "Economic Deregulation: Days of Reckoning for Microeconomists," *Journal of Economic Literature*, vol. 31 (1993), pp. 1263–89.

101. For example, Steven Morrison and Clifford Winston, "The Dynamics of Airline Pricing and Competition," *American Economic Review*, vol. 80 (1990), p. 390, estimate that airline deregulation has resulted in annual savings for travelers of approximately $6 billion, in 1988 dollars.

102. Winston, "Economic Deregulation," table 3.

In the 1978 Airline Deregulation Act, Congress incorporated a direct subsidy provision for airlines serving eligible small communities, called the Essential Air Service, which remains in effect.[103] Since deregulation, however, there has been virtually no need for this provision.[104] The primary reason why service to small communities has remained stable, and in many cases improved, is the massive reorganization of route structures that the airlines have pursued since 1978.

While passengers have made significant gains from deregulation, the fate of individual airlines has been mixed. This factor has not been due entirely to deregulation. The 1979 oil price shock and the recession of 1982 reduced airline profits. After deregulation, new entry boomed and prices fell substantially, especially on long-distance routes. But then new entry fell, and many new firms and smaller carriers either merged with a major carrier or declared bankruptcy and ceased operations. Still, with route restructuring and large increases in air travel in the 1980s, Morrison and Winston have estimated that deregulation of the airline industry has produced an annual increase in profits for the airlines of about $2.5 billion (in 1977 dollars) per year.[105]

As a result of these mergers and failures, concentration in the airline industry has risen since deregulation,[106] affecting direct trips especially, in which the passenger does not change planes. This trip pattern reflects the growth of hub-and-spoke operations, which the airlines use to achieve economies of scale and scope.[107] An unanticipated consequence of deregulation is that the hub-and-spoke systems make possible nonstop and frequent service between relatively iso-

---

103. Section 419 of the Airline Deregulation Act of 1978, which amended the Federal Aviation Act of 1958.

104. Lawrence Cunningham and E. Woodrow Eckard, "US Small Community Air Service Subsidies: Essential or Superfluous?" *Journal of Transport Economics and Policy*, vol. 21 (1987), pp. 255–77.

105. Steven Morrison and Clifford Winston, *The Economic Effects of Airline Deregulation* (Washington, D.C.: Brookings Institution, 1986), p. 40.

106. See Severin Borenstein, "The Evolution of U.S. Airline Competition," *Journal of Economic Perspectives*, vol. 6 (1992), pp. 45–73.

107. For a concise explanation of the hub-and-spoke system, see Viscusi et al., *Economics of Regulation and Antitrust*, p. 535.

lated cities and hub cities.[108] Thus, passengers can fly between a wide variety of isolated cities (via the hubs) that in fact exchange only a few passengers each day. (The trade-off is that the hub-and-spoke system produces longer travel times.) Many more routes have become possible and affordable than before deregulation of airline routes.

Another byproduct of deregulation has been the strong growth of the air cargo industry, composed of airlines that specialize in providing air express or general freight service, or both. It is also made up of airlines, including passenger airlines, that provide contract, charter, or scheduled cargo services to the shipping public and to other cargo airlines. During the 1980s, competition and the need for greater efficiency spurred the creation of automated sorting hubs, supported by a network of aircraft and ground vehicles that are coordinated at the national level. During the 1980s, revenue ton miles in this sector of the airline industry grew at an annual rate of over 7 percent.[109]

Airline safety continues to be an item of debate related to deregulation. Nancy Rose notes that aggregate statistics on U.S. airline safety provide reassurance for air passengers.[110] There are many measures of airline safety, including the absolute number of fatal and nonfatal accidents; fatal and total accidents per million departures; passenger fatalities per million passengers or per million passenger miles; passenger death risk per million departures; and "incidents" (such as near midair collisions or other hazards) per million departures. Rose reports that "virtually all of these measures suggest that the long-term trend toward increased airline safety has continued since economic deregulation of the airline industry in 1978."[111]

---

108. Levine, "Airline Competition in Deregulated Markets," p. 411.

109. U.S. Department of Commerce, *U.S. Industrial Outlook 1994*, p. 40–42.

110. Nancy Rose, "Fear of Flying? Economic Analyses of Airline Safety," *Journal of Economic Perspectives*, vol. 6 (1992), pp. 75–94.

111. See also Clinton Oster and C. K. Zorn, "Airline Deregulation: Is It Still Safe to Fly?" in Leon Moses and Ian Savage, eds., *Transportation Safety in an Age of Deregulation* (Oxford: Oxford University Press, 1989). These authors demonstrate that between the "regulated" (1971–1978) and "deregulated" (1979–1985) periods, total accidents per million departures for trunk and local service carriers declined by 54 percent. Accident rates due to pilot or controllers' error, equipment failure,

In sum, airline deregulation has worked, and with considerable benefits for passengers and for airlines that adapted. Admittedly, the world of deregulated airlines is more complex than imagined by the original proponents of deregulation. The airline market will never evolve to a perfectly competitive or perfectly contestable market, but then almost no real-world market does. Thus sources of economic rent, such as strong positions at key hub airports, will remain.[112] As Alfred Kahn, Michael Levine, and others have concluded,[113] these market imperfections should not be seen as justification for any form of re-regulation of the airline industry. In many cases, such problems could be addressed through making better use of current policy or by seeking to bring market forces to bear on additional elements of the industry, particularly the management of airport operations and airspace.[114]

Railroads. Regulatory reform in the railroad industry provided a transition from one of the most heavily regulated settings in American industry before the 1970s to a largely market-oriented system afterward. The Staggers Act of 1980 substantially relaxed controls over rates, allowed railroads to enter into long-term contracts with shippers, eased merger guidelines, and facilitated abandonment of unprofitable branch lines. Some regulation remains, however, primarily to protect shippers of specific products, such as coal and grain, where sunk costs are considerable and the railroads still hold powers of a natural monopoly.

Several general trends and consequences have followed from

---

and other aircraft declined by this amount or more, topped by a 71 percent reduction in accidents due to causes under a carrier's control after deregulation.

112. For a useful discussion, see Elizabeth Bailey and Jeffrey Williams, "Sources of Economic Rent in the Deregulated Airline Industry," *Journal of Law and Economics*, vol. 31 (1988), pp. 173–202.

113. See, for example, Alfred Kahn, "Surprises of Airline Deregulation," *American Economics Review, Papers and Proceedings*, vol. 78 (1988), pp. 316–22; Robert Hahn and Randall Kroszner, "The Mismanagement of Air Transport: A Supply-Side Analysis," *The Public Interest*, vol. 95 (1989), pp. 100–11; and Levine, "Competition in Deregulated Airline Markets."

114. See also National Governors' Association, *Airport Expansion and Preservation: The State Role* (Washington, D.C.: NGA Center for Policy Research, 1990), for a discussion of the state role in airport facilities.

deregulation in the railroad industry. These include the effect on rates, shipper benefits, railroad organization and profitability, industry infrastructure, freight market share, and labor and safety issues. Here, we discuss briefly these consequences in turn.

The Staggers Act did not completely deregulate the railroad industry, and the ICC retained the ability to regulate maximum rates. The commission, however, reduced its authority in areas where competition limits railroad rates. Now, more than three-quarters of freight traffic is not subject to maximum rate regulation, either because competition has kept rates at levels below the threshold for ICC authority or because the ICC exempted the traffic altogether. Traffic moving in boxcars and trailers on flatcars, for example, is exempted. In addition, the commission exempted many agricultural and manufactured commodities (including most lumber and wood products and transportation equipment), after determining that competition protected shippers. In the past few years, an average of less than a dozen new rate complaints and protests have been filed per year, about 4 percent of the annual average rate of nearly 300 rate complaints or protests before the Staggers Act.[115]

The Staggers Act allowed railroads and shippers for the first time to enter into confidential, legally binding contracts covering rail rates and services. These contracts must be filed with the ICC, but the specific rates and conditions are not disclosed publicly. Only a very general summary is released to the public. Now, most rail traffic moves under contract.

Since 1980, freight rates have declined by an annual rate of approximately 1.5 percent, compared with increases of 3 percent per year in the five years before 1980.[116] As Wesley Wilson has shown, however, aggregate analysis of rates masks significant differences in rates across commodities.[117] Initially, the majority of commodity rates rose after deregulation, reflecting greater market power. By 1988, however, deregulation produced lower prices for most commodities and did not increase prices for others, suggesting that advances in

---

115. U.S. Department of Commerce, *U.S. Industrial Outlook 1990*, sec. 42, p. 14.

116. U.S. Department of Commerce, *U.S. Industrial Outlook 1994* (Lanham, Md.: Bernan Press, 1994), sec. 40, p. 45.

117. Wesley Wilson, "Market-specific Effects of Rail Deregulation," *Journal of Industrial Economics*, vol. 42 (1994), pp. 1–22.

productivity dominated any adverse market power effects. Wilson concludes that while differences exist across commodities, the effect of deregulation has generally been to lower rates.

According to studies by Winston et al., the major benefits from railroad deregulation have not come from rate reductions.[118] Rather, railroads have generated benefits by making significant *service* improvements, particularly in the speed of freight delivery. They estimated these improvements to be worth nearly $5 billion per year. According to their studies, railroad rate deregulation has resulted in a reorganization of rates; rates have fallen for grain shipments but risen for coal shipments.

Some shippers—particularly coal-consuming electric utilities—continue to lobby for tightened regulatory controls, through either ICC action or additional legislation. They fear that the present system of regulation will not effectively limit railroad rates or provide adequate competitive service options. Thus, bills have been introduced in Congress every year since 1983 to change railroad regulation, but with opposition from the railroads and the Federal Railroad Administration, these efforts to make legislative cutbacks in the Staggers Act have all failed.[119]

With deregulation and preemption of state regulation, the railroads have been able to abandon thousands of miles of track and to merge operations.[120] In 1994, there were just 10 Class I (large) railroads, down from 73 in 1975, which operated 82 percent of the system mileage and employed over 90 percent of the industry labor force.[121] At the same time, there has been remarkable growth in smaller railroads, from 212 in 1980 to 550 by 1994.[122] Many of these

---

118. Winston et al., *The Economic Effects of Surface Freight Deregulation*, p. 28.

119. U.S. Department of Commerce, *U.S. Industrial Outlook 1990*, p. 42-15.

120. For a detailed analysis of managerial practices, including mergers, and their impact on railroad firm performance, see Ann Friedlaender, Ernst Berndt, and Gerard McCullough, "Governance Structure, Managerial Characteristics, and Firm Performance in the Deregulated Rail Industry," *Brookings Papers: Microeconomics*, 1992, pp. 95–186.

121. See Winston et al., *The Economic Effects of Surface Freight Deregulation*, p. 11.

122. Lisa Burgess, "Both Sides in ICC Debate Cite Rail Role in Arguments," *Journal of Commerce*, July 14, 1994, p. 1A.

developed from sales by Class I railroads of lines upon which traffic had declined to the smaller, lower-cost operators who could make a profit on them, in part because of changes in labor protection rules. These short-line operators have improved service to local shippers, while continuing to feed traffic to the major railroads. [123]

Railroad productivity measured by revenue ton miles per employee continues to increase faster than almost any other industry, doubling between 1983 and 1992. Many of these productivity gains result from greater efficiencies in staffing, [124] allowing railroad companies to compete successfully with trucks and barges for the first time in decades.

Since the Staggers Act, both the number of railroad employees and their wages have decreased. In 1977, the Class I railroads (including Amtrak) employed almost 483,000 people; by 1993, employment fell by more than 50 percent, to 215,000. [125] Railroad labor has also suffered wage losses. [126] The Association of American Railroads estimates that, factoring in various work rule concessions and resulting improvements in labor productivity, wages under deregulation are at least 20 percent lower than they were under regulation.

The greater control that railroads now have over capital investment and disinvestment has allowed new innovations in infrastructure, [127] particularly in intermodal operations. These are shipments where freight is carried in a box that can be passed from one form of

---

123. U.S. Department of Commerce, *U.S. Industrial Outlook 1994*, p. 40-6.

124. Ibid., p. 40-5.

125. Employment figures are from the Annual Reports of Class I carriers to the ICC.

126. Winston et al., *The Economic Effects of Surface Freight Deregulation*, pp. 39–40.

127. Ronald Braeutigam, "Consequences of Regulatory Reform in the American Railroad Industry," *Southern Economic Journal*, vol. 59 (1993), p. 480, notes:
The new flexibilities afforded railroads in setting rates, in offering contracts tailored to shippers' needs, and in structuring routes and service offerings based on market conditions have helped many railroads escape the serious financial plight of the early 1970s. Rates of return on equity and on investment have risen. . . . To be sure, there are problems that remain. Most railroads are still revenue inadequate, and there is therefore still concern that railroads cannot attract capital they need to provide improved services in the long run at the current industry size.

transportation to another (for example, ship to train or train to truck or truck to train). Rail intermodal traffic more than doubled from 3.1 million trailers and containers in 1980 to 6.7 million in 1992. This is a direct result of deregulation, since in 1981 the ICC exempted intermodal traffic from rate regulation. The railroads in 1984 introduced specialized railcars with depressed platforms that double-stacked (two high) containers. According to one estimate, this innovation alone has reduced the cost of transporting a railroad container by 30–45 percent.[128] Containers from Pacific Rim shipping can now move rapidly through West Coast ports to inland destinations on such double-stacked trains, carrying exports and domestic traffic on the backhaul. Double-stacked cars now account for approximately 40 percent of total intermodal capacity and 80 percent of containers.[129]

Combined with the ability to enter into long-term contracts, the exemption of intermodal traffic from rate regulation has led to the emergence of third-party brokers, or intermodal marketing companies, that charter space from railroads and organize shipments to and from the terminals with small independent truckers.[130] Such competitive and efficient transportation service enables manufacturing firms to improve inventory management and implement just-in-time production techniques.

The management changes and technological innovations discussed here have allowed the railroads to stabilize their share of intercity freight transportation. From 1980 to 1990, the industry maintained an approximate share of 37 percent of intercity freight traffic, measured in ton miles.[131] While this is still far below the shares of earlier decades, the long-term decline has been stopped.

Despite fears voiced before deregulation, as with airlines, safety has improved in the railroad industry. The greater flexibility and control railroads were given led to more investment in plant and equipment, as well as technological improvements such as electronic

---

128. See *Economist*, November 27, 1993, p. 65. This figure is attributed to Ashok Boghani, a transport expert with Arthur D. Little.

129. U.S. Department of Commerce, *U.S. Industrial Outlook 1994*, sec. 40, p. 5.

130. See ICC Office of Economics, *The U.S. Motor Carrier Industry Long after Deregulation* (Washington, D.C.: 1992), pp. 92–93.

131. Braeutigam, "Consequences of Regulatory Reform in the Railroad Industry," p. 473.

switching. These technological improvements have reduced the potential for accidents. The safety statistics of the Federal Railroad Administration indicate that the number of accidents caused by track defects declined almost 50 percent between 1982 and 1987.[132]

Deregulation has allowed the railroads to improve their financial health and their facilities. Shippers and the general public have gained from reductions in freight rates as well as improvements in service. The only losers from deregulation are those who gained from tight regulation, primarily railroad workers and a small number of shippers, who might have done as poorly under a strictly regulated but continued weak railroad industry. Although the railroads are still not in perfect financial health, deregulation has certainly made them much more viable over the long run, which is reflected in their steady market share in the face of strong competition.

Conclusions

This historical overview of transportation regulation, deregulation, and federalism illustrates several common themes across different modes. The first is that the public sector, federal and state, has long played a role in these transportation industries and that a completely market-based transportation sector has never existed. Government subsidies were important for the initial promotion and subsequent development and expansion of most of these industries. Federal and state governments provided or purchased land for railroad tracks and for highways. They provided rights of way, and some federal and state governments have actually constructed highways and airport facilities. The federal government also funded research into transportation technologies and guaranteed markets to infant industries, such as railroads and airlines, through the use of postal routes. Today, however, governments have reduced or eliminated many of these roles, leaving the private sector to do most of what needs to be continued, and evidence strongly suggests that trend is working. To achieve this goal of reduced public involvement, the federal government has usually had to force or preempt the states from continuing their regulation.

---

132. General Accounting Office, *The Impact of the Staggers Act on the Railroad Industry*, pp. 29–30.

A second common theme is that economies of scale were used to justify government regulations of rates, routes, and services. Railroads created one of the first industries that exploited large-scale economies. Charles Francis Adams and others struggled with how to trade off efficiency issues for concerns about market concentration and pricing power. Their choice was rate and entry regulation in railroads and other industries (such as telecommunications and electricity) with these characteristics. Ironically, trucking did *not* show significant economies of scale, although larger trucking firms can handle backhaul and deadhead problems more efficiently. As Thomas Gale Moore noted: "Virtually from the date the Motor Carrier Act passed, economists have criticized the idea of regulating such an inherently competitive industry."[133] While there are some economies of scale in water freight and airline freight transport, these industries are clearly not monopolies.

Closely related to scale economies has been the issue of collective rate making, with firms trying to create and maintain cartels to stabilize their markets and profits. American regulation has often allowed and encouraged collective rate making, explicitly exempting these firms from antitrust laws in 1948, for example. These rate bureaus or rate conferences, as they are commonly called, are still used in trucking and in maritime shipping regulated by the Federal Maritime Commission.

Partly as a result of presumed economies of scale and partly because trucking and airlines in particular grew substantially in the 1930s when America's faith in markets was at a low ebb, the idea of "destructive competition" has often been used to justify regulation that sets rates and limits entry. Virtually all modern economists dispute this argument that firms will not operate safely in order to engage in price wars, resulting in frequent bankruptcies, service disruptions, and monopolies. While there have been periodic price wars and firm bankruptcies in transportation sectors, these phenomena show that they are risky industries, like many others in the American economy, but not necessarily that strict regulation is required.[134]

---

133. Thomas Gale Moore, "Deregulating Transportation: Tracking the Progress," *Regulation*, vol. 4 (1978), p. 41.

134. Although much recent evidence refutes this argument, it still is used, as it was in the debate over intrastate trucking re-regulation in California in the 1980s. See Dan Baker, "Your Letter of the Law," Transportation Lawyers Association.

Closely related to destructive competition is the safety issue. All these transportation modes can cause accidents that harm goods and people in transit, as well as people not being transported. Since the 1920s, for example, automobile motorists have been concerned about the safety of large trucks on the roads with incentives to drive fast to their destination. One fear of deregulation in all these industries was that firms would reduce maintenance of their vehicles, competition would spur unsafe transportation practices, and more accidents would result. As we noted in our discussion of the consequences of airline and railroad deregulation, and as chapter 3 illustrates for trucking, these problems have, in fact, *declined* since industry deregulation, in part due to continuing safety monitoring by federal agencies.

A motif that pervades several of these themes, and one that is often unrecognized by proponents of economic regulation, is that the market itself is an extremely rigorous regulator. The need to meet consumer demands on a range of dimensions forces suppliers to act competitively and to introduce innovations in their operations. As our discussion of the airline and railroad industries made clear, the increased managerial flexibility and competition that deregulation allowed have produced significant technological and organizational innovations that not even deregulation advocates foresaw. Deregulation works, and preemption or reduction of state regulation helps reduce regulation. This point has perhaps been best made by Alfred Kahn: "The essence of the case for competition is the impossibility of predicting most of its consequences. The superiority of the competitive market is the positive stimuli it provides for constantly improving efficiency, innovating, and offering consumers a diversity of choices."[135]

Several of these themes show that economic ideas evolved considerably over time and that these ideas influenced policy choices made in Washington, D.C., and in the state capitals. But politics also shaped regulatory and deregulatory choices at both the federal and state levels. As proponents of the economic theory argue, interest groups sought policy changes to their benefit at both levels, with

---

135. Alfred Kahn, "Deregulation and Vested Interests: The Case of Airlines," in Roger Noll and Bruce Owen, eds., *The Political Economy of Deregulation* (Washington, D.C.: American Enterprise Institute, 1983), p. 140.

some success at various times. Political institutions, including Congress, the president, the regulatory agencies they created, and the courts, actively influenced regulations. Transportation regulatory policies resulted from a complex interplay of interest groups, institutions, and ideas.

Bearing in mind these themes in regulatory federalism and lessons from other deregulated transportation sectors, in subsequent chapters we focus our discussion exclusively on the trucking industry. We begin our examination of the industry with an analysis, in the next chapter, of the evolution of interstate trucking, focusing on the changes stimulated by the deregulatory 1980 Motor Carrier Act.

3

Interstate Trucking Deregulation

Employment has plummeted from roughly two thousand to seven hundred, the number of commissioners has shrunk from eleven to five, and the budget has been cut by more than 60 percent in real terms. Stopping by the commission [ICC], with its rows of vacant offices and corridors of empty halls, is akin to visiting a dying relative: One often wishes for the end to come swiftly and painlessly.
—LAWRENCE ROTHENBERG, *Regulation, Organizations, and Politics*

In the previous chapter, we traced the early historical development of state and federal trucking regulation and linked it to the development of railroad and airline regulation. For the remainder of the book, we focus almost entirely on trucking and the effects of regulatory federalism. Thus, we begin this chapter with a brief overview of the nature of the trucking industry and how its various sectors are typically classified. Next, we discuss the main features of interstate trucking regulation as it was actually administered in the forty-odd years following passage of the Motor Carrier Act of 1935. Familiarity with the details of interstate trucking regulation during that period remains essential for understanding recent regulatory approaches, because, until the 1994 preemption, many *states* continued to emulate that federal regulatory regime in their imposition of *intrastate* trucking regulations. (We discuss intrastate trucking regulations extensively in chapters 4 and 5.) Having explored interstate trucking regulation as it was formerly practiced, we detail the criticisms of that regulatory regime that ultimately contributed to the Motor Carrier Act (MCA) of 1980.

Next, we outline the major provisions of the deregulatory MCA of 1980. We then discuss the effects of regulatory reform on the interstate trucking industry. These effects include important changes in industry structure, changes in the demand for and supply of labor in the industry, significant productivity gains, and improvements in the outcomes for shippers and consumers. Finally in this chapter, we discuss some important recent changes in interstate trucking regulation. The remaining interstate regulatory apparatus is considerably less problematic than that in force before 1980.

The Nature of the Trucking Industry

Since trucking developed into a reliable way to move freight in the early twentieth century, the technology of the industry has changed little. Sectors of the industry are differentiated primarily by management arrangements and institutional rules rather than by production techniques. Typically, the trucking industry is classified according to two main dimensions: types of contract and types of carriage. Interestingly, although these classifications have some relationship to technological issues, their origins can be traced directly to the regulatory regime in which the industry developed. Here, we explain briefly the meaning of these classifications, and we discuss the regulatory origins of these classifications in the section that follows.

Suppose a firm needs to ship freight by truck. The firm's shipping managers could consider several options before choosing the one that minimizes costs, or maximizes other values, such as speed of transportation or security of the transported goods. This decision leads to one of three main types of arrangements.

First, the firm could vertically integrate production and shipping by retaining its own fleet of trucks. This arrangement is classified as private trucking. Over 50 percent of American trucking is provided privately. Essentially, private trucking services are similar to within-plant transfers using conveyor belts or forklifts. Private trucking is the preferred arrangement when equipment is so specialized as to be useful only to a single purchaser of transportation services. In such cases, there are no savings in using this same trucking equipment to serve more than one shipper.[1] Specialized trucking equipment is often used, for example, in construction, lumbering, agriculture, and mining, as well as for transport of automobiles. Private trucking is also favored when firms have regular shipping patterns of full truck-

---

1. Kenneth Boyer, "Deregulation of the Trucking Sector: Specialization, Concentration, Entry, and Financial Distress," *Southern Economic Journal*, vol. 59 (1993), pp. 481–95.

load amounts and can fill their own trucks with their own goods for the backhaul.

Second, the shipper could enter a long-term contracting arrangement with a trucking firm that will integrate its trucking operations with the firm's day-to-day operations. This is called contract carriage.[2] As with private trucking, contract carriage is more likely to be used when the firm has specialized trucking needs. The initial decision whether to integrate vertically or to write a long-term contract would depend on demand and supply conditions in the trucking market, frequency of shipments, and the specificity of the required equipment. Contract-carrier trucking firms typically contract to just a few shippers at a time, and over the years before deregulation, regulations limited the number of contracts for a single carrier.

Finally, instead of using private trucking or a contract carrier, the firm could ship its goods using a general for-hire or common-carrier trucking firm. As Kenneth Boyer explains: "When there is no need for specialized equipment, it is generally less expensive for a firm to hire trucking services than to provide the service for itself. The for-hire industry exists for using transportation capacity on backhauls and for increasing the load factor on equipment that would be idle because of seasonal or stochastic shipping patterns. For-hire carriers are generally more able than private truckers to fill vehicles on their return trips. Thus, even if a shipper has a truckload lot to ship in one direction, it may still be worthwhile to hire a trucking company to perform the service than to use its own trucks."[3]

Thus, shippers who want to move freight by truck have three options. Private carriage has generally been unregulated, although the Interstate Commerce Commission (ICC) tried to regulate it at various times, as did a few states. As chapter 2 illustrated, contract and common carriage were both strictly regulated before 1980, and the distinctions between them were important to regulators.

The second dimension used to classify sectors of the trucking

2. According to Lawrence Rothenberg, *Regulation, Organizations, and Politics*, p. 56, the concept of contract carriage was developed initially in Texas and was subsequently incorporated into federal motor carrier regulation to prevent these carriers from gaining competitive advantage. This principle was upheld by the Supreme Court in *Stephenson v. Binford*.

3. Boyer, "Deregulation of the Trucking Sector," p. 483.

industry relates to the type of carriage, and it further differentiates common-carrier trucking firms. Industry classification of this dimension is determined primarily by the weight and volume of the freight to be shipped.

There are three important categories: truckload (TL), less-than-truckload (LTL), and small packages.[4] Carriers usually haul TL freight directly from sender to receiver, without going through sorting terminals. The freight itself ranges from raw materials to finished goods. The largest TL firms today include Schneider National and J. B. Hunt.

The LTL sector of the industry specializes in transporting shipments of less than 10,000 pounds. LTL shipments often involve five different activities: local pickup, sorting at a terminal facility, line haul, sorting at a destination terminal, and local delivery. The LTL market uses sophisticated sorting terminals, local pickup and delivery service, and regional and national networks. Many LTL carriers formerly carried packages as an element of their smaller LTL business, but most of this traffic has now been captured by small package and package express carriers. The largest LTL firms today include Yellow, Consolidated, and Roadway.

Carriers in the small-packages sector handle parcels that weigh less than 150 pounds. Most of these carriers use intermodal freight transporting methods such as truck to airplane to truck, or truck to train to truck. Small-package service includes the two–three day delivery market originated and long dominated by United Parcel Service (UPS). The "package express" market, similar to the small-package business, is essentially the next-day air delivery market for documents and other small shipments that Federal Express originated. Although it is dominated by air cargo companies or by firms with air cargo operations, it is similar in some ways to the LTL and small-package markets. And, to blur the limits of these classifications further, most major LTL firms have recently developed or purchased package express operations, with Roadway developing a subsidiary in 1985 and Consolidated purchasing Emery in 1989.

---

4. The following discussion of the various types of carriage is informed by Interstate Commerce Commission, *The U.S. Motor Carrier Industry Long after Deregulation*, A Report by the Office of Economics (Washington, D.C.: Interstate Commerce Commission, 1992), pp. 68–70.

This summary illustrates the different sectors of the trucking industry. Although there are further breakdowns that could be made, such as general versus specialized carriers or regional versus nationwide carriers, these major distinctions, even though they are themselves becoming less clear with deregulation, do provide an overview. Next, we examine in more detail trucking regulations, leading toward the changes in 1980.

Interstate Trucking Regulation after 1935

As noted in chapter 2, regulation of interstate trucking started with the MCA of 1935, which had four goals: (1) a stable trucking industry with controlled carrier competition; (2) minimal duplication of services and facilities; (3) reasonable, stable, and nondiscriminatory rates; and (4) dependable service by financially sound carriers.[5] To achieve these goals, the MCA granted the ICC broad authority to regulate carrier prices and to control entry into and exit from interstate trucking markets. For forty years, the ICC used this authority to limit competition within the industry. Furthermore, the MCA became a model for state-level policy makers to follow in developing intrastate regulations. Thus, the trucking industry evolved within the context of a strict regulatory regime, much of which still remained at the intrastate level until 1945.

The MCA gave the ICC three major forms of regulation: control over entry, rates, and mergers. Of the three carrier groups, common carriers faced the most regulation.[6] We now explore how each of these carrier groups was regulated.

---

5. Michael Pustay, "Deregulation and the U S Trucking Industry," in *The Age of Regulatory Reform,* Kenneth Button and Dennis Swann, eds. (Oxford: Clarendon Press, 1989), p. 237.

6. In developing the following discussion of the regulatory arrangements established under the Motor Carrier Act of 1935, we draw upon Rothenberg, *Regulation, Organizations, and Politics,* in appendix 2-1, pp. 55–57. For further details of the provisions of the 1935 MCA, see also Parker McCollester and Frank Clark, *Federal Motor Carrier Regulation: Analysis and Annotated Interpretation of the Federal Motor Carrier Act of 1935* (New York: Traffic Publishing Company, 1935); and Warren Wagner, *A Legislative History of the Motor Carrier Act, 1935* (Denton, Md.: Roe Publishing, 1935).

Treatment of Common Carriers. The MCA defined a common carrier as "any person which holds itself out to the general public to engage in the transportation by motor vehicle in interstate or foreign commerce of passengers or property or any class or classes thereof for compensation, whether over regular or irregular routes." The act required that all common carriers own operating certificates, to be issued by the ICC under a "grandfather clause" to all common-carrier truckers in operation in 1935. Certificates were to be granted in the future only if the applicant could prove that the proposed service would contribute to the "public convenience and necessity" and if the firm were "fit, willing, and able" to provide the service in question. This was meant to address concerns about "destructive competition."

This rule essentially required potential entrants to prove that incumbent carriers were unable or unwilling to provide the particular service.[7] If an incumbent carrier protested the application, as frequently happened, the applicant would face an expensive, if not impossible, task of proving the unwillingness and inability of the incumbent to provide service. Since most major markets were already being served, it was extremely difficult for new trucking firms to enter major trucking markets.

All ICC-issued certificates indicated the services common carriers could provide, including the commodities or classes of commodities that they could carry, over which particular routes. The ICC could also decide the exact highway routes carriers had to follow, including intermediate stopping points. These certificates could be bought and sold, and researchers estimated that $600 million in certificates had been transacted by 1977. They were estimated to have an aggregate market value of $2–4 billion.[8] John Snow and Stephen Sobotka estimated that 3–5 percent of rates that shippers paid went directly to pay for the value of these certificates.[9]

---

7. Pustay, "Deregulation and the U.S. Trucking Industry," pp. 238–39.

8. Thomas Gale Moore, *Freight Transportation Regulation* (Washington, D.C.: American Enterprise Institute, 1972) provided an estimate of $2–3 billion, which John Snow and Stephen Sobotka, "Certificate Values," in Paul MacAvoy and John Snow, eds., *Regulation of Entry and Pricing in Truck Transportation* (Washington, D.C.: American Enterprise Institute, 1977), p. 153, raised to $4 billion.

9. Snow and Sobotka, "Certificate Values," p. 153.

Entry was the really critical element of ICC control. Rothenberg argues: "Motor carrier entry occupied 80 to 85 percent of the commission's total time. In comparison, mergers required far less attention, while rates merited even less because they were largely self-governing."[10] Between 1935 and 1980, out of 89,000 initial entry applications, only about 30 percent were approved by the ICC.[11]

The MCA did give the ICC broad authority over common-carrier rates. All rates were supposed to be reasonable and not unjustly discriminatory. Common carriers had to file their tariffs with the ICC and had to give thirty days' notice before making rate changes. The ICC could investigate rate changes as a result of a protest or on its own initiative, and it could suspend rates for up to seven months. If the ICC determined that a rate violated the just and reasonable requirement, it could then force the rate to be changed.

In reality, the ICC did not actively regulate trucking rates.[12] Most rates were filed by regional trucking cartels, or "rate bureaus," which submitted to the ICC the rates approved by member firms. Because millions of rates were filed each year, ICC review was minimal. Thus, these cartels were often able to set prices at levels at which they could earn healthy profits. Legally, the rate-setting cartels avoided challenges because rate bureaus were granted immunity from antitrust laws under the Reed-Bulwinkle Act of 1948. And, economically, because of the ICC's strict entry policies, the rate bureaus were never subject to real competition.

The rate-making process that evolved out of the 1935 MCA severely restricted competition. After freight was "classified" by the truckers' classification conferences, rates for each type of class of freight were determined. This was the primary function of the rate bureaus. From time to time, truckers wanted to change rates. There were two main types of rate changes. General rate changes applied to all types of freight classifications, shifting prices across the board. Selective rate changes, which involved deviations from the general rate structure, usually applied to a particular movement for a single shipper or class of shippers.

---

10. Rothenberg, *Regulation, Organizations, and Politics*, p. 117.

11. Milton Friedman and Rose Friedman, *Free to Choose* (New York: Avon Books, 1979), p. 188.

12. Pustay, "Deregulation and the U.S. Trucking Industry," p. 239.

After 1971, when the ICC prescribed criteria and methodologies for justifying general rate increases, the procedures were standardized across all rate bureaus.[13] This usually entailed four steps. First, the bureau performed a traffic study, detailing the volume of movement for truckers over a given period. These figures were based on statistically stratified samples of responding carriers' freight bills. While carriers were not obligated to participate, most did, as they wanted to support rate increases. Second, average costs were applied to determine the level of profitability for various types of carrier traffic. Third, the rate bureau evaluated carrier needs, taking into account future projections of productivity and anticipated changes in fuel prices and in labor expenses. Finally, the bureau proposed rate changes to target prices to preset operating ratios. Upon completion of this process, the rate proposals were forwarded to a committee of member carriers, known as the general rate committee. They voted on these recommendations with majority rule, and, subject to typically minimal ICC overview, tariff changes would then be posted and implemented.

Individual carriers could propose selective rate changes at any time, and most such proposals involved requests for rate decreases. Before 1980, such proposals were forwarded to a rate bureau's standing rate committee, which set up a public hearing on the proposal, about which interested parties were informed through their subscription to the rate bureau's docket service. At the hearings, any party could participate, regardless of whether they were directly affected by the freight movement under consideration. The standing rate committee then issued a report recommending acceptance or rejection, which parties could appeal to the general rate committee. If approved and not appealed within five days, these changes were allowed.[14]

At any point during these procedures, a carrier could bypass the collective rate-making process and file an "independent action." Before 1980, most rate bureaus required that independent actions be advertised in their dockets for a short period before taking effect to

---

13. Ex Parte No. MC-82, *Proposed New Procedures in Motor Carrier Revenue Proceedings*, 339 ICC 324 (1971); 340 ICC (1971); 351 ICC 1 (1975).

14. See Motor Carrier Ratemaking Study Commission, *Collective Ratemaking in the Trucking Industry: A Report to the President and the Congress of the United States* (Washington, D.C.: Government Printing Office, June 1983), especially pp. 102–7.

allow time for "flag-ins," which were cases where other carriers decided to join in this new rate. After this period, the independent actions were published for both the initiating carrier and any subsequent joiners.

While both selective rate changes and independent actions were theoretically designed to be a competitive check on the bureau's rate structure, in reality the system rarely operated in this way. Requests to the standing rate committee frequently met with opposition from other carriers, sometimes causing the ICC to scrutinize the proposed rate, and making rate changes exceedingly difficult. The ICC might then choose to suspend the rate and call for a formal investigation of its legality. The possibility of getting involved in an expensive rate hearing often discouraged truckers from filing independent actions in the first place.[15] Similarly, by allowing other carriers to match rates, independent actions brought with them an implicit incentive not to lower prices. In fact, a greater proportion of independent actions were "rule" changes (adjustments to the applicability of certain rules to particular types of freight movements) or flag-ins than rate adjustments.[16] Joe Sims cites several stories of automatic protests of independent actions, even if protestants were not involved in the particular case. The most interesting story involved thirteen carriers protesting a proposed new rate for "yak fat," a nonexistent commodity.[17]

John Shenefield, assistant attorney general, testified to Congress in 1977 that

> because of this loaded regulatory scheme, trying to lower rates in the trucking industry is not merely a business decision; it is a decision to go to war—to litigate—for those who would lower rates will inevitably face vigorous protests from rate bureau members. The process guarantees great delay, cost, and uncertainty as to outcome, and serves to

---

15. Pustay, "Deregulation and the US Trucking Industry," p. 242.

16. U.S. Congress, Senate Committee on the Judiciary, *Federal Restraints on Competition in the Trucking Industry: Antitrust Immunity and Economic Regulation*, 96th Congress, 2nd sess. (Washington, D.C.: GPO, 1980), p. 6.

17. Joe Sims, "Inedible Tallow, the Maximum Charges Rule, and Other Fables: Motor Carrier Regulation by the ICC," *Transportation Law Journal*, vol. 10 (1978), pp. 55–66.

depress—indeed to strangle—the entrepreneurial initiative which has been the great strength of American business. For any intelligent trucker, this system carries with it a simple message: don't lower prices.

As a result, carriers adhered to the general rate structure most of the time. All of these complicated procedures and ICC involvement helped the truckers to achieve effective cartel management.[18]

Under the MCA, the ICC also had the power to oversee mergers and acquisitions of trucking firms. The commission was supposed to protect the public interest by considering the effects that mergers would have on the provision of services (both inter- and intrastate), operating costs, and the interests of all relevant employees. As a result of strict entry limitations, attrition, and mergers, the number of ICC-certified carriers actually decreased from about 18,000 in 1935 to 15,000 in 1977.[19] The ICC still holds the power to oversee mergers and acquisitions.

Treatment of Contract Carriers. The MCA gave the ICC less authority over contract carriers than it had over common carriers. Initial rights to be contract carriers were given to all those previously in operation when the MCA was passed. Mergers and acquisitions of contract carriers were also to be approved by the ICC if they were in the public interest.

Contract carriers had significantly more freedom in setting routes and rates than common carriers. Rather than the operating certificates needed by common carriers to serve specific routes, contract carriers needed only permits, for which they had to show that they were providing service in the public interest. Thus, contract carrier entry was easier than common carriage entry. Similarly, only minimum rates were subject to commission scrutiny.

The ICC upheld minimum rates for contract carriers to protect common carriers from their competition. In 1957, common carriers pressured successfully for legislation that required contractors to file

---

18. See Stigler, "The Theory of Economic Regulation"; and Friedman and Friedman, *Free to Choose*.

19. John Snow, "The Problem of Motor Carrier Regulation and the Ford Administration's Proposal for Reform," in MacAvoy and Snow, eds., *Regulation of Entry and Pricing in Truck Transportation*, p. 19.

their actual rates with the ICC, which allowed common carriers to file protests against these rates and get the ICC to overrule their implementation. Generally, the ICC favored the common carriers in these disputes with contract carriers.[20]

Treatment of "Unregulated" Carriers. Under the 1935 MCA, unregulated carriers were immune from all but safety regulations. Unregulated carriage has generally accounted for more than half the trucking market. These carriers included six main groups:

- private trucking fleets vertically integrated with manufacturers or retailers
- motor vehicles owned by railroads, water carriers, and freight forwarders
- carriers operating totally within local "commercial zones"[21]
- motor vehicles carrying unprocessed fish, livestock, or agricultural commodities
- trucks carrying newspapers
- trucks owned and operated by agricultural cooperatives when carrying farmers' goods to and from the cooperatives

Still, over time, the ICC often tried to limit the effectiveness of competition that private or exempt carriers provided for common and contract carriers. Rothenberg notes: "ICC antipathy for private carriers manifested itself in two ways. First, the agency reacted quickly whenever it believed that private operators were moving into the arena reserved for common and contract truckers. . . . Second, the ICC, urged on by its regulatees, constantly tried to extend the scope of regulated carriage."[22] This behavior provides further evidence of capture of the ICC by the regulated interests.

---

20. See Rothenberg, *Regulation, Organizations, and Politics*, p. 207.

21. Commercial zones have been changed and expanded over time. The current exemption is for trucking within a base municipality, within all contiguous municipalities, and other municipalities located within a certain distance from the base municipality. That distance varies depending on the size of the base municipality. For municipalities of 2,500 people or less, it is 3 miles, while it ranges up to 20 miles for municipalities with more than 1 million population.

22. Rothenberg, *Regulation, Organizations, and Politics*, p. 137.

Critiques of Interstate Trucking Regulation. The 1935 MCA and its implementation through ICC regulation produced monopoly profits, excessive costs, and inflexibility. With strong support from truckers, however, this regulatory regime stayed intact for almost forty years. In his discussion of ICC trucking regulation throughout this period, Lawrence Rothenberg notes:

> as a regulatory commission the ICC was characterized by progressive, and fairly quick, decline from an entity that merited great respect through most of the first half of the century to one that was the object of ridicule by the middle to late 1960s. . . . The agency was increasingly perceived by those in the regulatory and larger governmental arenas as an uninteresting, anachronistic establishment run by political dependents and an entrenched bureaucracy.[23]

Between 1935 and 1980, the ICC did not simply reinforce the relative positions of competing transportation modes. Rather, the ICC's rulings illustrated two major biases.[24] First, in addition to market forces pushing in this direction, the ICC favored the growth of the trucking industry at the expense of the railroads. The ICC made regulatory concessions to the railroads only after they began fading in importance. Second, within the regulated trucking industry, the ICC assisted most LTL carriers of general freight that ran over regular routes. Rothenberg suggests that the ICC had a three-level hierarchy with LTL carriers most favored, followed by railroads and contract carriers, with unregulated and private carriers at the bottom.[25]

In particular, the groups that received the greatest benefits from this regulatory regime were the original owners of ICC operating

23. Ibid., p. 63. For a history of presidential influence over the ICC, see also Richard Waterman, *Presidential Influence and the Administrative State* (Knoxville: University of Tennessee Press, 1989), chap. 4.

24. Marcus Alexis, "The Political Economy of Federal Regulation of Surface Transportation," in *The Political Economy of Deregulation*, Roger Noll and Bruce Owen, eds. (Washington, D.C.: American Enterprise Institute, 1983), chap. 7; and Rothenberg, *Regulation, Organizations, and Politics*, p. 64.

25. Rothenberg, *Regulation, Organizations, and Politics*, p. 66.

rights, and members of the Teamsters Union, who earned economic rents from industry cartelization.[26]

Thus, academic economists and other observers objected to this regulatory regime. Critics cited three different types of evidence against trucking regulation.[27] The first type was comparative studies of prices in regulated and unregulated environments; rates in unregulated intrastate markets were found to be lower than those in comparable interstate markets.[28] Second, the multibillion dollar market value of operating certificates reflected the present discounted value of the excess profits flowing from ownership of these rights. Third, the ICC seemed to be promoting umbrella rate making to prevent price cutting.[29]

It became increasingly obvious through the 1970s that interstate trucking regulation was forcing carriers to operate in ways that raised costs, wasted fuel, and reduced the quality of trucking services. As a result, market players acted to get around these regulations. Shippers sought to reduce their transportation costs, for example, by starting private truck operations, which developed into the fastest-growing sector of the trucking industry. ICC regulations also led to an inappropriate mixture of traffic between rail and truck carriers.[30]

---

26. Nancy Rose, "Labor Rent Sharing and Regulation: Evidence from the Trucking Industry," *Journal of Political Economy*, vol. 95 (1987), pp. 1146–78.

27. Pustay, "Deregulation and the US Trucking Industry," pp. 242–44.

28. See, for example, U.S. Department of Agriculture, *Interstate Trucking of Frozen Fruits and Vegetables under Agricultural Exemptions*, Marketing Research Report no. 224 (Washington, D.C., 1958); U.S. Department of Agriculture, *Interstate Trucking of Fresh and Frozen Poultry under Agricultural Exemptions*, Marketing Research Report no. 316 (Washington, D.C., 1959); D. A. Breen, "The Monopoly Value of Household-Goods Carrier Operating Certificates," *Journal of Law and Economics*, vol. 20 (1977), pp. 153–86; and W. Bruce Allen et al., *An Examination of the Unregulated Trucking Experience in New Jersey* (Washington, D.C.: U.S. Department of Transportation, 1978).

29. See, for example, E. W. Williams, *The Regulation of Rail-Motor Competition* (New York: Harper and Brothers, 1958); and George Hilton, *The Transportation Act of 1958* (Bloomington, Ind.: Indiana University Press, 1969).

30. For discussions of the leadup to the MCA of 1980, see Robyn, *Braking the Special Interests;* and Karen Borlaug Phillips and Laurence Phillips, "Research, Politics, and the Dynamics of Policy Development: A Case Study of Motor Carrier Regulatory Reform," *Policy Sciences*, vol. 17 (1984), pp. 367–84.

In the 1970s, economists in the U.S. Department of Transportation (DOT) prepared analyses clearly showing the potential economic gains from trucking deregulation.[31] At the same time, energy price increases, stagflation, and concern about big government provided an impetus for Presidents Ford and Carter to do something to improve the economy. Deregulation was a policy that appeared to hold substantial economic and potential political benefits, in trucking, as well as in other industries.

The Motor Carrier Act of 1980

With new presidential appointments, the ICC relaxed interstate regulations significantly in the 1970s. This prompted the American Trucking Associations to ask Congress for legislation restricting the ICC, claiming the new initiatives would result in destructive competition. This strategy backfired, however, as Congress in 1980 passed legislation that went further than the ICC's administrative deregulation.[32] While the 1980 act did not fully deregulate trucking, it did ease entry requirements, reduce collective rate making, and encourage greater flexibility in pricing.

Before the passage of the 1980 MCA, the ICC undertook considerable liberalization of trucking regulation in the late 1970s. Under President Ford, the ICC expanded the unregulated commercial zone around metropolitan areas. In 1977, President Carter's ICC chairman, Daniel O'Neal, relaxed the 1935 entry standards. Specifically, during this period the ICC used its rule-making powers to limit entry protests to directly affected firms only, to raise the burden on protestants, to consider rates as an important element in new service applications, to ease restrictions on dual common-contract carriers, to ease restrictions on agricultural carriers carrying regulated commodities on their backhauls, and to eliminate the limit of eight contracts for contract carriers.[33] In addition, reversing its long-standing opposition to private carriers, the ICC gave private trucking firms the authority to solicit freight as for-hire carriers in 1978.[34]

---

31. See Robyn, *Braking the Special Interests*, p. 74.

32. Motor Carrier Act of 1980, 94 Stat. 793, 49 U.S.C. 1101.

33. See Rothenberg, *Regulation, Organizations, and Politics*, p. 229.

34. *Toto Purchasing and Supply Co., Inc.* 128 MCC 873 (March 24, 1978).

These ICC administrative decisions, followed by the MCA of 1980, led to substantial deregulation of the trucking industry. The major reforms contained in the MCA of 1980 affected entry, rate making, and operating restrictions. For entry, the ICC was required to allow an applicant to enter the industry when the service was found to meet a "useful public purpose." This requirement was considerably easier to meet than the previous "public necessity and convenience" test. Further, the applicant was no longer required to prove why the new service was necessary. Instead, opponents were now required to prove why the new service was not beneficial. Thus, the burden of proof was reversed. Easing entry, however, significantly devalued ICC operating certificates. As a transition strategy, holders of ICC certificates were allowed to write off part of the certificate value on their corporate taxes, an approach later expanded by Congress and the Financial Accounting Standards Board.

The 1980 MCA permitted common carriers to raise and lower rates 10 percent annually without regulatory interference, and the ICC was granted the discretion to permit even greater price freedom in the future. The exemption against antitrust action for carriers discussing and voting on single-line rates was repealed. The MCA established a study commission to report to Congress on the feasibility and desirability of eliminating the remaining antitrust immunity for joint-line rates and general rate adjustments.

The 1980 act was not a complete victory for deregulation. The act did continue to require that trucking firms (both for-hire common carriers and contract carriers) file their rates with the ICC, which led to continuing administrative costs and problems. Rate bureaus retained their general antitrust immunity. Regulators had to provide studies to show that the impact of deregulation on small communities was not negative.[35] The ICC also implemented deregulation cautiously in the early 1980s under President Reagan's appointee, Reese Taylor, who was "reputed to have close ties with the Teamsters."[36]

---

35. See Rothenberg, *Regulation, Organizations, and Politics*, p. 240.

36. Reagan received support from the Teamsters in 1980, as they were displeased with President Carter's advocacy of deregulation. The slow implementation of deregulation under Taylor is documented impressively in Richard Waterman and B. Dan Wood, "What Do We Do with Applied Research?" *PS: Political Science and Politics*, vol. 25 (1992), p. 561.

Finally, although the MCA was a critical element of the wave of deregulatory legislation in the late 1970s and early 1980s, it differed from other legislation in one important area. While the Air Cargo Deregulation Act of 1977, the Airline Deregulation Act of 1978, the Staggers Rail Act of 1980, and the Bus Regulatory Reform Act of 1982 all contained provisions for the federal government to preempt the states in economic regulation of these industries, the 1980 MCA did not preempt state-level economic regulation of the intrastate trucking industry. We discuss in detail the reasons for this difference, and subsequent attempts to preempt, at the end of chapter 4. As a result of nonpreemption, until 1995 many states continued to regulate intrastate trucking in much the same way as the federal government regulated interstate trucking under the 1935 MCA. Considering the size of intrastate trucking, this omission weakened the impact of the 1980 MCA. We now turn to discussing the effect of those reforms on the interstate trucking industry, which have been positive in almost every case.

The Effects of the 1980 MCA on Interstate Trucking

The effects of the 1980 MCA have been considerable. Some have been obvious, while others have been much more subtle. Here, we discuss some of the broad changes in the interstate trucking industry since 1980. These include changes in entry into the industry, increases in independent tariff filings, productivity increases, estimates of the benefits to shippers and consumers, the effects of deregulation on various trucking firms and their employees, and service and safety effects. While certainly not exhaustive, this review provides enough evidence to show that the changes stimulated by the 1980 MCA have produced important benefits for the American economy as a whole. Only the few special interests who benefited from the old regulatory regime have faced difficult times in the years since 1980.

Increase in Interstate Carriers. Many new carriers have entered the trucking industry since 1980. By 1992, the total number of licensed carriers had jumped from 18,000 in 1980 to over 49,000. Unlike the limited authority granted to firms before 1980, the ICC

71

has also awarded full nationwide authority to carry any commodity, anywhere to about 16,000 firms.[37]

While few carriers specializing solely in LTL trucking have been newly formed since 1980 and the top four LTL firms doubled their market share from 18 percent in 1977 to 37 percent by 1987,[38] there has still been significant geographic expansion by existing LTL firms into other territories and entry by other carriers, including carriers from other modes.[39] Among these more recent entrants are newly formed subsidiaries of existing LTL firms and the expanded operations of truckload, small-package, package express, and air cargo carriers. Even railroads, ocean carriers, and third parties, such as freight consolidators, forwarders, and brokers, have expanded into market segments of the traditional LTL carriers. Thus, since deregulation, many important innovations have occurred, which have blurred the old distinctions among modes that were largely the artificial results of the old regulatory regime.

Increase in Independent Filings and the Demise of Rate Bureaus. Within fairly broad limits, the 1980 MCA allowed trucking companies to set their own rates within the rate zone provisions. As the MCA also eliminated the advertising period for independent actions, many trucking firms filed independent actions, which considerably increased price competition in the industry. There were only 27,000 independent rate-filing actions in 1979, before the 1980 act, for example, but that number increased by nearly ten times, to 230,000 independent actions by 1983.[40]

Congressional authors of the 1980 MCA also wanted to end ICC

---

37. See Testimony of Andrew Card, Secretary of Transportation, *Before the Subcommittee of the U.S. House of Representatives*, March 31, 1992. See also Thomas Gale Moore, "Trucking Deregulation," in *The Fortune Encyclopedia of Economics* (New York: Warner Books, 1993), p. 35.

38. Morrison et al., *The Economic Effects of Surface Freight Deregulation*, p. 61.

39. ICC, *Trucking Industry Long after Deregulation*, pp. 37–38.

40. This number fell back down to 42,000 by 1985 because by then truckers were using negotiated rates, discounts, and other mechanisms for lowering rates, rather than independent actions. See ICC Staff Report 10, "Highlights of Activity in the Motor Carrier Industry," Office of Transportation Analysis (Washington, D.C.: March 1986).

sanctioning of cartel price-fixing arrangements. Yet, while the MCA placed restrictions on rate bureau activities, prohibiting discussion or votes on single-line rates, it did not abolish the bureaus' antitrust immunity. Instead, it created the Motor Carrier Ratemaking Study Commission to examine the need for continuing immunity. The commission found that "collective ratemaking conflicts sharply with the National Transportation Policy which, as a result of the Motor Carrier Act of 1980, now calls for greater reliance on marketplace competition and, more specifically, for rate and service differentiation to meet changing market demands and the diverse requirements of the shipping public."[41] The commission recommended total elimination of antitrust immunity for collective rate making for all rates and for freight classification. Despite these recommendations, however, antitrust immunity remains in place.

As a result of expanded independent actions, the rate bureaus were reduced in importance, however, and have been reduced in number in recent years.[42] Several large national LTL carriers have dropped their rate bureau membership, which they regard as increasingly irrelevant in today's trucking environment.

Productivity Increases. Productivity changes can include prices, quality, quantity of outputs, the timeliness of services, and changes in the mixture of inputs. John Ying explored changes in the cost structure of trucking firms in the years immediately following the 1980 MCA and found that while deregulation actually raised production costs in the first year by 7 percent, because of adjustment and start-up costs, in the next year costs fell 1 percent.[43] After that, Ying's simulations indicate that deregulation caused substantial productivity growth. Two years after the passage of the MCA, the result-

---

41. Motor Carrier Ratemaking Study Commission, *Collective Ratemaking in the Trucking Industry*, A Report to the President and the Congress of the United States (Washington, D.C.: Government Printing Office, 1983), p. xii.

42. Since 1980, in part because of mergers, the number of rate bureaus has dropped from fifteen to nine. Interstate Commerce Commission, *The U.S. Motor Carrier Industry Long after Deregulation*, pp. 57–60.

43. John Ying, "The Inefficiency of Regulating a Competitive Industry: Productivity Gains in Trucking Following Reform," *Review of Economics and Statistics*, vol. 72 (1990), pp. 191–201.

ing cost savings already amounted to over 9 percent. These efficiency gains emerged as trucking firms filled more backhauls, used more efficient routes, and developed other cost-cutting techniques. By 1984, Ying estimates cost savings had risen to 23 percent.[44] The Department of Transportation substantiates these findings, reporting that trucking productivity grew from average increases of 3.2 percent from 1973 to 1979, to 3.7 percent from 1980 to 1990.[45]

Ying argued that the rationalization of route structures played an important part in these efficiency gains. As in the airline industry, deregulation resulted in realignment of the route and commodity structures that regulation imposed on carriers.[46] With deregulation, trucking firms, like the airlines, developed efficient hub-and-spoke systems for collecting, transporting, and delivering freight for a large enough group of shippers to ensure a consistently high load factor on each truck. After deregulation, it also became apparent to firms that those with the largest route structures would have an advantage.[47] Thus, hub-and-spoke systems and firm mergers have led to increased productivity as measured by increases in the average number of miles per year from trucking vehicles.

Estimated Shipper and Consumer Savings. Winston and others estimated the effects of the MCA on the economic welfare of shippers and thus on final consumers. According to this analysis, trucking deregulation has lowered operating costs for private trucking, generating $3 billion per year in benefits to shippers. The increased competition among common carriers has caused rate reductions that amount to $4 billion in benefits, mostly from the LTL sector. Service improvements have also produced an estimated $1 billion in benefits to shippers.[48]

The ICC contends that, in addition to the cost savings illustrated here, shippers have received substantially more responsive and de-

---

44. Ibid., p. 197.

45. Card, Testimony to U.S. House of Representatives, p. 4.

46. See also Nicholas Glaskowsky, Jr., *Effects of Deregulation on Motor Carriers,* 2d ed. (Westport, Conn.: Eno Foundation for Transportation, 1990).

47. Boyer, "Deregulation of the Trucking Sector," p. 486.

48. Winston et al., *The Economic Effects of Surface Freight Deregulation,* p. 28.

pendable service as a result of the new market discipline imposed by competition.[49] Such benefits include reductions in the time between a shipper's request for service and the arrival of a carrier and more frequent service. According to Winston and others, improvements in these other dimensions have allowed shippers to develop just-in-time inventory management by transporting smaller shipments more frequently.[50] This has reduced inventory costs. In an earlier study, Robert Delaney estimated that the interstate deregulation of trucking had enabled logistics gains of more than $50 billion per year for shippers, an estimate that was controversial and later reestimated to be closer to $38 billion.[51] In any case, analysts agree that the kinds of contracts and flexible arrangements that the 1980 MCA allowed, combined with new information technologies, encouraged firms to use far more efficient inventory management systems.

Some of these gains for shippers have come at the expense of some of the trucking firms and employees who existed happily under the pre-1980 regulatory regime. The outcome has been far different from that associated with a zero-sum game, however, as our discussions of the emergence of new firms and changes in the demographics of employees in the trucking industry make clear.

The analysis presented by Winston and others also shows that deregulation has had a small positive impact on the profits of truckload carriers, about one-half billion dollars per year, but a fairly large negative impact on the profits of LTL carriers of almost $3 billion annually. The reason for this difference is that before deregulation the TL sector had far more firms and less disciplined rate bureaus than the LTL sector. Cost savings have resulted from the

---

49. See, for example, the testimony of Edward J. Philbin, chairman, Interstate Commerce Commission, before the House Committee on Public Works and Transportation Subcommittee on Surface Transportation, March 24, 1992, pp. 13–14.

50. Winston et al., *The Economic Effects of Surface Transportation Deregulation*, p. 27.

51. Robert Delaney, *The Disunited States: A Country in Search of an Efficient Transportation Policy*, Cato Institute Policy Analysis no. 84 (Washington, D.C., March 10, 1987). See also discussion of subsequent debate on sources and magnitudes of logistics savings in U.S. Department of Transportation Report to Congress, *Impact of State Regulation on the Package Express Industry*, DOT-P-16 (Washington, D.C., September 1990), pp. 45–46.

development of highly efficient carriers. In contrast, the LTL sector has suffered both declines in revenues and increases in costs related to better service provision under deregulation. The competitive battle for shippers has also forced LTL carriers to spend more on advertising and to carry lower average loads.[52]

Bankruptcies. As in any competitive market, not all trucking firms have prospered as a result of, or even survived, deregulation. Although shippers have been large beneficiaries, most carriers, as well as independent owner-operators, have experienced intense financial pressure. Many have gone bankrupt. The failure rate among trucking firms, however, is no higher than among firms in the economy more generally. Thus, the authors of the ICC report conclude:

> Competition among freight transport firms is a given, and there is nothing to suggest that this condition will change. Consequently, although many competitors will survive and prosper, failure and other turnover will be permanent features of the industry—as with most industries. By the same token, there is no evidence to suggest that shippers will not continue to demand and receive high quality transportation service. The implication for public policy is to let this competitive marketplace continue to determine winners and losers among the carriers and, in the process, allow shippers to be well served.[53]

Labor Issues. Since deregulation, the number of jobs in the trucking industry has grown by over 500,000.[54] But not all groups have gained from this expansion in the industry. Along with the owners of trucking firms that went bankrupt after deregulation, unionized trucking employees have been the big losers from deregulation. Under regulation, unionized labor in the LTL sector extracted rents from carriers as excess wages and were able to maintain high levels of employment. Rose calculated that union wages in 1977 were at least 20 percent

---

52. Winston et al., *The Economic Effects of Surface Freight Deregulation,* pp. 36–37.

53. Interstate Commerce Commission, *The U.S. Motor Carrier Industry Long after Deregulation,* p. 57.

54. Card, Testimony to U.S. House of Representatives, p. 6.

higher than they would have been had the industry been deregulated.[55] Even in 1994, unionized truckers earned an average wage of $45,000–50,000 per year, while drivers in the nonunionized sectors earned an average of $35,000–40,000.[56]

Since deregulation in 1980, employment levels and wages in the LTL sector have fallen dramatically. As Boyer argues:

> The key to understanding why trucking deregulation is seen as such a success is not found in large net benefits of the policy but rather in the identity of the parties from whom the transfers inherent in trucking regulation came. The Teamsters Union had a long history of forceful organizing, using bare-knuckle intimidation tactics. . . . So it seems only just that the institution that had used regulation so successfully for its own benefit should be punished through deregulation.[57]

The problem for unionized labor is that after deregulation, competition in the LTL sector has become intense and the LTL sector itself is decreasing in size.[58] Today, the LTL sector makes up less than 10 percent of the total trucking industry, and its business has been eroded by competition from TL carriers, as well as nonunionized third-party consolidators, and small-package carriers. After 1980, LTL carriers without nonunion subsidiaries to handle truckload freight quickly lost much of that business to lower-cost, nonunion TL carriers.

Thus, deregulation has created many nonunion jobs, while it has led to the steady decline of unionized positions. In 1980, for example, there were 210,000 unionized truckers employed in the industry. In 1994, that number had declined to about 120,000.[59] While the unionized sector is experiencing cutbacks, according to

---

55. Rose, "Labor Rent Sharing and Regulation," pp. 1146–78.

56. Daniel Pearl and Robert Frank, "Trucking Firms Face a Problem with Congress," *Wall Street Journal*, April 8, 1994. The earnings estimates are attributed to Wheat, First Securities, Inc.

57. Boyer, "Deregulation of the Trucking Sector," p. 492.

58. ICC, *The Motor Carrier Industry Long after Deregulation*, pp. 103–5.

59. John Schulz, "Teamsters Return to Work at LTL Carriers, but Greetings Include Layoffs, Closed Terminals," *Traffic World* (May 9, 1994), pp. 10–11.

Department of Labor estimates, long-term employment growth in the trucking industry will continue to be strong, with over 27,000 new trucking industry jobs being created each year.[60]

These changing employment patterns in the trucking industry have had different effects for different groups. John Heywood and James Peoples analyze the impact of trucking deregulation on the prevalence of black truck drivers.[61] Despite the relatively low human capital requirements needed to drive a truck, racial minorities, and blacks in particular, have historically been underrepresented among truck drivers and owners.[62] Further, of the few blacks in the trucking industry, most were in the more competitive local and private-carrier market, rather than in the protected long-distance, for-hire market, which, until deregulation, offered far better earnings.

The Teamsters' historically hostile attitude toward minorities was a significant reason for such underrepresentation. The strict ICC regulatory regime operating up to 1980, however, also froze entry into the industry and made it difficult for any new trucking entrants. Heywood and Peoples report that deregulation of interstate trucking "seems to have brought with it a substantial increase in the hiring of blacks in the traditionally and still central for-hire sector. This fits with [the] suggestion that the limits to competition provided by regulation allowed managers latitude to discriminate which, when reinforced with union preferences, resulted in underrepresentation."[63]

Although blacks are still underrepresented in the trucking industry, Heywood and Peoples suggest that "in the regulated period, the increased prevalence of black truckers was held back by institutional barriers of entry, regulation, and the union. In the deregulated period, the increased prevalence of black truckers seems held back by entry barriers, not necessarily racially based, into business more

---

60. This estimate is based on figures provided in the ICC report, *Trucking Long after Deregulation*, p. 74.

61. John Heywood and James Peoples, "Deregulation and the Prevalence of Black Truck Drivers," *Journal of Law and Economics*, vol. 37 (1994), pp. 133–58.

62. See, for example, Charles Perry, *Deregulation and the Decline of the Unionized Trucking Industry* (Philadelphia: University of Pennsylvania/Wharton School Press, 1986).

63. Heywood and Peoples, "Deregulation and the Prevalence of Black Truck Drivers," p. 151.

generally."[64] This analysis illustrates that economic regulation can produce patterns of privilege and discrimination within an industry that have implications extending well beyond more obvious price effects. As with other elements of this analysis, it confirms that deregulation can have a liberating effect on society.

Effect on Service to Small Communities. A particular concern raised in the deregulatory debate in the late 1970s was the supposed negative impact of reform on service to small communities. Studies conducted since 1980, however, show that this fear was unwarranted. In terms of rates, regulatory reform appears to have benefited small community shippers to a slightly greater extent than larger community shippers.[65] After surveying firms in smaller communities, the ICC concluded that there was little change in the quality or availability of service since deregulation, and most such changes were positive for small communities.[66] The ICC also found that there was a decline in both the number of small community complaints and the proportion of complaints coming from small communities. Field surveys conducted by Department of Transportation staffers yielded a similar picture.[67]

John Due and others conclude a review of the evidence on small community trucking service by stating:

> The majority of the studies of the impacts of trucking deregulation on the quantity, quality, and cost of regulated trucking service to rural communities have found the impacts to be neutral or positive. Given these findings, it is reasonable to find few governmental strategies to maintain service. The trucking firms have already employed strategies consistent with profit maximization that have enabled

---

64. Ibid., p. 152.

65. Pustay, "Deregulation and the US Trucking Industry," pp. 230–31.

66. Interstate Commerce Commission, *Small Community Service Study* (Washington, D.C.: Interstate Commerce Commission, 1982).

67. See Karen L. Borlaug, *A One-Year Assessment of the Motor Carrier Act of 1980: Small Community Trucking Service in Nevada and Oregon* (Washington, D.C.: U.S. Department of Transportation, 1981).

rural communities to maintain adequate trucking service at reasonable rates.[68]

Yet, as we shall see in chapter 4, the projected loss of service to small communities was used by opponents of intrastate deregulation until the 1994 preemption.

Safety Issues. Another goal of both economic and noneconomic regulation of the trucking industry was to guarantee the safety of trucking service. Regulation proponents claim that deregulation compromises safety in two ways.[69] First, it has caused financial distress for some carriers, and, discounting the future more heavily, they may be less likely to maintain their vehicles well. Second, deregulation has decreased some drivers' wages, which could cause them to increase the number of miles they drive.

While these arguments may have some theoretical merit, traffic safety statistics do not show an increase in accident rates following deregulation. One study, for example, suggests that truckers operating before the passage of the MCA had accident rates in 1977 and 1984 that showed no statistically significant difference.[70] Another possible source of problems stems from carriers that came into existence after enactment of the MCA. In one study, these new entrants were found during 1985–1986 to have significantly higher accident rates than carriers that had been in business before deregulation.[71] Only those carriers in business for less than two years, however, had statistically higher accident rates than established carriers. Further, it is not clear that the safety records of these new entrants would have been any different under the old regulatory regime.[72]

---

68. John Due, Benjamin Allen, Mary Kihl, and Michael Crum, *Transportation Service to Small Rural Communities: Effects of Deregulation* (Ames: Iowa State University Press, 1990), p. 68.

69. Boyer, "Deregulation of the Trucking Sector," pp. 491–92.

70. Thomas Corsi, Philip Fanara, Jr., and Judith Jarrell, "Safety Performance of Pre-MCA Motor Carriers: 1977 versus 1984," *Transportation Journal*, vol. 27 (1988), pp. 30–36.

71. Thomas Corsi and Philip Fanara, Jr., "Effects of New Entrants on Motor Carrier Safety," in *Transportation Safety in an Age of Deregulation*, Leon N. Moses and Ian Savage, eds. (New York: Oxford University Press, 1989).

72. Winston et al., *The Economic Effects of Surface Freight Deregulation*, p. 62.

Trucking deregulation could also have had indirect effects on highway safety, with more trucks on the road and drivers going faster to meet competitive deadlines. Careful analysis, though, tells a different story. Thomas Traynor and Patrick McCarthy, for example, conclude that economic deregulation of the trucking industry has not had significant effects on highway safety.[73] Further, Donald Alexander concludes that deregulation yielded several benefits that policy makers had probably not anticipated. He found that fatality and injury rates were lower after deregulation than before it, despite the large increase in truck traffic.[74] No careful analysis has discovered a positive relationship between deregulation and trucking accidents.

Summary. The deregulatory MCA of 1980 has spurred intense competition in virtually every element of the interstate trucking sector. Combined with technological and service innovations, this competition has produced a dynamic and expanding industry. As the ICC has noted, the benefits of interstate trucking deregulation are widespread and likely to be long term. The vast majority of shippers and many members of the trucking industry are pleased with deregulation. According to the ICC, the critics

> appear to be a narrowly focused group consisting primarily of smaller and financially distressed LTL carriers, organized workers in the LTL sector, and representatives of motor carrier rate bureaus. These groups have fared poorly under deregulation compared with their favored high-cost positions prior to 1980. However well intentioned these groups are, their views are often self-serving and lacking in theoretical, legal, economic and evidentiary merit.[75]

Interstate Regulation after 1980

Although the deregulatory stimulus of the 1980 MCA resulted in considerable success for the interstate trucking industry, the MCA

---

73. Thomas Traynor and Patrick McCarthy, "Economic Regulation and Highway Safety in the Trucking Industry: A Limited Dependent Variable Analysis," *Quarterly Review of Economics and Finance*, vol. 33 (1993), pp. 141–53.

74. Donald Alexander, "Motor Carrier Deregulation and Highway Safety: An Empirical Analysis," *Southern Economic Journal*, vol. 59 (1992), pp. 28–38.

75. Interstate Commerce Commission, *The U.S. Motor Carrier Industry Long after Deregulation*, p. v.

did not go all the way toward completing the deregulatory agenda. Consequently, some vestiges of the old regulatory regime established in the 1930s remained in the 1990s. Of special interest are the continuing presence of the ICC itself, despite having a greatly reduced role, and the need for tariff filings by trucking firms, which was finally eliminated in 1994.

Under the provisions of the MCA of 1980, interstate common carriers still had to file tariffs with the ICC. This filing provision was retained to prevent trucking firms from discriminating against certain customers. According to the chief of the ICC Section of Tariffs in 1994, however, no one had made a rate-discrimination complaint in more than a decade.[76] Rather, if shippers believed they were being overcharged by a trucking company, they could simply turn to another carrier. Despite this, every day some fifty ICC clerks filed an estimated 16,000 paper pages from the nation's trucking firms.[77] Thus, an average of about 1 million tariffs, including tariffs for household goods movement, were filed with the ICC each year.[78] Only between 4,000 and 8,000 of these were rejected for any reason, each year, which was less than 1 percent of the total filed.

The filing costs for the companies involved were not trivial. Each of the 1 million filings required a $10 fee. But the real costs of filing were often much higher. One trucking firm, for example, assigned four staff members and paid $20,000 in annual filing fees to record its rates with the ICC.[79] Thus, tariff filing at the ICC involved unnecessary administrative work that could have been eliminated in 1980.[80] Shippers hardly ever consulted these rates. And ICC filing did not provide protection for shippers against pricing problems but, until its elimination in 1994, created new problems, as the "undercharge crisis" discussed below illustrates.

---

76. Daniel Pearl, "ICC Keeps Truckin' Though It Has Lost Much of Its Authority," *Wall Street Journal*, April 27, 1994.

77. Ibid.

78. Lisa Burgess and Stephanie Nall, "Reduced Role Seen for ICC in Trucking," *Journal of Commerce*, July 14, 1994, p. 1A.

79. Ibid.

80. See Winston et al., *The Economic Effects of Surface Freight Deregulation*, pp. 59–60.

Negotiated Rates and the Undercharge Crisis. In the spirit of deregulation, the ICC revised its tariff filing procedures after 1980, permitting shipping and trucking firms to negotiate discounts from the tariffs on file for specific movements on as little as one day's notice. Faced with increased competition, truckers adopted a number of creative rate structures to secure more business. Some of these discounts were not readily apparent to shippers, such as range tariffs, which offer a series of rates for services that vary by transaction, or trigger tariffs, which provide discounts to shippers who specifically request participation in them. Other discounts were sometimes deceptive, such as off-bill discounting, which occurred when shippers sold products to consumers on a collect-on-delivery (COD) basis. Shippers secured a discount with trucking firms for transport, but they arranged for the trucking firm to bill the customer the full rate and refund them the difference. Regardless of which form of discounting was used, though, trucking companies were still required to file an amended tariff with the ICC reflecting the negotiated rates. Frequently, however, trucking firms failed to notify the ICC of these rate reductions, and the ICC, as guided by Congress, did not observe this situation closely, as competition seemed to be working well.

As noted, in the more competitive environment after deregulation, many trucking firms faced severe financial difficulties, and thousands had to file for bankruptcy. Some bankruptcy trustees recalled that a series of court decisions earlier in the century had ruled that shipping companies were liable for differences between published tariffs and the price they actually paid, even if the trucking firm misquoted the tariff rate or the shipper was unaware of the published tariff. This was known as the "filed-rate" doctrine.[81] Bankruptcy trustees hired auditors to search company records for instances where the rate charges billed were different from the actual tariffs on file at the ICC. When they found discrepancies, they sent bills to the shippers to recover the differences. Shippers usually refused to pay these "undercharges," claiming that they had made a valid agreement with the trucking company and should not be penalized for that firm's neglect in filing the tariffs.

As a result, many of these cases landed in court, where shippers

---

81. U.S. House of Representatives Report No. 103-359 (Washington, D.C.: U.S. Congress).

were repeatedly found liable for these claims based on the filed-rate doctrine. Since the statute of limitation for filing undercharge claims was three years, and bankruptcy rules at times allowed this to be extended for an additional two years, shippers faced potential undercharge actions long after the actual movements took place.[82]

In an effort to reduce such claims, the ICC issued a series of policy statements arguing that a strict interpretation of the filed-rate doctrine inhibited innovation and was no longer necessary to prevent rate discrimination against shippers. They found that collecting undercharges was an "unreasonable practice" and only negotiated rates between shippers and trucking firms should be permitted to be collected.[83] Five circuit courts reviewed and upheld this ICC position.

The Supreme Court reversed these findings in its 1990 *Maislin* decision, however, in which the Court found that the "unreasonable practice" approach violated the language and intent of the 1935 MCA.[84] The Supreme Court concluded that Congress had stated the filed-rate doctrine was paramount and necessary to protect shippers from price discrimination. Filed tariffs were found to supersede rates negotiated between shippers and trucking firms, even those rates that were not properly filed.

After this decision, the number of undercharge claims submitted by trustees of bankrupt trucking firms soared, numbering in the thousands each year. In one case alone, the ICC reported that the trustees of Transcon Lines intended to sue 340,000 shippers for undercharges totaling more than $1 billion.[85] Not only did the number of undercharge claims grow, but so did the scope of these actions. In particular, lawyers developed two more questionable forms of undercharge claims. First, rates filed under shipper *account codes* were argued to be invalid and undercharged because they did not designate the *name* of the customer, even though they were reported in compliance with ICC rules.[86] Furthermore, some trustees for bankrupt firms that

---

82. Interstate Commerce Commission, "Motor Carrier Undercharge Claims: A Brief Statement on ICC Practice," ICC Report, 1993, pp. 3–4.

83. Ibid., p. 3.

84. Maislin Industries, U.S. v. Primary Steel, Inc., 497 U.S. 116 (1990).

85. David Cawthorne, "ICC Finally Decides to Take Charge of Mushrooming Undercharge Crisis," *Traffic World*, June 8, 1992, p. 7.

86. House Report No. 103-39.

possessed both common- and contract-carrier authority attempted to collect undercharges for traffic moved under contract carriage, arguing that contracts for alleged movements were not valid and consequently the firm's higher common-carrier rate applied.[87] In total, the ICC Office of Economics estimated that shippers' exposure to undercharge claims could reach as high as $27 billion, with another $5 billion in interest on overdue bills.[88]

To resolve this problem, after years of bargaining, Congress passed the Negotiated Rates Act (NRA) in late 1993.[89] This legislation addressed four major dimensions of the undercharge crisis. First, the NRA exempted shipments by small businesses and charitable organizations from liability for undercharges. It also exempted shipments made before September 30, 1990, from undercharge collections, if doing so would be an "unreasonable practice." The NRA granted the ICC authority to make these judgments based on criteria similar to those used before the 1990 *Maislin* decision.

Second, the NRA instituted settlement procedures to satisfy genuine undercharge claims. For shipments weighing more than 10,000 pounds, a claim can be settled by payment of 15 percent of the differences between the filed and the negotiated rate. Shipments weighing less than 10,000 pounds require 20 percent of the difference. And if the claim involved a public warehouseman, the dispute could be settled by paying 5 percent of the undercharge.

Third, the NRA revised tariff filing procedures to prevent the appearance of certain types of undercharge claims. The name of the shipper for each account code must now be revealed in the tariff, and range tariffs must identify the specific rate employed in each shipment. Off-bill discounting is no longer allowed. And contract carriers are required to have written contracts with their customers, containing certain basic information.

---

87. Interstate Commerce Commission Decision no. 40945.

88. Statement of Karen B. Philipps, commissioner of the Interstate Commerce Commission, before the Subcommittee on Surface Transportation of the Committee on Public Works and Transportation, March 24, 1992.

89. Information on the contents of the 1993 Negotiated Rates Act was compiled from P.L. 103-180 and Interstate Commerce Commission, "Motor Carrier Undercharge Claims: A Brief Guide to the Negotiated Rates Act of 1993," prepared by the ICC Office of Public Assistance, 1993.

Finally, this legislation changed the statute of limitations for filing civil actions involving undercharges. Instead of three years, after December 3, 1994, litigation had to be brought within eighteen months.[90]

Thus, the 1993 NRA took a number of positive steps to alleviate the undercharge crisis that was plaguing the shipping industry. In 1994, however, trucking firms challenged aspects of this legislation in court. A North Carolina judge issued a decision that the settlement procedures adopted in the NRA were invalid because they "interfered with the property rights of bankrupt estates without changing bankruptcy laws."[91] While this decision was only a recommendation and has no effect unless adopted by a federal court, it was the first of what may be many legal tests of the NRA. By leaving the filed-rate doctrine intact, Congress left open the possibility that the undercharge problem could surface again in the future.

Shippers have mixed feelings about the NRA. Ed Emmett, head of the largest shipper group, the National Industrial Transportation League, stated: "While we support a lot of what the commission does, the root cause of their current problem is the filed rate doctrine. Many good things are being overshadowed by rather glaring examples of archaic regulation."[92] The league also argued that the ICC's proposed procedures are "much more involved, complex, and formalistic than what is contemplated or is appropriate under the statue enacted by Congress."[93]

The Trucking Industry Regulatory Reform Act of 1994 (TIRRA), passed by Congress and signed by President Clinton on August 26, 1994, further addressed the tariff filing issue. As a result, individual trucking firms no longer need to file tariffs. Some tariff filing will continue, however, largely for political reasons, to make the legislation passable. Tariffs will still be filed for joint-lines, rate bureaus,

---

90. During the interim period between late 1993 and December 1994, claims must be filed by the end of two years.

91. Stephanie Nall, "Undercharge Law Invalid, Bankruptcy Judge Rules," *Journal of Commerce*, February 4, 1994, p. 1A.

92. Rip Watson, "Most Transport Interests in Washington Support ICC," *Journal of Commerce*, June 20, 1994, p. 7A.

93. See National Industrial Transportation League, *Notice: The Shipper's Voice since 1907*, vol. 58 (April 15, 1994), p. 123.

and classified freight, which also retain their antitrust immunity, although shippers do not have to pay these rates. Household-goods carriers still file tariffs. Some shippers are concerned that this situation will lead to problems for shipments when freight is classified and bureaus file tariffs but individual carriers charge discounts.[94]

The End of the ICC. With these changes in place and several events that took place in 1994 and 1995, the ICC as an agency is likely to be eliminated by the end of 1996. The symbolic politics of eliminating a federal agency, as well as budget savings, are important. Doing away with a whole agency, especially one with such a long history, gives congressional budget cutters more political points than simply cutting the entire ICC budget of $53 million, a miniscule portion of the federal budget. The ICC budget included $17 million for truck tariff filing, $13 million for other trucking issues, and $23 million for regulation of other transportation modes. To cover part of this, the ICC collected $8 million in annual fees, largely from trucking filings. In mid-1994, the ICC had a total of 656 cases pending before it. Undercharge issues accounted for 335 of these, while rail cases accounted for 239. Of the undercharge cases, 175 were close to a decision, while 91 were in settlement negotiations.[95]

Representative Kasich of Ohio, who now spearheads the Republican House Budget reform effort, was the "budget entrepreneur" who, along with three other representatives in 1993, had their staffs go through old Reagan budgets and the 1983 Grace Commission report for ideas to reduce the federal government. One alternative that seemed especially ripe was the elimination of the ICC. They started a heavy publicity campaign to abolish it, using creative "Dear Colleague" letters to inform congressmen about some of the more absurd aspects of ICC policies. Anecdotes such as the existence of separate ICC tariffs for curved and straight candy canes were invaluable in demonstrating that the ICC, at times, exercised almost Soviet-like command-and-control regulation. These efforts led to a 1993 House vote to eliminate the ICC's budget, which came within twenty

---

94. John Schulz, "Shippers Bemoan 'State of Confusion' in Wake of Truck Regulatory Reforms," *Traffic World*, September 19, 1994, pp. 11–14.

95. Stephanie Nall, "Undercharge Cases over Half Agency's Load," *Journal of Commerce*, July 13, 1994, p. 10A.

votes of passage. The closeness of this outcome shocked observers and made it clear that the ICC was vulnerable.

Since 1980, interest group support for the ICC as an institution has waned, largely in response to the state of competition in most freight transportation markets. As a result, most trucking and railroad firms, as well as most shippers, would not expend a large amount of political capital to save the ICC. One of the ICC's largest and most visible supporters, the Teamsters' Union, became an increasingly ineffective voice as its membership declined, partly as a result of the 1980 MCA, and as its leadership divided over how to respond to this changing regulatory environment. The ICC itself has been opposed to its termination, but its influence has diminished over time as the agency and its activities have shrunk. Thus, as Congress has pushed to eliminate the ICC to show constituents its commitment to downsizing government, the agency's major proponents have not had the resources to stymie congressional efforts.

In June 1994, with an election looming, the House of Representatives voted 234 to 192 to eliminate funding for the ICC for fiscal year 1995. The voting was largely along party lines, but the bill had some bipartisan support as Republicans voted 168 to 8 in favor, while Democrats voted 66 to 183. A Senate Appropriations Committee voted in July to cut the ICC budget by one-third, and in August 1994 Congress passed TIRRA, which ended truck tariff filing and cut the ICC budget by one-third. The debate turned on budgetary considerations, not on charges of agency inefficiency. Although the policy arguments had been raised previously, they proved less essential than the simple notion that the ICC is an outmoded bureaucracy that has to be cut to show resolve on budget control. As chair Gail McDonald characterized it, the ICC "is an easy target."

Congress cannot eliminate the ICC without also passing legislation to address issues that remain on the books as law but would have no agency to handle them. Without this intermediate step, some unanticipated consequences could arise, as the undercharge problem illustrates. For example, a rule from the 1930s that bars interline operations between common and contract carriers remains in the regulations, but is routinely ignored. As Ed Emmett noted: "This is another of those examples of an outdated regulation that has been left on the books which people assumed was harmless. But like many

88

things related to truck regulations and rates, it can jump up and bite you."[96]

Section 210 of TIRRA required the ICC to issue a report on its future role in October 1994. This detailed (173-page) ICC report recommended elimination of the distinction between common and contract carriers, and thus the particular problem alluded to above.[97] The ICC also recommended elimination of all trucking-rate regulation and a narrowing of the antitrust exemption for the rate bureaus. Not surprisingly, these recommendations pleased shippers, but not the Teamsters Union. For railroad activities, the ICC recommended maintenance of its oversight activities: "We conclude that federal economic regulation of the rail industry should continue, without significant change." To perform these remaining duties, the ICC contended that either it must continue to exist or an independent, bipartisan ICC-like body should be placed within the Department of Transportation. At roughly the same time, though, the Congressional Research Service issued a study challenging the necessity of even these functions. It argued that the ICC wasted $3 million per year through its market-dominance oversight of the 10 percent of the railroad industry that falls into that category and recommended its elimination.

As also mandated in the TIRRA, the Department of Transportation studied these ICC recommendations and issued its own report in February 1995 on the future direction of the ICC. According to the department: "This report reflects a different view from that taken by the ICC and generally concludes that government should retain fewer functions."[98] Specifically, this report recommends: (1) elimination of all antitrust immunity; (2) elimination of all specific railroad rules, letting regular rules apply; (3) transferring railroad maximum rate regulation and abandonment oversight to the Department of Transportation; (4) elimination of all trucking regulation except Department of Transportation licensing and undercharge resolutions, having the

---

96. This quote appears in Gregory Johnson, "It's a Crime: Despite Flaws, ICC Honors 60-Year-Old-Law," *Journal of Commerce*, June 28, 1994, p. 3B.

97. Lisa Burgess, "Teamsters Pan ICC Report; Shippers Like Decontrol," *Journal of Commerce*, November 1, 1994, p. 3B.

98. U.S. Department of Transportation, *Report on the Functions of Interstate Commerce Commission*, February 1995, pp. 3–4.

Federal Trade Commission oversee household-goods carriers; (5) elimination of all intercity bus regulation; (6) transferring all truck licensing and insurance monitoring into the Department of Transportation; and (7) having no separate ICC body remain within the Department of Transportation, as they see little need for "insulated" decision making. This last element is perhaps the most significant, as the ICC had argued that an arrangement could be made like that of the Federal Energy Regulatory Commission, which stands as an independent regulatory agency but is housed within the Department of Energy. The Clinton administration, and most likely Congress, saw no great advantage to maintaining the ICC and simply putting it into the Department of Transportation. Only eliminating the agency completely could generate the kind of political support that these actors hoped to gain.

The Clinton administration proposed the complete elimination of the ICC by mid-FY1996. Some budget-cutters in Congress wanted to see it eliminated before FY1996. In either case, Congress was addressing the specifics in 1995. Thus, a small battle remains over how to eliminate the ICC and what to do with the few remaining residual functions that may be necessary for some transportation agency to perform. Interested groups disagree about exactly what those functions are. Even the railroads themselves have been split on this issue. Some shippers have supported the maintenance of an independent ICC. The most likely scenario is for the ICC to end sometime in 1996, and for the Department of Transportation and other agencies to take over most of the functions listed in the Department of Transportation's 1995 report.

Thus, the more-than-a-century-old ICC will end its reign as a transportation regulator and as the nation's oldest regulatory agency. Users of deregulated transportation services will rely largely on market competition as a regulator, with some remaining assistance from the Department of Transportation.

Conclusions

This chapter provides an overview of the trucking industry and the economic regulations under which the interstate sector of the industry operated following the MCA of 1935. We discussed the changes that resulted from ICC administrative deregulation in the 1970s and from the provisions of the deregulatory MCA of 1980. The interstate sector of the trucking industry has improved its performance substantially in the past fifteen years. Today it is clear to all but the most self-interested observer that interstate trucking deregulation has worked well. Entry into the market has increased dramatically, firms have worked successfully to develop highly efficient route structures, and other innovations, such as the use of intermodal operations, have surged sharply. Further, there is now a high degree of price competition in the industry, leading to lower costs for shippers. In these respects, the pattern of deregulation of interstate trucking since 1980 parallels the evolution of the deregulated airline and railroad industries that we reviewed in chapter 2.

Yet despite the enormous gains for freight transportation that resulted from the deregulatory agenda of the 1970s and 1980s, a few more steps have to be taken. The ICC, as an agency, is likely to be eliminated and the Department of Transportation will pick up the few remaining regulatory tasks. This transition has to be handled smoothly. The remaining important part of the deregulatory agenda not addressed by the 1980 act was the issue of state regulation of intrastate trucking. The rest of the book is devoted to this topic. In the next chapter, we address economic regulation and analyze what the states did after 1980, why they did not deregulate more, and what it cost the U.S. economy. We also analyze why the 1980 act did not preempt the states, and we examine other efforts since 1980 to preempt, including the reasons behind the success of the preemption effort in 1994.

4

State Economic Regulation
of Trucking

With the unarguable benefits of federal trucking deregulation—improved service levels at greatly reduced rates—why is it that the great majority of state governments keep their archaic entry control regulations? I can only conclude that at the state level, truckers have more political clout than they had at the federal level.[1]

—JAMES JOHNSON AND K. SCHNEIDER

As chapter 3 illustrated, interstate trucking deregulation proved to be a remarkable success, evaluated by virtually any criterion. Rates for shipments dropped, competition and the number of trucking firms increased, trucking's share of the freight transportation market grew, safety did not suffer, minorities increased their role in the industry, and shippers were given substantially more options in moving their freight. While some regulations remain, interstate trucking deregulation has been at least as successful as deregulation in the other freight transportation sectors.

In contrast to these deregulatory moves on the federal level, until 1994 the large intrastate trucking industry remained heavily regulated by state agencies in all but a handful of states. Further, complete deregulation, when it did come about, was initiated by the congressional decision of 1994 to preempt state-level regulation. Until this preemption occurred, many states still regulated their intrastate trucking sector in a manner inconsistent with the success shown by relying more on the market and less on government regulation.

The differences could not be more stark between federal deregu-

---

1. James Johnson and K. Schneider, "The 1980 Motor Carrier Act: A Ten-Year Retrospective by Traffic Executives," *Transportation Practitioners Journal*, vol. 58 (1991), p. 371, citing a corporate shipping manager surveyed in 1990.

lation of most sectors of the freight transportation industry after 1980 and the heavy state regulation of intrastate trucking that continued right into 1994. These differences raise vital questions about regulatory federalism and how we should distinguish between the political forces that shape economic institutions and organizational forms at the federal and state level. Here we have evidence of "an idea in good currency"[2] at the federal level that received short shrift at the state level. Further, in the years after 1980, it took a series of congressional attempts before the various regulatory regimes were aligned. Over these years, all interested policy analysts and practitioners came to realize that full state deregulation of the trucking industry would come only through federal preemption.

It is important that we reflect on the implications of this situation for theories of federalism and policy innovation. Frequently, scholars of the innovation process have characterized the states as "laboratories of democracy."[3] In this characterization, states are seen as the crucible of new policy ideas. Indeed, as our discussion in chapter 2 made clear, states frequently led the way in the nineteenth-century development of railroad regulations. Yet, in the case of *deregulation*, states did little to promote a policy innovation from which the economic efficiency gains were large and obvious. For the most part, instead, they obstructed this change. To gain more insight into the political processes that generated this apparent anomaly, we carefully examine state economic regulation over intrastate trucking in the period from 1980 to 1994.

In the next section of this chapter, we describe what happened in the states following the Motor Carrier Act of 1980, which largely deregulated interstate trucking but left the regulation of intrastate trucking to the states. Following this, we present an index of regulatory strictness in the states as of mid-1994, just before federal pre-

2. Donald A. Schon, *Beyond the Stable State* (New York: Norton, 1971), p. 124.

3. David Osborne, *Laboratories of Democracy* (Boston, Mass.: Harvard Business School Press, 1988). The classic work in this field is Jack L. Walker's "The Diffusion of Innovations among the American States," *American Political Science Review*, vol. 63 (1969), pp. 880–99. For a comprehensive review of the relevant literature, see Robert L. Savage's "Diffusion Research Traditions and the Spread of Policy Innovations in a Federal System," *Publius: The Journal of Federalism*, vol. 15 (1985), pp. 1–27.

emption. We next consider why it was that the process of regulatory reform moved so slowly at the state level. This part of our discussion is divided into two sections, one dealing with state regulatory institutions and the other dealing with the politics of state regulation. After that, we devote another section to examining the costs of continued state regulation. Our focus here is on how intrastate trucking regulations benefited incumbent trucking firms at the expense of shippers and consumers. We follow this with a section in which we review the alternatives that emerged during the 1980s and 1990s to overcome the costs of state regulation. We focus here on showing how changing economic and political forces (linked closely to technological innovations) finally came together to result in federal preemption of state-level economic regulation of the trucking industry.

What the States Did after 1980

Before federal deregulation in 1980, most states regulated in a manner consistent with the Interstate Commerce Commission, with a few exceptions. New Jersey and Delaware, both of which are dense states where the commercial metropolitan exemption zones cover much of state territory, had never regulated intrastate trucking comprehensively. A few other states regulated in a relaxed manner. But for the most part, intrastate regulation was as strict as or stricter than federal regulation before ICC reform in the 1970s.

Trucking deregulation did pick up some momentum in the states after the federal 1980 MCA. Partly in response to a sunset law and disagreement about how to regulate, Florida, a state in which about 80 percent of its for-hire trucking tonnage moved within the state, deregulated the industry in 1980.[4] Trucking regulation in Florida before 1980 was characterized by strictly controlled entry and rate bureaus that set prices subject to the approval of the Public Service Commission. As the deregulation policy evolved, it worked well, and there was little pressure to go back to the old regime. Shippers

---

4. W. Bruce Allen, Arayah Preechemetta, Gary Shao, and Scott Singer, *The Impact of State Economic Regulation of Motor Carriage on Intrastate and Interstate Commerce*, Report prepared for the U.S. Department of Transportation, 1991, p. 8, using 1977 data. All figures quoted for individual state intrastate for-hire tonnage come from this source.

reported satisfaction with the new competitive environment. Florida's experience has been the subject of a number of studies that have documented its great successes, with rates dropping an average of 15 percent. Thus, just as California was a policy model for an unregulated airline market, Florida acted as a policy laboratory for trucking deregulation.[5] But even while these laboratory results proved highly positive, they did not lead to the expected policy diffusion. As we shall see, only a few states followed Florida's lead.

In 1981, Arizona deregulated trucking with Governor Babbitt's strong support, as the voters approved a referendum on the issue, with more than a two-to-one margin. Arizona also had a large amount of intrastate traffic, as 71 percent of its for-hire market was intrastate in 1977, and it had also been one of the strictest states in trucking regulation. Deregulation required a referendum because Arizona differs from most states in that its regulatory framework is actually part of the state constitution and can therefore be amended only with voter approval.[6] Afterward, Arizona truckers indicated their persistence in opposing deregulation: "We've got two more legislative sessions before the law takes effect—we'll be working hard to get legislation passed to modify the way the bill is currently written."[7] Although they did not succeed in overturning the referendum in Arizona, as we discuss below, a similar strategy by truckers in Indiana was successful later in the 1980s.

Continuing this pattern, Maine, a state with 88 percent intrastate traffic, followed the lead of Florida and Arizona and deregulated trucking in 1982.

Wisconsin was a state with a smaller percentage of intrastate

5. See, for example, Keon Chi, "Intrastate Motor Carrier Deregulation: The Florida Experience," *Innovations* (Lexington, Ky.: Council of State Governments, 1982), p. 6; and Roger Blair, David Kaserman, and James McClave, "Motor Carrier Deregulation: The Florida Experiment," *Review of Economics and Statistics*, vol. 68 (1986), pp. 159–64.

6. See Cassandra Moore, *Intrastate Trucking: Stronghold of the Regulators*, Policy analysis no. 204 (Washington, D.C.: CATO Institute, February 16, 1994), pp. 7–10, for more detail on Arizona's deregulatory battle and the positive results that have been reported afterward.

7. Fleet News Report, "Arizona Voters Ask for, and Get, Dereg," *Fleet News*, December 1980, p. 86.

traffic, at 29 percent. With the support of the governor and high-level regulators, Wisconsin largely deregulated trucking in 1983, though the state maintained regulatory power over trucking insurance and the fitness of carriers.

This one-state-per-year pattern continued in 1984, when the Libertarian party successfully promoted trucking deregulation in Alaska, a state where nearly 100 percent of the for-hire truck tonnage moved intrastate. It was a one-issue campaign for a party that was looking for issues, and it happened to be successful.

On the other side of the scale, Vermont had a very small percentage of intrastate traffic, with only 5 percent, the lowest in the nation. Vermont deregulated in 1985, seemingly because of a lack of interest by any major party in continuing the regulations.[8]

After 1985, state trucking deregulation in the states slowed considerably. Between then and 1994, only Maryland, where 22 percent of trucked tonnage moved intrastate, deregulated comprehensively (in 1992). A few more states passed partial deregulation bills that reduced regulation or deregulated certain segments of their trucking industry. But aside from the nine states mentioned here, all other states continued to have legislation providing for the regulation of intrastate trucking that was little different from the pre-1980 rules. Thus, the spread of the idea of legislative trucking deregulation was very slow, despite the federal success and several years of documented state successes in Florida and elsewhere. As one observer noted: "Complete intrastate deregulation got off to no more than a snail's pace which soon fizzled out completely."[9]

In this section, we will examine the trends in state regulation between 1980 and 1994, relying partly on data gathered by the Transportation Lawyers Association (TLA), headed by the efforts of Daniel Baker, in his annual "Your Letter of the Law" report. These surveys were filled in by more than one respondent in each state, in almost every year, from 1983 through 1993. These are the best and most comprehensive data available on economic regulation in the states over time.[10]

---

8. Daniel Baker, "Your Letter of the Law," Transportation Lawyers Association, 1989, p. 2.

9. Dabney Waring, "The Downside of Motor Carrier Deregulation," *Transportation Law Journal*, vol. 21 (1993), p. 427.

10. These surveys were prepared by the Transportation Lawyers Association and

To update the issues and to provide more in-depth information about how the states were actually regulating right up to the point of federal preemption, in June 1994 we conducted our own telephone survey of all forty-one states that then continued to regulate intrastate trucking. In each state, we spoke to an official, sometimes more than one, with responsibility for trucking regulation. We received useful responses from all forty-one states. When we asked similar questions, the responses we received are essentially similar to those of the TLA. In the sections that follow, we use these data sources to paint a comprehensive picture of state regulation as of mid-1994.

Although only a few state legislatures deregulated trucking comprehensively, over 100 bills were introduced and considered in the fifty states between 1983 and 1994. Some of these bills addressed comprehensive deregulation, while others focused on deregulating part of the trucking industry. The timing of these bills, however, suggests that the idea was most popular in the early 1980s and faded somewhat later. As table 4–1 illustrates, partial or comprehensive deregulatory bills were considered in twenty-two state legislatures in 1983, but this figure fell to single digits in most years after that.

Our own 1994 survey confirmed that twenty-five of the forty-one states considered some form of deregulation legislation in the years 1987 through 1994. Some of these addressed only a few shipped items, such as mining items in Nevada, sludge in Colorado, and open-top dump carriers in Alabama. Others were more comprehensive, but most of these bills failed to pass the legislature. Over 85 percent of our respondents (thirty-five of forty-one) reported that they did *not* expect major legislative changes in their states in the near future.

As we saw on the interstate level, with ICC administrative deregulatory action in the 1970s preceding congressional action, legislative action is not the only way to achieve effective deregulation. State regulators themselves implemented more relaxed trucking rate

---

provided to us by Daniel Baker. TLA performs a comprehensive survey of the states, relying on up to five sources in each state to answer a series of questions about intrastate trucking deregulation. The survey was prepared nearly every year from 1983 to 1993. Most of the questions are asked in exactly the same fashion each year. There are a few questions that change slightly or that were added over the years, based on changes in trucking regulations.

TABLE 4–1
SURVEY RESULTS ON STATE REGULATION OF TRUCKING, 1983–1994
(number of states)

	Legislatures Considering Deregulation Bills	Strict Rate Regulation States	Strict Entry States	States with "Effective" Application Protests
1983	22	—	—	—
1984	9	33	41	40
1985	11	32	40	36
1986	5	31	36	36
1987	7	25	35	36
1988	—	—	—	—
1989	11	24	34	33
1990	8	24	34	29
1991	—	—	—	—
1992	11	23	35	29
1993	12	24	35	30
1994	6	25	36	28

NOTE: Empty cells indicate no data from those years.
SOURCE: Authors' tabulations from Transportation Lawyers Association annual surveys.

regulation in a larger number of states after 1980. Table 4–1 shows that while about two-thirds of all states reported that they regulated intrastate rates strictly in 1984, this number was reduced to about half the states, twenty-five, in 1994.[11] Still, this raises the question of a "half-full or half-empty glass"; half the states still regulated intrastate trucking rates strictly in 1994 despite fifteen years of evidence showing gains from deregulation. Either the other twenty-five states did not regulate rates at all, which was virtually true in the nine deregulated states, or their regulators played a limited role in rate regulation. It is important to note that, unlike more permanent legislative changes, administrative enforcement could change as dif-

11. Respondents are asked whether their rate regulation, as practiced, is strict, relaxed, or not applied at all.

ferent top administrators come into office, a point we discuss further below.[12]

In our 1994 survey, we gained a more detailed understanding of how states really performed strict or relaxed rate regulation of common carriers. One way that some states partially relaxed rate regulation was to allow "rate windows" or "zones of rate flexibility" explicitly, so that carriers could lower or raise rates by up to a specified percentage, without extensive regulatory approvals. But, as of mid-1994, only eight states allowed such rate windows, which ranged from as low as 10 percent to as high as 100 percent.

Tariffs, which detailed the specific rates for a particular commodity over a particular route, had to be filed in most states. They were typically filed by rate bureaus or by the carriers themselves. While twenty states had fewer than 1,000 tariffs filed in 1993, in eleven states more than 1,000 tariffs were filed, with a high of 18,000 in Indiana. Obviously, as with interstate trucking under the filed-rate doctrine (discussed in chapter 3), filing, maintaining, and using these filed rates were major regulatory tasks in the states.

In our 1994 survey, we found that for carriers to be allowed general rate increases, regulators required explicit cost justification in thirty-three states, and in twenty-nine of these states the regulatory commission could hold hearings on general rate increases. Thirteen states reported that they still used operating ratios, which we discuss below, to determine appropriate rates, with a range in these ratios from 90 percent to 95 percent.[13]

We also found in our survey that independent actions on rates were allowed in thirty-nine of the forty-one states still regulating. This sounds as though most states had effective flexibility in rates, but it is somewhat misleading, as we noted it was in chapter 3 for

---

12. We do not believe that small changes from year to year, of one state or two, for example from 1987 to 1994, are particularly significant in illustrating a general pattern, because of possible minor errors with the surveys or the respondents. Thus, there has not necessarily been a trend toward more strict regulation in the past few years.

13. NARUC (National Association of Regulatory Utility Commissioners) reported in 1987 that state operating ratios ranged from 89 percent to 96.5 percent. See Allen et al., *The Impact of State Economic Regulation of Motor Carriage*, p. 28.

interstate independent actions before deregulation. Most of the states, thirty-two, required these actions to be advertised, usually for more than a week but less than a month (although four states required that independent actions be advertised for more than a month). After these independent actions were advertised, other carriers were able to protest them in thirty-eight states. In thirty-seven states, competitors were able to join in these independent actions. While this may sound as if it promoted competition and the ability to lower rates, instead the combination of long advertising periods, protests, and the possibility of competitors' charging new rates promoted cartel-like behavior (especially as most carriers were members of antitrust-immune rate bureaus). In this environment, it did not pay for individual firms to offer lower rates through independent actions. In the end, if the independent actions taken by firms survived these lengthy processes, their rates were usually matched by competitors anyway.

In 1994, rate bureaus existed and were immune from state antitrust action in thirty-one states. This number actually increased after 1980, because in 1985, in the *Southern Motor Carrier Ratemaking Conference* case, which the U.S. Department of Justice had started as an antitrust suit in 1977, the U.S. Supreme Court ruled that intrastate collective rate making did not violate national antitrust laws as long as it was sanctioned and actively supervised by regulatory bodies. These bureaus were immune from interstate antitrust action based on Reed-Bulwinkle, but lower courts held that national antitrust laws did apply to intrastate rate making, until the Supreme Court reversed these decisions.

Rates for *contract* carriers were still regulated in thirty states in 1994, although usually with fewer requirements than for common carriers. Often, the main regulation of contract carriers was that their rates could not be below those of common carriers. This regulation fitted with the long-standing pattern, described in chapter 3, of regulating contract carriers to protect common carriers rather than shippers.

Officials in seven states indicated to us that the undercharge problem that plagued interstate shippers in recent years was beginning to emerge on the state level. Officials in Arkansas, California, Connecticut, Michigan, New Hampshire, and New York reported some problems with undercharge filings related to intrastate rates.

In addition to rates, the ability of new firms to enter intrastate markets as common carriers is a critical aspect of a regulatory regime. Again, between 1980 and 1994, state regulators eased entry requirements somewhat, as fewer states required a full-blown "certificate of public convenience and necessity," the traditional burden on entrants to show that their service was needed. Table 4–1 shows a somewhat similar pattern of relaxed entry requirements as for rates, although fewer states reported that they relaxed their entry requirements over this period. In addition to the seven states that deregulated legislatively after 1980,[14] five states moved out of the "strict" entry standards category into easier-to-meet requirements or none at all. It is important to note that many states also exempted the shipping of certain commodities from entry and rate regulation requirements. As with interstate trucking, by 1994 agricultural products were exempt in almost every state, while individual states often favored important elements of their economy with exemptions, such as lumber in New Hampshire, newspapers in New York, and coal in West Virginia.

Following the pre-1980 pattern at the federal level, in 1994 when new entrants applied, incumbent firms were allowed to protest and try to block the new common-carrier entrant in forty of the forty-one states. In addition to the requirements cited above, such protests sometimes made it very difficult for new firms to get into the market, even when there was a demand for their service. Table 4–1 shows the number of states in which protests of new carrier applications were considered "effective" (that is, they "sometimes" or "often" resulted in denial of entry for service). This number dropped from forty in 1984 to fewer than thirty in 1994. Still, even on the eve of federal preemption, in 60 percent of the states incumbent trucking firms could often effectively protest and block new entrants. Of course, the numbers of states with effective protests are fairly similar to those with strict entry, as high entry barriers and protests typically worked in tandem to prevent full-blown competition.

Whether these protests of new entrants actually blocked entry was often contingent on which party held the burden of proof. Did applicants have to demonstrate gaps in current service, or did incumbents have to show that their service was adequate? In 1994, the

---

14. As we have noted, New Jersey and Delaware had not regulated intrastate trucking comprehensively.

burden of proof was on the applicant in twenty-four states, while it was on the protester in sixteen states. In five states, the protest period was relatively short, a week or less, but in the other thirty-three states the protest period was longer than a week but less than a month. In 1994, sixteen states reported that virtually all, that is 95–100 percent, of the applications for entry were approved. Another ten states reported that most, 80–95 percent, were approved, while in eight states less than 80 percent of new applicants were approved, with some considerably below that number. [15]

Entry into *contract* carriage was easier in most states than for common carriers. Still, in 1994, nineteen states required contract carriers to show public convenience and necessity, and such entry could be denied in those nineteen states. Nearly all the states, thirty-seven, allowed protests of contract-carrier entry.

Clearly, these trends indicate that the states showed some tendency toward deregulation over the years 1980 to 1994. More states did not regulate at all, some relaxed the manner in which they regulated rates, and some relaxed market entry requirements. Again, the question is whether to read this pattern as a half-full or a half-empty glass. Just as the number of complete deregulations leveled off after 1985 or 1986, so most other deregulatory trends leveled off after 1986. Very little deregulatory momentum built over the eight years before 1994. By the time of federal preemption of state regulation, about half the states still regulated rates strictly, and more than half still made entry very difficult.

Another important point to emphasize is that most of this relaxed regulation resulted from actions taken by regulatory staff. In the absence of legislation taking it off the books, future regulators could have enforced it more strictly once again. To make the point, we note that, over the past decade, California and Indiana *reversed* their regulations from more to less relaxed. In addition, at the time of federal preemption in 1994, there were still huge filing requirements in most states, as illustrated by the 18,000 tariffs filed in Indiana in 1993. These burdens, as well as the efforts of carriers and shippers to avoid the impacts of state regulation, were frequently left out of economic welfare studies, because such studies typically focus on

---

15. Note that these percentages are self-reported by the regulators, are not open to easy confirmation, and may tend to be biased upward.

direct costs. When analysts did attempt to measure those *indirect* costs, however, they found the estimated costs of state regulation increased substantially, as illustrated below.

It is difficult to interpret the maze of state economic regulatory requirements that existed before the recent preemption. Clearly, more states than just the nine that had comprehensively deregulated had relaxed their entry or rate regulations. A number of the most strictly regulated states had relaxed somewhat and had considered going further, as our case studies below illustrate.[16] In 1993, Allen et al. reported the details of their analysis of economic regulation in four states—Iowa, Kansas, Missouri, and Nebraska.[17] The authors found that, of these four states, only Nebraska still regulated in a manner that could be described as strict. On the basis of these results, the authors argued that the economic welfare costs from deregulation may be much smaller than several earlier studies had estimated. But they also pointed out that any possible benefits of remaining economic regulation, for safety or for small communities, were not very important either.

To get a more accurate sense of regulations both on the books and in practice, we developed an index of regulatory strictness, based on several questions from our 1994 survey.[18]

Index of Regulatory Strictness

We used four measures for strictness of entry and four measures for strictness of rate regulation. These could also be assessed separately,

---

16. Though it did not detail which ones, the American Trucking Associations estimated that about one-third of the states were largely or effectively deregulated. See U.S. Congress, House of Representatives, Subcommittee on Surface Transportation of the Committee on Commerce, testimony of Tom Donohue, president of the ATA, *Hearings on Legislation to Preempt State Motor Carrier Regulations Pertaining to Rates, Routes, and Services*, 103d Congress, 1st session, July 20, 1994.

17. Benjamin J. Allen, T. H. Maze, and Clyde Walter, "Intrastate Trucking Deregulation: Have Both the Negative and Positive Impacts Been Overstated?" *Transportation Journal*, vol. 33 (1993), pp. 30–39.

18. Our telephone survey attempted to confirm and go beyond the surveys of the Transportation Lawyers Association. We asked for the official most familiar with trucking regulation within the state regulatory body. We asked that person several questions, many of which were specific follow-ups to questions that the TLA had asked. We received useful responses from all forty-one states that still regulated, during the month of June 1994.

but we combined them to yield an index of total state regulatory strictness ranging from zero to eight.[19]

The most critical aspects of entry regulation were the requirements entrants had to meet and the possibility for incumbent firms, or the regulators themselves, to resist entry. Thus, we gave a state one point if it required an entrant to show the traditionally used proof of "public convenience and necessity," and zero otherwise. If the burden of proof concerning the need for entry was on the applicant, we gave the state one point, and zero if the burden was on the protestant. If the protests of entry were sometimes effective or successful, according to our respondents, we give the state one point, and zero otherwise. Finally, if the percentage of applicants actually approved was 80 percent or less, that state received one point, and zero for percentages greater than 80 percent. Thus, the forty-one states that still regulated in 1994 ranged the entire length of our entry scale, from zero to four, with the largest number of states (fourteen) receiving a score of three on the index.

We developed a similar scale for rate regulation. The key issues in rate regulation were how rates were set and how much flexibility carriers had to change rates to meet market conditions. If a state reported that it regulated rates strictly, we gave the state one point, and zero otherwise. If a state had rate bureaus with antitrust immunity we gave the state one point, and zero otherwise. If a state required carriers to cost-justify all rate changes *and* could require regulatory hearings on such rate changes, then the state received one point, and zero otherwise. Finally, if the state did not allow rate windows or zones of rate flexibility, it received one point, and zero if it did allow such rate flexibility. These questions yielded a scale for rates that covered the entire range from zero to four, with the largest number of states (fifteen) receiving a score of four points, as strict as possible.

---

19. We chose the questions for their theoretical accuracy in capturing the regulatory concept, and we also chose questions on which there was real variation among the states. We chose to develop an additive measure, giving equal weighting to each factor. Our rationale for this approach was that, although we know that strictness depends on a number of factors, it is unclear how these various factors should be weighed. Thus, by adding them together, we make the assumption that all of them contribute equally to making a strict regime.

To yield an index accurately reflecting the degree of state regulation over both entry and rates as of mid-1994, we combined these two scales. Our combined scale ranged from zero to eight and we observed at least one state at every level, except for the one point score. Figure 4–1 is a map of the states with their index scores. The deregulated states are indicated with cross-hatching. The moderately regulated states are shaded, while the states still regulating strictly in 1994 are shown in white.

Five states received the maximum score of eight points: Colorado, Kentucky, Oklahoma, Pennsylvania, and Nevada. Eleven states scored seven points (Texas perhaps the most prominent among them), while ten states scored six points. We consider scores of six points or higher to indicate strict regulation of rates and entry. Another fourteen states received scores between two and five, which indicates partial deregulation, while one additional state, Idaho, received a score of 0 points.

We believe this index is an accurate portrayal of the manner in which states reported that they regulated and how they actually regulated trucking on the eve of federal preemption. Thirteen of the twenty states in which Allen et al. found higher intrastate rates than interstate rates are in our category above six points.[20]

This correspondence suggests that about half the fifty states still regulated entry and rates strictly in 1994. This finding is consistent with those of the Transportation Lawyers Association's surveys, over time, which showed a fairly flat trend from 1986 to 1993. After fifteen years of very successful interstate deregulation and fifteen years of Florida's successful state policy model, half the states still regulated intrastate markets strictly. Clearly, as of August 1994, when Congress moved to preempt intrastate trucking regulation, there was little sign from the states themselves that they were about to complete the deregulatory agenda on their own volition.

A question naturally arises from the discussion to this point. That is, following passage of the MCA of 1980, why was progress toward state-level deregulation so slow? To develop an answer to this question, we must consider a number of factors. For convenience, we categorize these factors under two broad headings: state regulatory

---

20. Allen et al., *The Impact of State Economic Regulation of Motor Carriage.*

FIGURE 4–1

INDEX OF STATE ECONOMIC REGULATION, 1994

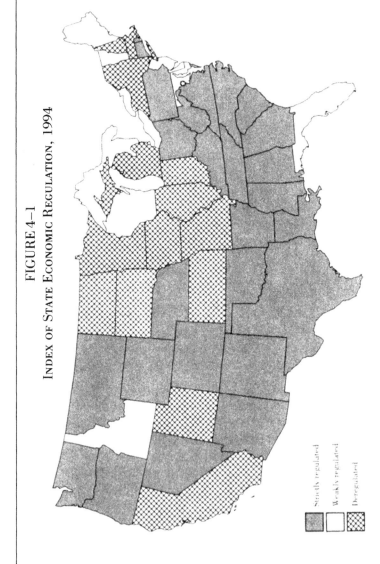

Strictly regulated

Weakly regulated

Deregulated

NOTE: Alaska is not regulated, and Hawaii is strictly regulated.
SOURCE: Authors.

institutions and the politics of state regulation. The following two sections are devoted to exploring these factors in turn.

State Regulatory Institutions

While legislative provisions regarding how to regulate were critical for shaping the practice of intrastate trucking regulation, it is important to note that the regulators themselves often had some discretion to implement and apply those laws in a strict fashion or in a more relaxed manner. This administrative discretion had serious implications for the way that these regulations affected truckers in the states.

In thirty-one of the forty-one states that still performed economic regulation of intrastate trucking in 1994, the policies were administered by the public utility commissions, or PUCs.[21] These PUCs have also usually regulated a state's electricity and telecommunications firms, which are generally more salient political issues and which, therefore, usually involve a far greater investment in staff and other resources. PUC commissioners (ranging in number from one to seven in the states) are appointed by the governor in about three-fourths of the states, and these commissioners are judged to have a considerable degree of independence from governors and legislators in making their regulatory choices.[22] In the other one-fourth of the states, mostly in the South, PUC commissioners are elected directly by voters. Studies are inconclusive on whether elected PUC regulators make consistently different policy choices from appointed regulators.[23]

In the other ten states that regulated trucking in 1994, the implementation of regulations was done by a department of transportation, a revenue department, or other similar bureaucracy. Usually these agencies are headed by a single gubernatorial appointee, rather

---

21. State regulatory agencies are also sometimes called public service commissions, utilities boards, corporation commissions, and other similar names.

22. See Paul Teske, "The State of State Regulation," in David Rosenbloom and Richard Schwartz, eds., *Handbook of Regulation and Administrative Law* (New York: Marcel Dekker, Inc., 1994), for an update on what academic studies of the independence of state regulators have discovered.

23. See Paul Teske, *After Divestiture: The Political Economy of State Telecommunications Regulation* (Albany: SUNY Press, 1990).

than a multiheaded PUC. In states where the PUC performed the economic regulation, departments of transportation and highway departments were often (and continue to be) responsible for safety and related police-power enforcement activities in trucking (see chapter 5).[24]

In either kind of bureaucracy, the daily aspects of state trucking regulation (both economic and noneconomic) have always been handled largely by staff members; commissioners have not been regularly involved in trucking. Legislators have become involved from time to time, for instance when legislation has been considered or passed, but most important activity has taken place within the regulatory agencies. In smaller states with very small numbers of staffers, the actual amount of economic regulatory activity was limited regardless of the state statutes.[25]

Of course, trucking regulators get their authority delegated from state legislatures, and this delegation of powers from the legislature has typically varied across states. Allen et al. argue: "Most statutes are written ambiguously with the intent that the appointees to the regulatory agency will make de facto law depending on their judgment."[26] But some states have traditionally delegated more power than others; high-delegation states have given their public utility commissions and departments of transportation more scope to regulate, a greater number of instruments to wield in regulating, and minimal oversight requirements, while other state legislatures have delegated less to their regulators and retained more powers.

A recent quantitative analysis of why the states vary on these dimensions revealed that party differences among the legislative houses and the governor's office, or "divided government," led to more delegated scope and instruments, as this form of political conflict encourages politicians to pass trucking regulation on to state

---

24. Comparing scores from our index, the thirty-one states using PUCs to regulate trucking average a 5.58 score, while the ten states using departments of transportation average a somewhat more relaxed 4.8. While there is a difference between the two institutional forms of regulators, then, the difference is not statistically significant at high levels, so we cannot say with statistical confidence that states using different kinds of bureaucratic institutions regulate intrastate trucking differently.

25. See Allen et al., "Intrastate Trucking Deregulation."

26. Allen et al., *The Impact of State Economic Regulation of Motor Carriage*, p. 41.

regulators. At the same time, states with greater turnover in their legislatures have been more likely to impose fewer oversight requirements on their trucking regulators, as the political uncertainty about future legislative coalitions encourages the current legislative majority to insulate regulators more. Finally, greater delegated scope has usually been associated with greater oversight requirements, suggesting that even though politicians often pass aspects of this contentious issue on to regulators, they retain oversight to determine how it is being handled, so that they might intervene in the future.[27]

As the case studies below illustrate, the state regulatory institutions, and the powers they held, were often very important to the development of regulatory and deregulatory policies.

The State Regulatory Process. Given some amount of delegated authority to the regulators, how did state regulation actually operate? Traditionally, the regulatory process at the state level was much like that at the ICC before the 1970s but often performed with fewer resources. Only in the states that reformed regulation after 1980 did these processes change much. Our survey findings illustrated in some detail how entry applications were processed. Now we turn to the details of state rate regulation as it was in mid-1994, on the eve of federal preemption.

Rate setting. In a majority of states, trucking rates for freight shipments along specified routes were regulated. For general common carriers, shipped commodities were classified by the National Motor Freight Traffic Association (NMFTA).[28] States either published the rates themselves or established a set of guidelines for rates by which truckers were bound. Generally, operating ratios were used to determine minimum rates for specific lines. In some states, this ratio was

---

27. For the full quantitative evidence and analysis of the theories suggesting the hypothesis that political conflict and uncertainty lead to varying degrees of delegation, see Mallika Bhattacharya, *Testing Theories of Legislative Delegation: Evidence from the States* (Ph.D. diss., SUNY at Stony Brook, 1994).

28. William Pugh, "Intrastate Regulation," *Transportation Practitioners Journal*, vol. 60 (1993), notes that some carriers have been using the NMFTA's classification schemes without paying membership dues, or free riding. The Oregon PUC staff, for example, has sided with the NMFTA and argued that carriers should be forced to pay their share of such a collective process.

the same for all routes, regardless of the type of truck, the length of haul, or the nature of the shipment. Other states determined the ratio on a case-by-case basis. Some states no longer formally used operating ratios.[29]

An operating ratio is the proportion of operating costs to operating revenues. If this ratio is greater than one, costs are greater than revenues, resulting in losses for firms on designated routes. Conversely, a ratio below one produces profits for trucking firms. The key for regulators is to define a ratio that allows firms to operate efficiently (less than 1.00), without generating excess profits, which have historically been viewed as an operating ratio below .90. Before 1980, at the federal level, the ICC generally applied a target operating ratio of .93. In our 1994 survey, we found that most states maintained ratios in the range of .90–.95. Thus, in theory, rates were set to the lowest threshold at which motor carriers could still achieve a normal rate of return on their investment.

In practice, though, such operating efficiency was rarely achieved; instead, the generation of operating ratios was plagued with flaws, resulting in inflated prices and noncompetitive behavior. Determining rates that reflected the target operating ratio required regulators to estimate the operating cost function for truckers. Since most states based their estimates on the operating costs of firms observed in practice, either as an average of the cost parameters of all firms or of the most efficient firms, estimates of operating costs were necessarily no better than those produced by the most efficient firm and more likely were substantially removed from the theoretically lowest cost. Thus, at the outset, most rates were set above the theoretically optimal point.

The situation worsened as more complications were added over time. Cost functions of firms, for example, were frequently subject to fluctuations due to shifting fuel prices, labor wages, and technology. If states were to maintain their specified operating ratio, they needed to readjust their estimates of costs continually. But because few states' regulatory agencies had enough resources to compile such information in a sound and timely fashion, even greater differences

29. See also John Felton and Dale Anderson, *Regulation and Deregulation of the Motor Carrier Industry* (Ames, Iowa: Iowa State University Press, 1987), pp. 99–102, for more information on the use of state operating ratios.

between estimated and true costs developed. Furthermore, since trucking firms knew in advance that regulatory bodies would ensure a certain rate of return, through the operating ratio, they had no incentive to curb costs that would affect all carriers, such as labor demands for higher wages.[30]

Exemptions. Because regulation often raised rather than lowered prices, state legislators had exempted certain critical commodities from regulated rates in their states. Just as the 1935 MCA exempted agricultural products from interstate regulations, in 1994 most states exempted agricultural products from intrastate regulation. Sometimes other products shipped were exempted for political reasons. Kentucky, for example, exempted coal, and Oregon exempted potatoes. Those exemptions show that legislators realized that trucking regulation did not help shippers and that critical elements of the state economy needed "protection" from the regulation. Some states went further than others; North Carolina statutes exempted sand and gravel, newspapers, insecticides, farm co-ops, livestock, fish, and raw lumber products.[31]

Of course, the state regulatory process of setting rates and exemptions, like all other regulatory processes, was inherently subject to political influence of various kinds. As in electricity and telephone regulation, many scholars believe that capture by regulated firms was the dominant pattern in state trucking regulation. Stigler provided the classic theoretical statement of this view and, interestingly, tested it empirically using data from state trucking weight requirements.[32]

But capture was often too simple a story. Even the ICC in its most protective days from the 1940s to the 1970s did not show the simple capture pattern that was often ascribed to it. Rothenberg, in the most comprehensive quantitative analysis of ICC decision making, showed that entry, rate, and merger decisions were influenced

---

30. For an excellent discussion of the generation of operating ratios and their problems see Allen et al., *The Impact of State Economic Regulation of Motor Carriage*, chap. 2.

31. See James Freeman and Richard Beilock, "State Regulatory Responses to Federal Motor Carrier Reregulation," *Florida Law Review*, vol. 35 (1983), p. 61, n. 31.

32. George Stigler, "The Theory of Economic Regulation," *Bell Journal of Economics and Management Science*, vol. 2 (1971), pp. 3–21.

by labor, government officials, and shippers, as well as by truckers. A more captured ICC did emerge over time, as presidential appointees became more favorable to the truckers in the 1950s and 1960s.[33] Still, several interested parties attempted to influence federal and state trucking regulation throughout the years.

The Politics of State Regulation

From this discussion and the history of trucking regulation presented earlier, it is clear that several interest groups played a role in shaping regulatory policy. Truckers themselves largely favored continuing state regulation of entry and the use of rate bureaus to set prices. The economic theory, anecdotal evidence, and quantitative evidence on the efficacy of Senate PAC contributions by the ATA in 1980,[34] all indicate that truckers were the most important interest group opposing deregulation at all levels. This is the classic cartel argument, and trucking firms have also been supported by Teamsters Union drivers, who, as noted above, have managed to obtain wages 10–20 percent higher than nonunion drivers, partly because of protective regulation. The International Brotherhood of Teamsters claims over 1.4 million members nationwide, of which a few hundred thousand are truck drivers.

As regulation began to unravel in some areas, some truckers realized that they could gain from further deregulation and began to support it. Thus, it is not appropriate to say that all truckers opposed deregulation at the state level; it depended on which firms in which markets, the extent of deregulation, and the rise of other competitors, like the air cargo carriers.

Other interests managed to influence trucking policy throughout the years, as illustrated in chapters 2 and 3. The railroads, for example, long influenced regulation of their trucking competitors at

---

33. Lawrence Rothenberg, *Regulation, Organizations, and Politics* (Ann Arbor: University of Michigan Press, 1994).

34. See John Frendreis and Richard Waterman, "PAC Contributions and Legislative Behavior: Senate Voting on Trucking Deregulation," *Social Science Quarterly*, vol. 66 (1985), pp. 401–12.

the federal and state levels.[35] As noted above, agricultural interest groups influenced trucking regulation by gaining exemptions from regulation for their products to gain lower transportation prices.

Shippers almost uniformly favored deregulation. The National Industrial Transportation League long favored total deregulation of trucking.[36] Members of the National Private Truck Council, which also favored deregulation, are mainly shippers as well as carriers of their own products.

Testing the power of these interest groups at the state level, we performed a quantitative regression analysis using regulatory data from the Transportation Lawyers Association to determine which interest groups influenced whether a state continued to regulate intrastate trucking in the 1990s. We used independent variables to measure the power of truckers, shippers, railroad interests, and farmers, controlling for the extent of the metropolitan commercial exemption zone in each state.[37] The results of this analysis provide strong statistical evidence of the economic theory of regulation. The political power of truckers at the state level translated into continuing economic regulation to protect them. At the same time, when the political power of shippers was higher, the state was more likely to deregulate. These quantitative results accord with the conventional wisdom and anecdotal evidence that regulations benefited established trucking firms and their employees at the expense of shippers and, ultimately, consumers.

---

35. See Donald Harper, *Economic Regulation of the Trucking Industry by the States* (Urbana, Ill.: University of Illinois Press, 1959), as well as Charles Carter, *State Regulation of Motor Carriers in North Carolina* (Chapel Hill: University of North Carolina Press, 1958); and Andrew Hacker, "Pressure Politics in Pennsylvania: The Truckers versus the Railroads," in A. Westin, ed., *The Uses of Power: Seven Cases in American Politics* (New York: Harcourt, Brace and World, 1962), for detailed discussions of how railroad interests have influenced state trucking regulation.

36. They may favor some continued light regulation of railroad lines that are effective monopolies for some shippers. Even here, they believe that the regulation should not be strict.

37. These details of this analysis, as well as additional results for the question of state rate regulation, are reported in Paul Teske, Samuel Best, and Michael Mintrom, "The Economic Theory of Regulation and Trucking Deregulation: Shifting to the State Level," *Public Choice*, vol. 79 (1994), pp. 247–56.

Case Studies. To examine in more detail the political tug-of-war between trucking firms and shippers at the state level, we now present four case studies of state regulatory politics. We chose these particular cases because they highlight how differences in the balance of interests at the state level can produce divergent outcomes. In Texas, truckers dominated for a long time, but shippers and institutional actors recently began to force some changes. The Indiana case points to the importance of the trucking firms, even to the point of reversing reforms. The case of California emphasizes the role played by shippers. And the Michigan case demonstrates the important role that labor unions sometimes played in influencing the configuration of the regulatory regime. These cases show that, even though each state regulated strictly, there was not a single way that they all got to that point. The details in these cases largely support the quantitative results we have just reported. But quantitative results draw our attention to broad patterns, while these case studies show the important, and often idiosyncratic, individual-level differences that broader patterns can disguise, as well as the roles played by institutional actors.

Daniel Baker, who followed state regulation for the Transportation Lawyers Association, argued that deregulation was *never* successfully passed in a state when trucking interests were organized and opposed it actively, especially if they could gain support from small communities that feared a reduction in service under deregulation and from smaller shippers who were often cross-subsidized by state regulatory practices. Advocates of deregulation, mainly large shippers and sometimes trucking firms that were not advantaged by state regulation, were only successful when they gained the support of a governor or strong legislators *and* when truckers did not actively fight against them.

Of course, not all states were equal in the importance of state regulation of intrastate trucking. The Gellman report, analyzed below, estimated the costs of regulation by state in 1989. It found that the states with the largest efficiency costs from trucking regulation were, in descending order, Texas, Illinois, Pennsylvania, Michigan, California, Georgia, Washington, New York, Louisiana, Oregon, Minnesota, and Indiana. This list matches fairly well with internal ICC data that Allen et al. analyzed from the mid-1970s, when they found that Texas had 19 percent of all intrastate trucking revenue in

114

the United States and California had 13 percent, followed by Ohio with 8 percent, Michigan with 5 percent, and New York with 4 percent. These top five states thus made up 50 percent of all intrastate revenues, and the top ten states held 67 percent.[38]

Thus, case studies of these states are critically important. We provide brief analyses of trucking politics in Texas (rated first above), Michigan (fourth), California (fifth), and Indiana (twelfth).[39]

Texas. For more than fifty years, Texas transportation regulators were among the most stubborn in the United States in maintaining their regulatory authority, regulating strictly and resisting and challenging federal preemption efforts. Some 64 percent of all for-hire trucking tonnage in Texas has moved intrastate.[40]

The Texas Railroad Commission (TRC), which also regulated trucking, played a featured historical role in many court cases documented in chapter 2. The commissioners are elected by the voters and wield extraordinary power. After 1980, the TRC opposed the preemption elements of the Staggers Act in court but lost. The TRC was prominently featured in the 1986 ICC preemption-related *Armstrong* and the 1992 ICC *Texas Warehousemen* trucking cases analyzed below. In recent years, the TRC retained its status as one of the strictest trucking regulators.

In the past dozen years, several shipper groups organized in Texas to challenge restrictive regulation. In 1982, more than 200 shippers banded together to form the Texas Association to Improve Distribution (TEX-AID). Their efforts also received support from Common Cause, the consumer group, and from the Shippers Oilfield Traffic Association and the Texas Association for Competitive Transportation. TEX-AID spent over $500,000 in the mid-1980s to try to achieve intrastate deregulation. While they did not achieve that goal, TEX-AID did succeed in convincing the legislature to introduce a zone of "rate reasonableness."[41] Full deregulation was not imple-

---

38. Allen et al., *The Impact of State Economic Regulation of Motor Carriage.*

39. See Moore, *Intrastate Trucking*, pp. 7–21, for more detailed case studies of several states.

40. Again these figures are from Allen et al., *The Impact of State Economic Regulation of Motor Carriage*, from ICC data from the mid-1970s.

41. This began in 1987. The state legislature passed a bill that allowed rates to deviate from the state-prescribed levels by up to 15 percent for truckload shipments and by up to 5 percent for less-than-truckload. See Robert Bowman, "The Great

mented because of strong opposition from the Texas Motor Transport Association (TMTA).

TEX-AID argued that 80 percent of intrastate common carriage was controlled by only six firms—Brown Express, Central Freight, Herder Truck Lines, Meridian Express, Red Arrow Freight Lines, and Southwestern Motor Transport.[42] According to another estimate, two of these common carriers controlled 55 percent of the Texas market, and the top four together controlled more than 70 percent. More recently, a transportation consultant estimated that one firm, Central Freight Lines, with 4,000 employees, three hubs, and fifty-three terminals, controlled 75 percent of the *general commodities* Texas intrastate market.[43]

Whatever the exact market share of these privileged carriers under Texas state regulations, the extreme difficulty of gaining approval for new entrants into the Texas market drove up prices, and carrier opposition to regulatory change became entrenched. In 1983, shippers won some relief from the legislature, in shifting the burden of proof on entry, so that an incumbent needed to show adequate service, not an entrant. Previously, applicants could spend as much as $30,000 on legal fees trying to get an operating certificate and still fail to obtain one. But this change did not have a profound impact on entry or on rates.

To illustrate the effect on rates of TRC regulation, for example, in 1994 moving a shipment of tobacco products the 125 miles from Shreveport, Louisiana, to Sulphur Springs, Texas, cost $450. The same shipment traveling from Sulphur Springs to Dallas—two Texas points only 85 miles apart—cost $714.[44] The Gellman Report and other studies of the cost of state regulation suggest that intrastate trucking regulations in Texas were costing the U.S. economy $1–2

Deregulation Debate Is Alive and Well in Texas and California," *Traffic World*, October 30, 1989, pp. 18–19.

42. See James Cooke, "Deregulation Update: Showdown in Texas," *Traffic Management*, June 1984, p. 63. In legislative hearings, estimates have been offered that these six carriers control 96 percent of the Texas market.

43. See Debra Beachy, "Texas Cargo Deregulation Could Backfire, Critics Say," *Journal of Commerce*, April 12, 1994, p. 2B.

44. From "Trucking in the States," editorial, *Journal of Commerce*, January 20, 1994, p. 6A.

billion per year, most of which was a cost to the Texas economy directly.

Shippers responded to these high rates and the lack of intrastate competition in ways other than political action. Some warehouses formerly based in Texas moved just out of the state to avoid intrastate hauls at higher rates, moves that harmed the Texas economy. Some shippers also adjusted in other ways, as a recent report made clear: "High intrastate truckload costs not only encourage shippers to look out of state for services, they also have prompted Texas shippers to use private fleets wherever possible. TEX-AID's current president, Ron E. Cummings, says that it's less expensive for his company, Anderson Clayton Foods, to operate a private fleet than to use for-hire trucking in Texas."[45]

After a decade of bitter fighting, shippers began to see some regulatory relief in the 1990s as the balance of control of the TRC shifted to a more deregulatory position. And the legislature began to shift as the economic harm of strict regulation became more apparent. In 1993, legislators introduced the Transportation Regulatory Reform Act, supported by the Texas Association for Competitive Transportation, made up of 300 shippers. The bill would have reduced the power of the TRC to limit market entry and would have allowed negotiated rates up to 20 percent above or 50 percent below tariffs filed with the TRC.[46]

Not surprisingly, the Texas MTA opposed the bill, offering the traditional argument that safety would suffer, as would service to small communities.[47] Interestingly, Central Freight, which was purchased in 1993 by national less-than-truckload giant Roadway Services, formerly opposed rate deregulation but after this change of ownership began to favor it. The TRC had approved rates based on the average operating costs of all general freight truckers. Central asked for a 10 percent operating profit margin to be required in rates.[48] But Central still did not favor free entry, which was also

---

45. Cooke, "Deregulation Update," p. 63.

46. See Pugh, "Intrastate Regulation," pp. 326–27.

47. Quoted by Beachy, "Texas Cargo Deregulation Could Backfire," p. 2B.

48. Transport Topics Statelines (no author), "Texas Fleets Ask for Rate Flexibility," *Transport Topics*, April 11, 1994, p. 12.

critical to deregulation in the limited Texas market. Even this regulated trucking firm preferred some rate flexibility, so long as it did not face entry pressure.

As a result of a compromise bill drafted by Lt. Gov. Bob Bullock, the TMTA, and the Texas Association for Competitive Trucking and passed by the legislature in the spring of 1993, the TRC implemented the following relaxation in rate regulation. Truckload rates for general commodities, which include manufactured goods, retail goods, boxed goods, and apparel, could be discounted up to 40 percent below established base rates (compared with an allowed 15 percent deviation for less-than-truckload shipments). Contract carriers would not be limited in the number of contracts they could negotiate. The TRC also widened backhaul rights for specialized commodities, but backhauls of general commodities still required difficult approvals.

The TMTA argued that the TRC had gone too far with these rules. Hampton Rogers, government affairs director of TMTA, said: "This is a revolution. It looks more like deregulation."[49]

In another set of decisions pushing more deregulation in 1993, the Fifth U.S. Circuit Court of Appeals in New Orleans interpreted ICC rulings that shipments from outside Texas going to a Texas warehouse were not subject to intrastate regulation. The TMTA argued that this decision affected up to 70 percent of general commodities shipped to Texas.

Related to the air cargo carrier situation documented below and the Ninth Circuit decision in the California case, the Texas attorney general then decided that the TRC did not have the authority to regulate the intrastate trucking activities of air package carriers.[50] To illustrate the link between regulation and economic development, three days after Texas dropped regulation of air cargo carriers, Federal Express announced that it would establish a new hub at the Dallas–Fort Worth airport.

As a result of all these recent changes, trucking firms in Texas began to realize that tight regulation may no longer have been possi-

---

49. See Thomas Strah, "Regulatory Reform Comes to Texas: Some Truckers Say Changes Amount to Deregulation, *Transport Topics*, September 1993, p. 3.

50. See Dan Morales, attorney general, State of Texas, Letter Opinion no. 93-112, December 14, 1993.

ble and that a half-regulated industry may not have served their interests. In April 1994, the TMTA called for legislative deregulation in 1995. Central's president Tom Clowe stated: "The Texas intrastate common carrier freight market is substantially deregulated and the marketplace today is determining rates and, we believe, will continue to do so in a deregulated environment."[51]

Despite these actions, the Americans for Safe and Competitive Trucking argued that

> intrastate shippers are held hostage by a few large intrastate carriers. These carriers, fearful of deregulation and competition, are now saying that they will support deregulation for Texas. What they really support is piecemeal deregulation—next year—that would allow freedom of pricing, but not freedom of entry. Where only a few are allowed to operate, freedom of pricing (unaccompanied by freedom of entry) is almost meaningless. If history is any indication it could be decades before Texas removes economic regulation.[52]

Texas, one of the largest intrastate markets in the country, had perhaps the strictest regulation, particularly for common-carrier entry; and, after ten years of fierce political battles, regulations started to be relaxed, but only little by little. Thus, congressional approval of federal preemption of state trucking regulations in 1994 signaled some long-sought relief for Texas shippers (and some trucking firms) that had previously had difficulties operating effectively in this large, but highly regulated market.

Michigan. Michigan was also one of the strictest states in intrastate trucking regulation. It was important because 48 percent of for-hire trucking tonnage in Michigan moves intrastate. Trucking politics in Michigan pitted the power of the Teamsters Union against Big Three automobile firms and other shippers. Political battles over regulation were fought for many years.

---

51. Staff Report, "Texas Fleets Press for Deregulation," *Transport Topics*, April 18, 1994, p. 3.

52. Statement of F. S. Garrison, chairman of American Freightways Corporation, for the Americans for Safe and Competitive Trucking; U.S. Congress, House of Representatives, Subcommittee on Surface Transportation of the Committee on Public Works and Transportation, Washington, D.C., July 20, 1994.

Gradually, after contentious battles, deregulation made a little headway in Michigan. After Public Service Commission assaults on collective rate making, a compromise law passed in 1994 restored the power of rate bureaus and retained strict common-carrier entry restrictions. It eased temporary entry for contract carriers but made permanent entry even harder.[53] The 1994 Michigan law also prohibited contract carriers from getting into the less-than-truckload market.

The Teamsters pressed hard for this bill. While happy with some of the provisions, Governor Engler, a Republican, signed it reluctantly, as he favored full deregulation, arguing that the bill "makes our job climate more unfavorable and is another roadblock to luring job providers to Michigan."

Essentially, the law was a compromise between shippers, mainly the Association for Safe and Competitive Transportation, and regulated carriers, who had used the acronym MCARTS, for Michigan Citizens Allied for Responsible Transportation Safety.[54] As in other states, but here with more clout, organized labor was aligned with MCARTS.

The critical element of the compromise was more flexibility for new and existing contract carriers but more rigorous regulation of common carriers. One-year contracts were required, with exclusive trucks, but carriers could be both common and contract carriers at the same time. Protests against new contract carriers were quite limited by this law.

At the same time, the entry standard for common carriers was made stricter. "Useful public purpose" was upgraded to the tougher "required public purpose" requirement, which compelled service to meet a demonstrated public necessity without creating excess service.

In 1992, the PSC had restricted the antitrust immunity of the Michigan Intra-State Motor Tariff Bureau and the Greater Detroit Movers Association to set rates jointly.[55] The 1994 compromise law

---

53. See Mark Solomon, "Michigan Governor Signs Truck Deregulation Bill," *Journal of Commerce*, January 31, 1994, p. 2B.

54. See William Pugh, "Intrastate Regulation," *Transportation Practitioners Journal*, vol. 61 (1994), pp. 345–49.

55. Traffic World Special (no author), "Michigan Cuts Antitrust Immunity on Collective Intrastate Ratemaking," *Traffic World*, August 24, 1992, p. 35.

recognized and allowed collectively set rates. The Michigan PSC would no longer try to investigate the antitrust actions of these rate bureaus.

The filed-rate doctrine was to continue in Michigan, with prohibitions against rebates and discriminatory rates. The zone of rate flexibility was increased from 10 percent to 20 percent, and existing carriers were allowed to meet rates of competitors without cost justification.

Thus, although some aspects of trucking regulation were relaxed in Michigan in 1994, others were strengthened. Therefore, on the eve of congressional preemption of state economic regulation, Michigan's regulatory regime for the intrastate trucking industry was a long way from full deregulation.

California. California was one of the most important states for trucking regulation because 83 percent of its trucked tonnage moves intrastate, it has the nation's largest population, and the state was prone to restrictive regulation. The California regulators first proposed trucking deregulation before federal deregulation, in 1975, but opposition from truckers forced them to act slowly. In 1980, when the federal MCA was passed, the California Public Utilities Commission (PUC) adopted an experimental regulatory program that paralleled the provisions of the federal deregulation and, in particular, allowed for more flexible pricing.[56] The California Trucking Association, the California Manufacturers Association, and the Teamsters Union argued for changes in this policy in 1983, suggesting that "destructive competition" was taking place.

After investigations in 1986, the California PUC, with a new balance of power, adopted a re-regulatory regime, in part "to prevent competitive forces in the industry from becoming destructive."[57] This policy allowed for small rate windows of plus or minus 5 percent. Any additional rate changes required detailed cost justification, which could cost from $200 to $3,000 to prepare for a single shipment. In addition, a 10 percent general rate increase was established to aid the industry.

---

56. For details, see California Public Utilities Commission, Strategic Planning Division, *California's Trucking Industry: A Review of Regulatory Policies and Objectives* (Sacramento, Calif.: CPUC, 1988).

57. See Baker, "Your Letter of the Law, 1987," p. 42.

These re-regulation policies received widespread criticism. Major shippers organized to oppose them; Baker estimates that the California Coalition for Trucking Deregulation spent over $500,000 between 1986 and 1989, fighting for deregulation.[58] As a result, the California PUC in 1989 opened the rate window to 10 percent. California PUC staff appraisals of this policy were highly favorable.

More recently, in June 1993, the California PUC expanded the rate window to 30 percent and reduced the time for and ability of carriers to protest special rate agreements. In addition, the 1991 Ninth District Court decision to preempt regulation of air cargo carriers helped to change the regulatory environment in California.

To address the air cargo issue directly, a compromise bill, A.B. 2015, was signed by Governor Wilson in October 1993. While many described it as deregulation for the air cargo carriers, Baker noted that it added safety regulation requirements for those carriers.[59] The bill also included a compromise pushed by the Teamsters, to limit to 10 percent the amount of subcontracting that these firms could use, which nearly caused Governor Wilson to veto the bill.

In 1994, the California PUC considered whether the air cargo carrier exemption had disrupted "the competitive balance between carriers." Larry Farrens, a consultant to the California Trucking Association, which favored complete economic deregulation, said at this time: "I believe total deregulation will become a reality within a year."[60] At the time that Congress approved federal preemption of state-level regulation of the trucking industry, the California PUC was considering whether filed rates could be eliminated and whether they could give more freedom from regulation to contract carriers.[61] They sought comments from interested parties about how best to proceed with further deregulation. Options included small-package rate freedom, shipper-specific tariffs, expanded special contracts, and nonfiled tariffs.[62]

---

58. Baker, "Your Letter of the Law, 1991," p. 14.

59. See Daniel Baker, "The Anatomy and Effects of UPS's California 'Deregulation' Legislation," *Transportation Lawyer*, vol. 3 (1994), pp. 39–40.

60. Quoted in Robert James, "Calif., Texas Continue Deregulation Drive," *Traffic World*, April 11, 1994, p. 15.

61. CPUC Dockets No. I94-03-036 and R94-03-037.

62. John Schulz, "NIT League 'Strongly Backs' Calif. Deregulation," *Traffic World*, June 6, 1994, p. 34.

Thus, over the past twenty years, California has gone back and forth on intrastate trucking deregulation. In 1994, the state appeared to be moving toward more substantial deregulation.

Indiana. Indiana provides another illustration of how the power of truckers could reverse state regulatory reform, in a state where 28 percent of for-hire trucked tonnage moves within the state. A 1987 Indiana law, based largely on recommendations of governmental officials rather than on shipper or public outcry, allowed for administrative reform of trucking regulation starting in 1988 and free entry into the industry in 1990.[63] Federal Express saw these policy moves as encouraging enough to plan a major hub in the state to take advantage of relaxed regulations.

The state Motor Truck Association (MTA) was not active at first. Once the law actually passed, however, the MTA successfully lobbied the Republican-controlled legislature to repeal the free-entry provision. The bill had two goals; first, it transferred administrative responsibility for trucking regulation from the Public Service Commission (PSC) to the Revenue Department, and, second, it established the end of entry regulation as of 1990. Rates would have continued to be regulated, but applications for rate changes were to be approved routinely. Passage of the law would have meant that intrastate trucking would be subject only to safety and insurance regulation.

The bill had its genesis in a standard investigation conducted by the House Sunset Committee, which suggested that the PSC should examine whether to continue to have entry barriers. The committee staff argued that consumers would benefit greatly from deregulation.

When the bill was introduced in the House, the Indiana MTA took a neutral stance, as was often the case in states where different kinds of carriers had different interests in regulation and deregulation. Some members of the MTA that were integrated with air freight operations supported deregulation. Leadership changes at the MTA also promoted neutrality at that time. The MTA supported the first part of the bill, the transfer of regulatory administration to the Revenue Department, which it hoped would be more aggressive in enforc-

---

63. See Peter Boerger, *Motor Carrier Regulation in Indiana: Sunset Audit* (Indianapolis: Indiana Legislative Services Agency, 1987).

ing trucking regulation than the PSC had become. (This perception was accurate as the PSC staff wanted to get completely out of trucking regulation.)

For all these reasons, the MTA decided to wait for passage before attempting to exert substantial influence. Given the long lead times for implementation built into the bill, this strategy was not inappropriate. After passage of the bill, the MTA called on members to lobby legislators, each of whose districts had at least one trucking firm. This strategy proved effective. Although some shippers opposed the MTA lobbying, it was not symmetric political pressure.[64]

Thus, in 1989, the new legislation was repealed, dramatically illustrating the political power of the truckers at the state level. The transfer of administration to the Revenue Department continued, but the entry barriers remained in place through 1994. Air cargo carriers operating intrastate trucking service, particularly Federal Express, were exempted from entry regulation as long as they maintained an operating hub in the state and moved goods through that facility.

Our 1994 survey found that incumbent firms in Indiana could protest the application of new entrants, who had to show proof of public convenience and necessity and to show that existing service was satisfactory. This process could take up to 180 days, far longer than the protest period allowed any other state. Approval for contract-carrier service was considerably easier. Rate regulation rejected common-carrier rates that seemed too low (defined as one-third below the standard), unless carriers could demonstrate profitability, through a cost justification. Independent actions required thirty days' notice, which was at the high end of state time periods, and 18,000 tariffs were filed in 1993, by far the highest reported number in our survey.

While these four states were among the strictest regulators, their regulatory actions represented only part of the costs imposed on shippers and ultimately on consumers in this country as a result of intrastate regulation of the trucking industry. The next section illustrates and compares the results of several studies of these costs.

Costs of Continued State Regulation

Over the past three decades, numerous studies showed the efficiency losses from state regulation. Some focused narrowly on first-order

---

64. See Daniel Baker, "State Regulation and Federal Preemption," Your Letter of the Law, Transportation Lawyers Association 1990, p. 58.

efficiency costs, while others took a more expansive view to include the changes in logistics and inventory operation that shippers needed to make to compensate for state regulation-induced problems. In the appendix to this chapter, we summarize twenty studies of state regulation of trucking, performed in different states at different times.[65] Almost all these studies show that deregulated or unregulated markets produce lower rates and equally good or better services than those subject to state regulation.

For the studies prepared for the nation as a whole, the benefits from intrastate deregulation were in the range of $3–8 billion per year. These include the Allen et al. 1990 study for the U.S. Department of Transportation, the 1990 Gellman Associates study for Federal Express, and the 1990 Winston et al. study for the Brookings Institution.[66] The Gellman Research Associates report estimated that state regulations led to $128 per year in increased costs for every American family of four people.

Although it is harder to document such costs accurately, some studies looked beyond the first-order economic efficiency effects of regulation. In the best example of taking a broader perspective on costs, including logistics, Robert Delaney of Cass Logistics estimated an additional $15 billion per year in costs related to altered logistics to avoid or get around inefficient state regulations.[67]

In addition to these general studies of the costs of state economic regulation, many shippers cited compelling specific examples of these costs. Georgia-Pacific argued that state regulation cost the company more than $5 million per year. Norman Langberg, former director of traffic and distribution, argued:

> Georgia-Pacific manufactures tissue products in Palatka, Florida, and LaGrange, Georgia. An intrastate move from LaGrange, Georgia, to Atlanta, Georgia (63 miles), costs $228. An interstate move from Palatka, Florida, to At-

---

65. Other studies in the literature are largely similar in approach and conclusions.

66. Allen et al., *The Impact of State Economic Regulation of Motor Carriage*; Gellman Research Associates, *The Economic Cost of Intrastate Trucking Regulation*, Final report, June 5, 1990; and Winston et al., *The Economic Effects of Surface Freight Deregulation* (Washington, D.C.: Brookings Institution, 1990).

67. Robert Delaney, "The Disunited States: A Country in Search of an Efficient Transportation Policy," Cato Institute Policy Analysis no. 84, March 10, 1987.

lanta, Georgia (354 miles), costs $265. Georgia-Pacific manufactures a wide variety of paper and building products at Crossett, Arkansas. An intrastate move from Crossett, Arkansas, to Texarkana, Arkansas (131 miles), costs $350. An interstate move from Crossett, Arkansas, to Texarkana, Texas (135 miles), costs $250.[68]

Frito-Lay estimated that state regulation cost the company over $8 million per year. Shipping manager Rittenmayer said in 1992:

Right now it is as much as 40 percent more expensive for us to truck our products within State borders than across State lines. When one of the carriers that we would hire picks up a load at our Jackson, Mississippi, plant and would deliver it to New Orleans, which is 179 miles away, it costs us approximately $2.23 per mile. But if we take that same truck and we deliver that load 170 miles across the State of Mississippi to Biloxi, we will spend $6.79 per mile.[69]

Finally, in 1990, F. Sprague Exley, vice president of distribution for Savannah Foods and Industries, Inc., observed:

In the state of Michigan, where we have 4 beet sugar plants, a packaging facility and consignment warehouses, regulation is costly. Michigan limits operating authority to a select few carriers, and rate publication is both slow and restrictive. . . . The cost to ship a truckload of sugar intrastate from our plant in Sebawaing, Michigan, to Monroe, Michigan, a distance of 154 miles, is $2.65 per mile. However, from the same plant, we can ship to Toledo, Ohio, 174 miles away, for $1.63 per mile. That cost is 38% less, but it is 20 miles further into another state. From our Carrollton, Michigan, plant to Coloma, Michigan, the cost is $2.64 per mile (186 miles); but we can ship from

---

68. U.S. Congress, House of Representatives, Subcommittee on Commerce, Consumer, and Monetary Affairs of the Committee on Government Operations, *Hearings on Consumer Cost of Continued State Motor Carrier Regulation*, 101st Congress, 2d session, March 29, 1990, p. 180.

69. U.S. Congress, House of Representatives, Subcommittee on Commerce, Consumer, and Monetary Affairs of the Committee on Government Operations, *Hearings on Regulatory Issues: Intrastate Regulation, Negotiated Rates, and Overweight Containers*, 101st Congress, 2d session, April 2, 1992, p. 1256.

Carrollton to Southbend, Indiana (206 miles), for $2.21 per mile, 16% less cost. . . . The reason for the lower rates, of course, is that these are deregulated interstate shipments, and the carriers have open access, allowing them to run more efficiently. Similar examples could be cited for every state with a regulatory structure where we have facilities.[70]

Obviously, state trucking regulation did not benefit large shippers in states, and, according to Allen et al., nearly 80 percent of the costs of state regulation stayed within each state. The other 20 percent of the costs of state regulation was exported to businesses and consumers in other states, a finding that helped to illustrate the burden on interstate commerce from intrastate regulation.[71] The shipper group, Americans for Safe and Competitive Trucking, produced a chart to illustrate the increased intrastate costs (see table 4–2). In almost every case, the shorter intrastate trip cost considerably more for a wide range of shipped goods.

The most recent study of the costs of state regulation, by Daniels and Kleit for the Federal Trade Commission, came out just in time for the final stages of congressional debate in 1994.[72] These economists distinguished the separate effects of regulation of rates, entry, and the antitrust immunity. They found that for the less-than-truckload sector, state entry restrictions raised rates 20 percent, rate regulations raised rates 5 percent, and antitrust immunity raised rates 12 percent. In the truckload sector, rate regulations raised rates 32 percent, while the other regulations were not found to have a consistently significant effect on rates. This study was important for its timing and also because the antitrust immunity of rate bureaus was not eliminated by 1994 congressional action.

---

70. U.S. Congress, House of Representatives, Subcommittee on Commerce, Consumer, and Monetary Affairs of the Committee on Government Operations, *Hearings on the Consumer Cost of Continued State Motor Carrier Regulation*, 101st Congress, 2d session, March 29, 1990, p. 170.

71. Allen et al., *The Impact of State Economic Regulation of Motor Carriage.*

72. Timothy Daniels and Andrew Kleit, *Disentangling Regulatory Policy: The Effects of State Regulation on Trucking Rates*, working paper no. 205 (Washington, D.C.: Bureau of Economics, Federal Trade Commission, July 1994).

TABLE 4–2
COMPARISON OF INTERSTATE AND INTRASTATE SHIPPING COSTS, 1992

Cargo	Interstate Route	Cost	Intrastate Route	Cost
Filters	Dallas, Tex.– Kansas City, Mo. (495 miles)	$495	Dallas, Tex.– Houston (245 miles)	$632
Paper products	Richmond, Va.– Raleigh, N.C. (146 miles)	$204	Richmond, Va.– Danville (146 miles)	$539
Sugar	Sebawaing, Mich.– Toledo, Ohio (174 miles)	$284	Sebawaing, Mich.– Monroe (154 miles)	$408
Tissue	Palatka, Fla.– Atlanta, Ga. (354 miles)	$265	LaGrange, Ga.– Atlanta (63 miles)	$228
Tobacco products	Shreveport, La.– Sulphur Springs, Tex. (125 miles)	$450	Dallas, Tex.– Sulphur Springs (85 miles)	$714

SOURCE: Americans for Safe and Competitive Trucking, 1992.

Preemption of State Economic Regulation

The evidence presented in the previous sections of this chapter shows that, from an economic efficiency perspective, state regulation was extremely costly, both to state economies and to interstate commerce. At the time Congress passed the 1980 MCA, considerable evidence was available on the costs of interstate trucking regulation. Further, in other vital deregulatory legislation of the period, explicit provision was made for federal preemption of state-level economic regulations. Thus, a puzzling question emerges: why was it that the 1980 MCA did *not* preempt the states? A related question then follows: why did it take until 1994 before other efforts to preempt the states finally succeeded?

In response to our first question, there are several possible reasons why the 1980 MCA did not preempt the states on trucking regulation. We will consider each of these in turn and develop the most likely answer. We will then address our second question.

First, policy makers and concerned parties may have had a sense that state regulation of intrastate trucking was not important and therefore not a worthwhile issue. ICC policy changes in the 1970s pushed Congress to pass the 1980 MCA, and the ICC had jurisdiction over interstate commerce. In support of this view, several analyses of trucking deregulation do not even mention the role of states in trucking regulation.[73] At that time, few studies had been prepared showing harm from state regulation.[74] But this view of the intrastate traffic as minimal was not accurate, as more than half of trucking tons carried and nearly half of all trucking revenues were generated intrastate as of 1980. Intrastate railroad revenues were far smaller in absolute and percentage terms in 1980 (less than 10 percent), but the 1980 Staggers Act explicitly preempted any independent state role.

In addition, some knew that the state issues were important. Before the MCA passed, the ICC held a federal-state workshop on trucking regulation that explicitly discussed state regulation.[75] The 1980 MCA itself (section 19) provided for a study of the effects of regulation, including regulation by the states, by 1982.[76] Congress expressed concern that differing state regulations could create prob-

---

73. See, for example, Martha Derthick and Paul Quirk, *The Politics of Deregulation* (Washington, D.C.: Brookings Institution, 1985); and Dorothy Robyn, *Braking the Special Interests* (Chicago: University of Chicago Press, 1987).

74. Karen Phillips, vice chairman of the ICC, recently suggested to us that in 1980 the ICC felt unable to make the case that state regulations were particularly harmful. Few studies existed at the time that demonstrated the benefits of removing state regulations (compared with the situation in mid-1994). NARUC argued that Congress could not keep taking regulatory powers away from the states and expect little resistance.

75. See Garland Chow, "Studies of Intrastate Trucking Regulation—A Critique," *Transportation Journal*, vol. 19 (1980), p. 32. The document developed was *Proceedings of the Federal-State Workshop on Motor Carrier Regulation* (Washington, D.C.: U.S. Government Printing Office, 1980).

76. This study focused more on operating restrictions than on the economic cost of state regulations.

lems, stating: "It is in the national interest to minimize the burdens of such regulation while at the same time preserving the legitimate interests of the States in such regulation."[77]

Second, as illustrated in the above quotation, on ideological or "states' rights" grounds, congressional actors may not have wanted to overstep their power and preempt the states. But this is a weak argument, as the other four transportation deregulation bills from 1978 to 1982 all explicitly preempted the states in the face of this same issue. As an analyst of intercity bus regulation noted, "Congressional power to delegate authority to the Interstate Commerce Commission so as to allow the ICC to preempt state regulation of intrastate activities is vast and well grounded in precedent."[78] Intrastate trucking does not offer any additional theoretical or practical argument about why the states should have retained power.

Third, some policy makers may have believed that interstate and intrastate freight movements were truly separate and separable and that state oversight was appropriate. This argument is not any more applicable to trucking than to the other transportation sectors. Furthermore, over seventy years of legal battling, some at the U.S. Supreme Court level, as illustrated in chapter 2, had shown that inter- and intrastate distinctions were complex and that cases were decided in very arbitrary ways, depending on the precise details of a particular situation.

Fourth, the Teamsters Union and trucking firms opposed to deregulation may have had more political power than opponents of deregulation in the other transportation sectors.[79] While they were unable to overcome the pro-deregulation forces on the interstate level, they effectively kept preemption of intrastate regulation off the agenda. Larger political compromises and presidential politics may also have contributed.[80]

---

77. Freeman and Beilock, "State Regulatory Responses to Federal Motor Carrier Reregulation," p. 59.

78. Jeremy Kahn, "The Bus Regulatory Reform Act of 1982 and Federal Preemption of Intrastate Regulation of the Intercity Bus Industry," *Transportation Law Journal*, vol. 14 (1986), p. 185.

79. Teske et al., "The Economic Theory of Regulation and Trucking Deregulation."

80. Rothenberg, *Regulation, Organizations, and Politics*; and Waterman and

Fifth, pro-deregulation supporters may have realized that while intrastate issues were important, a compromise for interstate deregulation was the most that could be achieved at that time. Given strong opposition, it was difficult enough to achieve substantial interstate deregulation without pursuing intrastate preemption at the same time.[81] Thus, advocates did not address the state issue directly but instead included a provision to study and revisit it.

Finally, some may have believed that the states would deregulate intrastate trucking on their own. Swept up by interstate success and by successful deregulation in other industries, perhaps many thought the states would themselves deregulate, as six states did over the next six years. But, as we have seen, most states were still actively regulating their intrastate trucking sector in 1994.

We believe that the best explanation for the lack of preemption in the 1980 MCA is a combination of the last three reasons. The first three explanations are not convincing. In contrast, it seems plausible that the political power of deregulation opponents and the desire by proponents to achieve at least interstate deregulation kept preemption of the states off the immediate agenda in 1980. Deregulation supporters may have hoped the states would act on their own and, if not, that preemption could be revisited later. As we shall discuss, preemption was revisited, both in explicit congressional form and through attempts by the ICC to redefine intrastate movements into a trivial category. While these two efforts were persistent in recent years, they did not succeed in eliminating state regulation, and, eventually, preemption came in 1994 from a somewhat surprising source—the pressure of air carriers for whom trucking provided a key element in their intermodal operations.

Three Different Attempts at Preemption. After 1980, Congress considered several bills that would directly preempt the state role in intrastate trucking deregulation. The ICC tried to preempt effectively by leaving the states with authority over a very minor, truly intrastate commerce sector. And intermodal air and truck carriers, such as Federal Express and United Parcel Service, led a "backdoor," and

---

Wood, "What Do We Do with Applied Research?" *PS: Political Science and Politics*, vol. 25 (September 1992), pp. 559–64.

81. Rothenberg, *Regulation, Organizations, and Politics*.

ultimately successful, assault on intrastate regulation through the preemption provisions of the Federal Aviation Act.[82] We will consider each of these three efforts in turn.

Given the success of the 1980 MCA and the persistence of state economic regulation of trucking, Congress subsequently considered several proposals to preempt state regulatory authority. Often these proposals were attached to other transportation bills or budgetary appropriations, rather than standing completely on their own. Some of this activity was stimulated by the 1982 joint Department of Transportation–ICC report that examined state regulation under section 19 of the 1980 MCA.[83]

Under President Reagan, a few explicit proposals were made to preempt the states. Asked for predictions about 1985, Reagan's ICC chairman Reese Taylor noted in 1984: "One issue that will have to be resolved before you can have any further deregulation is the issue of federal preemption of the states. You cannot have an essentially deregulated environment on the federal level and a very highly regulated situation at the state level."[84]

In 1985 the Reagan administration submitted the Trucking Deregulation Act of 1985, which aimed to eliminate tariff filings, the ICC itself, and the antitrust protection for rate bureaus, as well as thoroughly preempting state regulation.[85] That bill did not succeed in Congress. Similarly, the Reagan administration proposed the Trucking Productivity Improvement Act of 1987, which became H.R. 2591. This did not pass either. Late in 1987 a bill introduced by

---

82. The organization of this section is modeled after Samuel Ewer Eastman's excellent article, "Three Shots at State Economic Regulation of Interstate Motor Carriers," in *Transportation Practitioners Journal*, vol. 61 (1993), pp. 31–38.

83. Allen et al., *The Impact of State Economic Regulation of Motor Carriage*. But there were disputes about whether the congressional mandate meant for this study to focus on economic regulation or simply on safety, weights, taxes, and the like. See U.S. Department of Transportation and Interstate Commerce Commission, *Options for Uniform State Regulation*, section 19, Motor Carrier Act of 1980, working paper no. 1 (1980).

84. *Transport Topics*, December 17, 1984, "The ICC in 1984: Where Has It Been, Where Is It Going?" p. 12.

85. See Allen et al., *The Impact of State Economic Regulation of Motor Carriage*, p. 6.

Senator Packwood and Congressmen Moody and DeLay would have preempted the states by allowing truckers operating in three or more states to be called "national carriers," freed from both federal and state regulation. This bill also allowed for elimination of antitrust exemptions. This, too, was unsuccessful, as state regulators, trucking firms, and labor unions mounted strong opposition.

As further evidence of the harm of intrastate regulation accumulated and as it became clear that state deregulation was not an accelerating phenomenon (with some states actually reversing themselves on deregulation), efforts to preempt the states increased in the 1990s. The 1991 Department of Transportation report by Allen et al. documented impressively both the importance of intrastate trucking and the costs of such continuing regulation, not only to consumers within regulated states but to consumers in other states as well (which, of course, is the definition of *interstate* commerce).[86]

Thus, every legislative session in the 1990s featured at least one and sometimes more bills that aimed to preempt the state role in trucking regulation. With continued opposition from state regulators, the National Association of Regulatory Utility Commissioners, the Teamsters Union, and protected intrastate carriers, none of these bills passed. Direct preemption was simply not possible because of this opposition in Congress, much as the politics of regulation within the states prevented much deregulation.

To highlight just a few of these recent bills, H.R. 4261 in 1990 would have completely preempted intrastate economic regulation. Introduced in 1991, H.R. 3021, the Intermodal Carriers Competitiveness Act, would have preempted state regulation of any carrier that by itself or with an affiliated carrier provided national interstate intermodal air-ground transport service. In both 1991 and 1992, H.R. 4406, the Trucking Regulatory Reform Act, was introduced to follow the format of the railroad's 1980 Staggers Act, which preempted any important state trucking role that differed from ICC regulation but allowed state regulation to continue. In 1992, H.R. 1064, the Safe and Competitive Trucking Act, would have preempted nearly all state regulation. Also introduced in 1992, H.R. 4334 would have exempted private carriers from state regulations.

Several other versions of related or combined bills were also

---

86. Ibid.

introduced unsuccessfully in the early 1990s. As we discuss in chapter 5, bills did pass that tried to make state operating arrangements more compatible and tried to deal with issues such as transportation of hazardous materials. Until 1994, however, bills promoting the preemption of state economic regulation were unsuccessful despite many efforts by different sponsors.

ICC Redefinitions of Intrastate Truck Movements as Interstate Commerce. The second way that federal government officials attempted to reduce the power of state trucking regulation in recent years was through administrative and legal means. The ICC used its decision-making authority in the area of jurisdictional questions of interstate versus intrastate commerce to expand the category of interstate commerce at the expense of state regulators. This attempt started most recently in 1986 with the *Armstrong* decision and followed a long history of legal questions related to interstate commerce, some of which we chronicled in chapter 2.[87]

In the *Armstrong* decision, the ICC argued that when carpet was moved from out-of-state into Texas, stored temporarily in a warehouse, and later moved intrastate, the intrastate movement was part of a larger interstate movement and thus not subject to Texas regulation. Court rulings initially reversed the ICC, but then higher courts upheld it on this narrow case.

Not surprisingly, other cases with other commodities, other lengths of stay in warehousing, and other pertinent facts were brought to the ICC and to the courts to test the extent of this effective preemption of state authority over "mixed" interstate and intrastate carriage.[88] Thus, in 1992, the ICC produced a more general policy statement to clarify the issue and to inform state commissions on where they had now drawn these boundaries.[89] This statement was

---

87. Armstrong, Inc.-Transportation within Texas, 2 ICC 2d 63 (1986), aff'd sub nom, Texas v. ICC, 886 F.2d 458 (5th Cir. 1989).

88. One of the more prominent was No. MC-C-30006-The Quaker Oats Company-Transportation within Texas and California-Petition for Declaratory Order, 4 ICC 2d 1033 (1987).

89. Ex Parte No. MC-207, Policy Statement—Motor Carrier Interstate Transportation—From out-of-State through Warehouses to Points in the Same State, 8 ICC 2d 470, 471 (1992).

seen as quite purposefully pushing the boundaries of interstate commerce at the expense of state control. One analyst argued: "As a result of its disagreement regarding this issue with certain state PUCs (particularly the Texas Railroad Commission), the ICC has openly announced its plan to join forces with and assist the parties who are resisting regulation by the state PUCs."[90] The Bush administration stated that it would use the powers of the U.S. Department of Justice to enforce these legal distinctions.

A few days after the policy statement, the ICC issued its *Texas Warehousemen* decision, by a 3–2 vote, in which the ICC supported the warehousemen and others against the Texas Railroad Commission.[91] The ICC ruled that almost any products shipped into warehouses from outside the state remained in interstate commerce on their next movement within the state. This decision was based on older rulings that analyzed the "essential character" of the shipment[92] and the "fixed and persistent intent" of the shipper at the time of original shipment,[93] but it also went well beyond those cases and established a more general ruling that the ICC had previously resisted.

As one analyst noted: "The ICC's 3–2 decision, while characterized as simply a follow-up on its *Armstrong* series, represented a substantial change in the criteria which distinguish interstate from intrastate commerce."[94] Under this ruling, plans for future shipment did not need to be in place when the interstate movement was made, the exact shippers did not need to be described, and mixing of interstate and intrastate products in the same warehouse did not alter the interstate character of a particular shipment.

In addition, in its *Pittsburgh-Johnstown-Altoona Express, Inc.* *(PJAX)* decision, the ICC ruled that an intrastate movement from

---

90. William Pugh, "Intrastate Regulation," *Transportation Practitioners Journal*, vol. 59 (1992), p. 430.

91. No. MC-C-30194, Association of Texas Warehousemen, et al.-Petition for Declaratory Order-Certain For-Hire Motor Transportation within Texas, 8 I.C.C. 2d 476 (1992).

92. From the case of Baltimore & O.S.W.R.R. v. Settle, 260 U.S. 166, 170 (1922).

93. See Armstrong decision.

94. Pugh, "Intrastate Regulation," p. 430.

storage by a for-hire carrier was a continuation of an interstate movement that had originated in *private* carriage, which explicitly reversed an earlier Supreme Court ruling from the New Deal era on mixed private and for-hire carriage.[95]

This series of administrative rulings by the ICC effectively preempted considerable state regulation. As Pugh summarized:

> Not only is *Texas Warehousemen* so vague and general that contrary facts would be much harder to find, but this decision, along with *PJAX*, eliminates important criteria which have served to distinguish intrastate from interstate commerce in particular circumstances. Clearly, the ICC's new policy, along with the threat of enforcement by the DOJ, is designed as a giant step forward in eliminating legally controlled state regulation.[96]

Next, in November 1993, the ICC used the Texas cases to expand further the interstate definition in MC-C-30198, *Advantage Tank Lines, Inc-Petition for Declaratory Order*. Here, gasoline was shipped via a "shipper-controlled" pipeline from Illinois to Michigan and then trucked to other sites in Michigan. The ICC ruled that the trucking portion was part of interstate commerce, not subject to Michigan's intrastate regulations. This decision reversed the ICC's long-standing ruling *Determination of Jurisdiction over Transportation of Petroleum and Petroleum Products within a Single State*, 71 M.C.C. 17 (1957). This case was also important because it showed that the general trend toward expansion of the definition of interstate commerce would not be reversed by the first Democratic-controlled ICC in a dozen years. As one analyst noted: "It is apparent that those who hoped that a new Democratic majority would change the Commission's direction on the broad jurisdictional issues covered by this case, will be disappointed."[97]

Some other related preemption decisions are important to consider here as well. On the more narrow issue of sale of operating

---

95. That decision was Pennsylvania Railroad Co. v. Public Utility Commission, 298 U.S. 170 (1936).

96. Pugh, "Intrastate Regulation," p. 432.

97. Ibid., p. 347.

authority from one company to another, the ICC made some decisions that expanded the ability of firms to purchase intrastate operating authority without approval by that state's regulators. The Interstate Commerce Act explicitly gave the ICC authority over transfers of both interstate *and* intrastate operating rights (without the need for approval by states of the intrastate transfer) where total revenues involved exceed $2 million. After several legal challenges and qualifications, the ICC, in its 1993 *Ex Parte No. MC-216* rule-making proceeding, expanded the definition of revenues broadly to preempt effectively the states in this area.

A prominent transportation lawyer summarized these efforts by noting:

> The ICC's latest incursion into the field of states' rights to regulate intrastate commerce within their borders negates, at least in part, the strict regulatory philosophy of many states. Permitting motor carriers greater freedom to transfer their intrastate operating rights issued by those states that restrict their issuance as well as their transfer enables the ICC, through its free-market administration of the Interstate Commerce Act, to bring more intrastate transfers into harmony with the ICC's own policy that has all but eliminated any regulatory obstacle to transfer of interstate operating rights.[98]

In June 1994, the ICC ruled on a case in which a trucking firm transported petroleum products over an interstate route, through New Jersey but connecting two Pennsylvania locations, that was 10 percent more circuitous than a strictly intrastate route. The firm could not obtain intrastate operating authority in Pennsylvania and the state PUC argued that this route was an "interstate subterfuge." The ICC ruled in favor of the trucking firm, although previous rulings had found against firms that use interstate routes twice as long as intrastate routes.[99] Thus, right up to the point when congressional ap-

---

98. See Kim Mann, "New Rules Govern Federal Preemption: Expanded Scope, but New Burden of Proof," *Transportation Lawyer*, vol. 3 (1994), pp. 33–39, for considerable detail on the legal issues involved in these cases.

99. The firm is C&K Carriers, Inc., and the ruling was MC-C-30215. See Traffic World Special Report, "ICC Allows Carriers Interstate Route for Pennsylvania Intrastate Shipments," *Traffic World*, June 13, 1994, p. 22.

proval of federal preemption finally occurred, the game of interstate and intrastate definitions continued to be played, much as it had since 1935. But in the past decade, Republican- and Democratic-controlled ICCs had greatly expanded the legal definition of interstate commerce and were not overturned in the courts. Still, state regulation over a considerable portion of the nation's freight movements remained in place.

Trucking Preemption through Airline Deregulation. While congressional attempts to preempt state regulations directly in the years after the 1980 MCA were all unsuccessful and while the ICC made slow (albeit notable) progress in unfastening the grip of state regulations on the trucking industry, in the end federal preemption came through an unlikely source—the efforts of intermodal small-package carriers. These carriers had developed into really powerful economic entities only as a consequence of the airline deregulation initiatives of the 1970s. Here we see clear evidence of how difficult it is to predict market-driven innovations and their consequences.

The prelude to the 1994 federal preemption was provided by several court cases. In 1991, the Ninth Circuit Court of Appeals interpreted federal preemption broadly and reduced the state role in transportation regulation. This interpretation was not revisited by the Supreme Court, which had just recently struck down efforts by the National Association of (state) Attorneys General to regulate airline fare advertising. That previous ruling was based on the preemption provisions of the Federal Aviation Act, which explicitly left no important role for the states.[100]

The related airlines deregulation law for cargo carriers led to congressional action in 1994 that finally succeeded in preempting intrastate trucking regulation. As we mentioned above, this third, and most surprising, approach to preempting state regulations came through the emergence of intermodal carriers. Air freight carriers, such as Federal Express, developed a new business over the past two

---

100. The case is Morales v. Trans World Airlines, 112 S.Ct. 2031 (1992). For an analysis of this case and its relationship to the Federal Express issue, see Pamela Williams, "Federal Express v. California Public Utilities Commission: The Ninth Circuit Court of Appeals, the Airline Deregulation Act and State Regulation of Intrastate Trucking," *Transportation Law Journal*, vol. 21 (1992), pp. 303–29.

decades that was more flexible and responsive for smaller packages than were many less-than-truckload trucking services. They were not subject to state *air* regulation as of the airline deregulation implemented in the late 1970s. Title 49 U.S.C. & 105(a)(1) states that "no State or political subdivision thereof . . . shall enact or enforce any law, rule, regulation, standard, or any other provision . . . relating to rates, routes or services of any air carrier having authority under subchapter IV of this chapter to provide air transportation."

Federal Express is now a huge firm, delivering packages in virtually all states and in many nations, with 456 airplanes and 30,000 trucks. Federal Express operates more than 2,600 trucks in California alone. The firm was extremely frustrated with California trucking regulations, including ones that prohibited it from offering such advantageous services to its customers as longer credit, providing telephone rather than written claims, and a money-back guarantee, all of which were unlawful in California. This frustration with state *trucking* regulation in California led Federal Express to challenge the applicability of state regulation to the firm under the Federal Aviation Act. Founder Fred Smith argued: "There has been no such thing as purely intrastate commerce since maybe when Daniel Boone was in Tennessee."[101]

Federal Express challenged California's regulation in 1987. The district court supported the California PUC's right to regulate Federal Express, but the Court of Appeals for the Ninth Circuit reversed that decision in favor of Federal Express.[102] The U.S. Supreme Court chose not to reconsider this decision, which then became applicable to Federal Express in states in the Ninth Circuit jurisdiction, including California, Alaska, Arizona, Hawaii, Idaho, Montana, Nevada, Oregon, and Washington.

While this legal action was taking place, Federal Express also pursued this issue in other political forums. To place the matter on the federal legislative agenda, Federal Express commissioned the report by Gellman Associates on the cost of such state regulation.

---

101. Quoted in John Schulz, "Strange Forces Coalesce to Support Broad Intrastate Trucking Deregulation," *Traffic World*, August 1, 1994, p. 11.

102. Federal Express Corporation v. California Public Utilities Commission (and others), 716 F. Supp. 1299 (D.C. Cal 1989), 936 F.2d 1075f (9th Cir. 1991), 112 S.Ct. 2956, *writ certiorari* denied (1991).

The firm also applied political pressure to have the U.S. Department of Transportation prepare an options report for congressional action. Section 341 of Public Law no. 101-614, the FY1990 Transportation Appropriations Bill, required that the Department of Transportation prepare this report, which was issued in September 1990; it recommended several possible options, focusing on preempting state regulation of air cargo carriers.[103] Air cargo carriers realized that congressional preemption was potentially a more fruitful effort than a direct political assault on regulations *within* a large number of state legislatures.

In the meantime, a few other states acted. As noted above, the Texas attorney general interpreted the California decision to apply to his state as well. In Kentucky, the state legislature passed a bill in April 1994 to exempt integrated intermodal small-package carriers from state regulation.[104]

UPS, unlike its rival Federal Express, is defined as a motor carrier and not as an air carrier, even though it now operates over 155 large cargo aircraft and charters over 300 more smaller planes each night. Thus, the court decision did not apply to this company directly. UPS was concerned that simply as a result of classification issues the competitive environment had become unfair, with Federal Express exempted from state trucking regulations. Thus, UPS began a strong political campaign to avoid the kinds of state economic regulations that had harmed it as well. In 1994, for example, the company proposed a nationwide rate increase that had to be approved in each regulated state. Thirteen states suspended the rate increase, six on the protest of only a single shipper, costing UPS $9 million in lost revenues. In Colorado, a state with strict regulations, only 1 of 19,000 UPS customers opposed the increase: that customer provided UPS with less than $150 of sales per week. According to state regulations, that one customer was enough to delay the increase for several months, at a cost to UPS of $230,000.[105] Recognizing the potential

---

103. DOT-P-16, *Report to Congress: Impact of State Regulation on the Package Express Industry*, U.S. Department of Transportation, Office of the Secretary of Transportation, September 1990.

104. Robert James, "Kentucky Deregulates Express Carriers," *Traffic World*, April 25, 1994, p. 15.

105. Daniel Pearl and Robert Frank, "Trucking Firms Face a Problem with Congress," *Wall Street Journal*, April 8, 1994.

costs of taking this state-by-state approach, UPS pushed for a congressional bill that was introduced in 1992 as a technical correction to airline law to address the California court ruling more broadly; the bill did not pass. To accelerate resolution of this issue, the political action committee for UPS contributed more than $1 million to members of Congress in 1994, more than any other PAC.[106]

Thus, although they are rivals in the marketplace, through their mutually reinforcing actions, UPS and Federal Express pushed the issue onto the 1994 congressional agenda. Exemption of these firms from state regulation was placed into an Airport Improvement Program bill that authorized money for important projects, which was considered "must pass" legislation. And, along the way, UPS and Federal Express received support from some of the traditional trucking firms that also began to see the competitive disadvantages that they might face as a consequence of a mismatch between regulatory regimes and the arbitrariness of the ways these regulations classified various freight transportation firms. As one observer noted, "Companies like Overnight signed on to state preemption bills two years ago and have led the contingent in the American Trucking Associations that believe more deregulation is needed."[107]

In effect, the circle of deregulation was widened throughout the progress of congressional legislation. The major less-than-truckload carriers realized the disadvantages of being regulated when Federal Express and UPS were deregulated at the state level. Yellow, the largest less-than-truckload carrier, which provides intrastate service in twenty-one states, argued that the court and state decisions provided an uneven playing field. Thus, they pushed for an expansion of the federal bill beyond just Federal Express and UPS, stating: "UPS and Federal Express are seeking to extend this uneven playing field to all intrastate markets through federal preemption. To do so would be unfair and would create severe market distortions, unless Yellow's intrastate operations are deregulated on an equal basis."[108] Yellow and others realized that if they had to continue to file tariffs

---

106. Jack Anderson and Michael Binstein, "Delivering a Senate Favor for UPS," *Washington Post*, July 7, 1994.

107. Robert James, "FedEx, UPS Try Backdoor Deregulation," *Traffic World*, March 28, 1994, p. 13.

108. Yellow Freight lobbying document, used in congressional hearings, 1994.

and go through sometimes lengthy state approval processes, they would not be able to compete effectively or nimbly with deregulated UPS or Federal Express.

As the process continued, other carriers came to hold a similar perspective. In effect, the point of political equilibrium moved from favoring the status quo to favoring complete deregulation. Since one or two major players in the field (UPS and Federal Express) would be able to work in a more deregulated environment, other large firms began to see that the state-level regulations from which some had benefited could now do them considerable harm because they inhibited organizational flexibility. Of course, as more firms came to see that they could maintain a competitive position only if they could escape the burden of full state regulation, the political forces sustaining the status quo dwindled.

Sensing this shift in the political equilibrium, in June 1994 the Executive Committee of the ATA made a historic, and internally controversial, decision to favor preemption of state regulation through this bill. Essentially, those members favoring preemption believed that some form of the bill would pass in 1994, that the courts were applying rulings in this direction, and that several states were moving in a similar direction. ATA's president, Tom Donohue, noted: "The world is changing. When all things are moving in the same direction, you can't stop water, you can only guide it."[109] To assert some influence, the ATA offered several specific changes to make the bill more palatable to its members.

The bill, officially section 211 of the Senate's version of the Airport Improvement Program Reauthorization Act, exempted certain air carriers from state regulation of their trucking operations if they carried a certain number of packages by air each year, a number originally set at 50,000. In June 1994, the Senate approved the bill by a voice vote, and the threshold for packages was lowered to 15,000 per year.[110]

In July House hearings on the bill, the Clinton administration came out in favor of the legislation, calling it "an important step in

---

109. Quoted in Rip Watson, "Carrier Interests Spar As Hearings Approach," *Journal of Commerce*, July 12, 1994, p. 2B.

110. Daniel Pearl, "Bill Exempting Many Trucking Firms from State Rules Is Approved by Senate," *Wall Street Journal*, June 20, 1994.

resolving conflicting laws that interfere with efficient intermodal cargo movements."[111] The Department of Transportation cited the previously noted 1994 FTC staff report that showed the regulations of entry, rates, and antitrust immunity increase intrastate less-than-truckload rates 37 percent above comparable deregulated interstate rates and truckload rates by 32 percent.[112]

When the bill went to a House-Senate conference committee, it made provisions to exempt all carriers from state-level regulations, not just those with affiliations to the air cargo industry.[113] The final version of the bill did not cover household goods carriers, nor did it bar states from regulating safety or insurance issues. It allowed states to set guidelines for uniform bills of lading, cargo liability or credit rules and preserved antitrust immunity for joint rates or routes, classifications, and mileage guides. Those regulations, however, could not be any more burdensome than ICC rules.[114]

The final provisions of the bill contained compromises designed to reduce areas of disagreement. While supportive of state preemption generally, in the House committee hearings the National Association of Manufacturers raised concerns about the unclear language of the draft bill: "Simple billing could become a nightmare for small businesses as well. Will there be different types of bills of lading for regulated versus non-regulated carriers in states that continue to engage in economic regulation of every carrier possible? In addition, the current language would put small private carriers at a disadvantage."[115] Concerns of this sort were addressed in the final bill.

111. Ibid.

112. Statement of Frank Kruesi, assistant secretary of the Department of Transportation for Transportation Policy; U.S. Congress, House of Representatives, Subcommittee on Surface Transportation, of the Committee on Public Works and Transportation, *Hearing on Preemption of State Regulation of Intermodal All-Cargo Air Carriers*, July 20, 1994, p. 5.

113. Section 211 of the Senate's version of the bill became section 601 of the conference report.

114. This information was reported in Robert P. James, "Truckers Prepare for New Era As Congress Orders End to State Economic Regulation," *Traffic World*, August 15, 1994, pp. 8–9.

115. Testimony of Norman Langberg on behalf of the National Association of Manufacturers; U.S. Congress, House of Representatives, Subcommittee on Surface Transportation of the Committee on Public Works and Transportation, *Hearings*

Reflecting on the passage of the bill, James Burnley, former secretary of transportation and attorney for Yellow Freight, told us: "The dynamic of [section] 211 had a real 'domino effect.' Before things began to fall though, there was real concern that if the bill went too far that the whole thing would collapse. Once it became clear that UPS and FedEx were going to be exempted, large LTLs [less-than-truckload carriers] wanted to be included. Once large LTLs were included, then smaller LTLs were, and so on down the line. Then, in one glorious afternoon on August 8 in one hour and 40 minutes, gridlock vanished." Eric White, executive director of Americans for Safe and Competitive Transportation, a 200-member coalition of truckers and shippers that had pressed for three years for intrastate and private carrier deregulation, said of the passage of the bill: "It's amazing. This bill is better than any I ever got introduced."[116]

Thus, Congress finally preempted the states through the vehicle of intermodal competition. To some extent, its hand was forced by court decisions, by an uneven playing field, and by other factors. And opposition to the bill was greatly reduced by the lack of influence of the Teamsters Union. The weakness of the Teamsters Union in 1994 was part of a long-term slide in its power, highlighted by the lack of impact of its nationwide transportation strike in April 1994 and partly by a short-run situation related to leadership and administrative turnover. Without this opposition, and with support from the dominant trucking interest group, the ATA, Congress was able to preempt the states.

Conclusions

With the 1994 federal preemption contained in the Airport Improvement Program Reauthorization Bill, state economic regulation of the trucking industry has now been all but dismantled. This was an important step in completing the deregulatory agenda. It is interesting, however, to reflect on what this experience tells us about policy making in a federalist system. Rather than serving as laboratories of

---

on Preemption of State Regulation of Intermodal All-Cargo Air Carriers, July 20, 1994, p. 7.

116. James, "Truckers Prepare for New Era."

democracy, the states can cast themselves as the last bastions of the regulated special interests.

In the period after the 1980 MCA, there was some action at the state level. Seven states removed their regulations of entry and rates for intrastate trucking, but this deregulatory momentum in the state legislatures stalled around 1985. Given that two states never regulated intrastate trucking, this left forty-one regulated states. While legislative initiatives were less than energetic in the years from 1985 through 1994, several states relaxed the rules for economic regulation, principally through bureaucratic exercise of administrative discretion. Even so, on the eve of the 1994 federal preemption of state economic regulation, about half the states still regulated according to the 1930s model of strict entry standards and filed rates. This regulation persisted despite wide and deep evidence that deregulation had substantial benefits. This evidence, and pressure by organized shipping groups, was not enough to overcome the entrenched state-level interests that benefited from regulation.

Recognizing this gridlock at the state level, the federal government stepped up several different efforts to preempt the states in the early 1990s. Particularly after 1985, when state-level deregulatory legislative initiatives stalled, many bills to preempt the states were introduced in the U.S. Congress, all of which failed. Over this period, the ICC acted to reduce the amount of intrastate commerce over which states had jurisdiction. Finally, in 1994 pressure from air package carriers provided the means by which most state economic regulation of trucking was ultimately preempted.

MAJOR ANALYSES OF INTRASTATE TRUCKING REGULATION, 1979–1991

Study, Author, Date of Publication	Years Studied	Market	Projected Impact	Methodology
"The Effect of Iowa's Regulatory System on the Interstate Motor Carrier Industry," by the Iowa Department of Transportation, Planning and Research Division, 1979.	1977	Iowa	Intrastate rates were 3–10% lower than interstate rates.	Study compares unregulated intrastate rates and regulated interstate rates for Iowa general commodity carriers holding both forms of authority.
"Examination of the Unregulated Trucking Experience in New Jersey," by W. B. Allen, S. Lonergan, and D. Plane. Prepared for U.S. DOT, 1979.	1978	New Jersey	Rates were 9–11% lower for small shippers and 10–15% lower for large shippers in the unregulated market.	Study compares rates for intrastate movements within New Jersey (which was unregulated) to interstate movements that either originated or terminated within New Jersey.

Study	Year	State	Findings	Description
"An Examination of Economic Deregulation of Intrastate Trucking in Michigan," by the Public Service Commission, Michigan Department of Commerce, 1979.	1979	Michigan	Rates for LTL shipments are 5–8% lower and rates for TL shipments are 10–20% lower inside the Detroit commercial zone.	Study compares rates within Detroit commercial zone, where no collective rate making exists, and areas outside this zone, where collective rate making is permitted.
"Intrastate Motor Carrier Regulation in Texas," by M. Pustay. Appeared in *Logistics and Transportation Review*, 1983.	1969–1981	Texas	Entry is found to be severely restrictive, with only 6 large, 12 medium, and 10 small general routes awarded to the sampled carriers from 1969 to mid-1981.	Study tabulates the number of general commodity operating authorities (by type of route) awarded to 6 of the primary intrastate carriers.
"Regulation of the Intrastate Motor Freight Industry of Ohio," by M. Pustay. Appeared in *ICC Practitioners' Journal*, 1983.	1978	Ohio	Tight entry policies enabled only 48% of entry applications to be approved and none without restrictive amendments to satisfy protestants.	Study analyzes the approval rate of common carrier entry applications.

(Table continues)

147

Study, Author, Date of Publication	Years Studied	Market	Projected Impact	Methodology
"The Effects of Intrastate Motor Carrier Regulation upon the Texas Agricultural Industry," by A. Schuster. Appeared in *Transportation Research Forum*, 1983.	1981	Texas	$38.4 million in savings to agricultural producers alone.	Study computes the difference between existing carrier rates and projected revenue needs in a deregulated environment for major agricultural commodities.
"Motor Carrier Regulation and Its Impact on Service: An Analysis of Texas Fresh Fruit and Vegetable Shippers," by L. Makus and S. Fuller. Appeared in *Southern Journal of Agricultural Economics*, 1983.	1981	Texas	For 11 out of 14 service attributes examined, shippers perceived interstate carriage to be superior to intrastate carriage, including lower rates, availability, fewer restrictions on in-transit services, and willingness to serve out-of-way markets.	Survey of fresh fruit and vegetable shippers.

148

Reference	Year	State	Findings	Methodology
"Effect of Intrastate Motor Carrier Regulation of Rates and Service: The Texas Experience" by S. Fuller, L. Makus, and J. Lamkin." Appeared in *Transportation Journal*, 1983.	1981	Texas	Regulated intrastate rates exceed exempt interstate rates for 5 commodities over comparable distances, while interstate rates are greater than intrastate rates for only 1 commodity.	Study regressed the rates (in cents per ton mile) of 9 agricultural commodities on trip distance and a dummy for the applicable form of regulation (regulated interstate or exempt interstate).
"Intrastate Motor Carrier Regulatory Reform in South Dakota," by M. Pustay. Appeared in *ICC Practitioners' Journal*, 1984.	1979–1983	South Dakota	Intrastate rates are approximately 70% of comparable interstate rates.	Study divides the South Dakota operating ratio by the nationwide operating ratio of the 3 largest regular route common carriers operating in the state over a 5-year period.
"Economic Regulation of For-Hire Trucking in the 1980s: The Case of Minnesota," by D.	1982	Minnesota	42% of manufacturers and 52% of grain elevator operators believed rates would drop if intrastate	Survey of shippers and grain elevator operators in the state.

(Table continues)

149

Study, Author, Date of Publication	Years Studied	Market	Projected Impact	Methodology
Harper. Appeared in *Transportation Practitioners Journal*, 1984.			rate regulation were eliminated.	
"The Small Community Service Issue: The Impact of State and Federal Regulation," by M. Pustay. Appeared in *Proceedings of the Transportation Forum*, 1985.	1976, 1982, 1984	Texas, Ohio, Minnesota, New Mexico, South Dakota, Florida, Maine, Wisconsin	Between 1976 and 1984, the average number of carriers offering interstate service to small communities rose in every state. During this same period, the mean number of carriers serving these same areas increased in only 3 states, each of which relaxed regulatory controls.	50 communities with populations less than 2,000 were randomly selected from each state and the National Highway and Airway Carriers Route guide was used to determine the level of service offered in each area.

Study	Date	Location	Findings	Methodology
"Effects of Reregulation of the California Intrastate Trucking Industry," by N. Frey, R. Krolick, L. Nidiffer, and J. Tontz. Appeared in *Transportation Journal*, 1985.	1984	California	64% and 55% of intrastate shippers report decreases in rates for TL and LTL shipments respectively after rate making had been liberalized.	Survey of intrastate shippers.
"Intrastate Regulation and Interstate Motor Carriers," by B. S. McMullan and P. Schary. Appeared in *Transportation Research Forum*, 1986.	1979–1984	Oregon	State regulations increase both rates and costs, ultimately resulting in a negative impact on operating profit.	Study regresses carrier rates, costs, and profits on differences in operating characteristics and the proportion of carrier operations conducted intrastate.
"Motor Carrier Deregulation: The Florida Experiment," by R. Blair, D. Kaserman, and J. McClave. Appeared in *The Review of Economics and Statistics*, 1986.	June 1980– Sept. 1982	Florida	Average reduction in rates, ceteris paribus, of 14.6% after deregulation.	Study regresses the price of individual shipments per ton mile on shipment characteristics and the timing of the movement. (4 time points)

(Table continues)

151

Study, Author, Date of Publication	Years Studied	Market	Projected Impact	Methodology
"The Impact of Motor Carrier Deregulation: California Intrastate Agricultural Products" by N. G. Frey, R. Krolick, and J. Tontz. Appeared in *Logistics and Transportation Review*, 1986.	1983 and 1984	California	60 and 70% of shippers report decreased rates for LTL and TL shipments of fresh fruits and vegetables respectively after deregulation. The figures rise to 90 and 93% for carriers.	Survey of fresh fruit and vegetable shippers and carriers.
"The Effect on Rate Levels and Structures of Removing Entry and Rate Controls on Motor Carriers," by R. Beilock and J. Freeman. Appeared in *Journal of Transport Economics and Policy*, 1987.	Jan. 1979– Oct. 1984	Arizona and Florida	During the period under examination, interstate rates along all routes are higher; however, on half the Arizona routes and all the Florida routes average intrastate rates are lower after deregulation in these areas.	Study compares average interstate and intrastate rates for particular movements before and after intrastate deregulation.

"Economic Regulation of Oregon Intrastate Trucking: A Policy Evaluation," by E. White. Prepared for the Oregon Public Utility Commission, November 1988.	1988	Oregon	$100 million in savings.	No evidence of estimate provided. Based on "some plausible assumptions."
"The Impact of State Economic Regulations of Motor Carriage on Intrastate and Interstate Commerce," by W. B. Allen, A. Preechemetta, G. Shao, and S. Singer. Prepared for the U.S. DOT, 1990.	1986	States that exercise some form of rate regulation	$2.8 billion (in 1988 dollars) in savings.	Study estimates the savings that would be accrued if those states with intrastate rates higher than interstate rates for comparable movements were deregulated.

(Table continues)

153

Study, Author, Date of Publication	Years Studied	Market	Projected Impact	Methodology
"The Economic Effects of Surface Freight Transportation," by C. Winston, T. Corsi, C. Grimm, and C. Evans. Brookings Institution, 1990.	1989	States that exercise some form of rate regulation	$1.7 billion (in 1977 dollars) in savings	Estimate a lower bound welfare gain by multiplying the total revenue generated by the regulated LTL sector by the average reduction in rates found in 60 LTL intrastate shipments within California and Nebraska.
"State Regulation of Motor Carriers in a Deregulated Transportation Environment," by E. Morash and G. Wagenheim. Appeared in *Transportation Journal*, 1991.	1986	Michigan	Estimated savings of $86.6 million or 20% of intrastate revenues.	Study estimates the revenue for each category of shipment, applies these to the differences between the discounted interstate and intrastate rates, and then aggregates the results.

SOURCE: Authors.

5

State Operating Restrictions on Trucking Firms

The problem which all federalized nations have to solve is how to secure an efficient central government and preserve national unity, while allowing free scope for the diversities . . . of the members of the federation. It is . . . to keep the centrifugal and centripetal forces in equilibrium, so that neither the planet states shall fly off into space, nor the sun of the central government draw them into its consuming fires.
—LORD JAMES BRYCE

In chapter 4, we focused on state economic regulation of trucking. While such regulation benefited a small number of actors at a large cost to society, a plethora of state operating restrictions that represent virtually all other regulations in the trucking industry has more complicated effects. Under the use of its police power, each state independently oversees the movement of freight within its jurisdiction, implementing and enforcing standards that cover every aspect of motor carriers' operations. Each state can enforce these standards as an interstate trucker moves through that state, and thus state actions affect interstate commerce. The federal government has not preempted much of this regulation out of respect for state police powers, but it has recently pushed harder for better coordination of these operating restrictions.

These restrictions are more like "social" regulations than economic regulations. Rather than economies of scale, the potential market failures addressed are those of negative externalities, such as pollution, and information asymmetries, such as safety concerns and

---

Lord James Bryce, "American Commonwealth," *Modern Democracies*.

155

insurance. We believe that these restrictions theoretically address legitimate concerns about the trucking industry but that their administration and implementation by the states have been lacking.

While the same theories of the political economy of regulation—the economic theory, institutionalism, and the politics of ideas—can be used to study the formulation of these regulations, they apply differently. Trucking firms, for example, are the strongest interest group, and they do not gain from many of these regulations, which is why they are often referred to as "restrictions." While truckers might prefer to avoid some of these regulations, they recognize, as do politicians, that there is broader support in society for maintaining safety and environmental standards. Thus, concentrated interest groups do not necessarily get what they want in this case. Instead, larger ideas like automobile safety and clean air mobilize broader, latent interests in society and dominate the politics of operating restrictions. For their part, state institutional actors seem most interested in gaining revenues from the taxes and fees associated with these operating restrictions to support their activities.

The structure of such requirements and the fees that typically accompany them often share little in common across the states. This lack of consistency frequently produces substantial inefficiency through excessive paperwork, wasteful overlap and duplication, and higher operating costs. While the politics of operating restrictions are often quite different from the politics of economic regulation, the outcomes for consumers are similar. In both cases, consumers suffer the consequences of an inefficient regulatory structure, paying unnecessary, excessive prices for products moved by the nation's trucking industry.

States typically apply three principal types of operating restrictions to motor carriers: vehicle operating taxes, vehicle size and weight requirements, and safety regulations. While historically each has been seen as a legitimate function of state government, these restrictions increasingly affect the flow of interstate commerce, raising questions about the acceptable boundaries of states' rights. For instance, should states be permitted to institute independent registration procedures for interstate carriers or impose different vehicle length and weight limitations? In the past decade, considerable progress has been made in coordinating certain state restrictions. Unfortunately, these advances usually necessitated federal intervention since voluntary compliance from all the states could not usually be achieved. Worse, many state operating restrictions that impede interstate commerce persist.

In this chapter, we highlight the major forms of operating restrictions within the states, explaining the rationale behind them and detailing the economic consequences for truckers, shippers, and consumers. We provide considerable detail not only to inform the reader but also to illustrate the length to which trucking firms must go to address these state operating restrictions. Furthermore, we outline different approaches that have been proposed or implemented to address them, examining the feasibility of these plans. Finally, we discuss continuing problems in the administration and implementation of state operating restrictions.

State Registration and Operating Taxes

Historically, states have collected revenue to cover the cost of construction and maintenance of their highways. What began as the simple registration of operating vehicles evolved into a complex set of directives and fees designed to cover the rising costs of such highway activities. Today, highway-related taxes fall into three general categories, differing on the basis of structure, incidence, and administration. Motor vehicle registration and licensing fees are known as first-structure taxes. Second-structure taxes refer to fuel-use taxes and reporting requirements. Third-structure taxes consist of weight-distance, ton-mile, or axle-mile taxes. While the components of each type of tax are different, each is generally designed to vary according to vehicle use, meaning that users are charged roughly in proportion to the cost responsibility of their vehicles.

As operating taxes multiplied over time, the burden of complying with these standards grew tremendously, especially for interstate carriers who needed to provide the necessary paperwork and fees for *each* state in which they operated. Moreover, little uniformity existed among the states. Filing procedures, tax rates, and enforcement agencies differed from state to state. One household goods carrier reported that "to legalize one typical tractor trailer for operation in 48 states for one year required filing 179 applications and permits and writing 76 checks. In addition, 290 fuel tax, third structure tax

157

and miscellaneous mileage-based reports had to be completed for 42 states involving 32 different formulas and 48 different forms."[2] The waste stemming from these requirements proved so egregious that the Department of Transportation estimated that filing the paperwork alone costs truckers between $1 billion and $3.2 billion per year,[3] and the American Trucking Associations complained: "The system of state road taxes, taken as a whole, is a tangle of mismatched tax laws and regulations that is a notorious embarrassment to good government and good tax administration."[4]

During the past two decades, several "base-state" agreements emerged to address the growing problem. For instance, the International Registration Plan and the International Fuel Tax Agreement were voluntary compacts among participating jurisdictions designed to reduce overlap and duplication in vehicle registration and fuel-use tax reporting. Under such plans, interstate carriers register with a single jurisdiction, which collects their liability for all jurisdictions and redistributes the fees based on the extent of their operations. While such agreements eased the paperwork burden to some extent, they fell far short of creating a uniform system of administration for state operating taxes, as some states failed to participate, while others did not always comply with the terms of the agreements. Responding to increasing pressures from the industry to do more, Congress passed the Motor Carrier Act of 1991 (1991 MCA) within the Intermodal Surface Transportation Efficiency Act, removing some of the more onerous state requirements and mandating that states join the principal base-state agreements by the middle of the 1990s.[5]

---

2. Written statement of Jeffrey N. Shane, assistant secretary for policy and international affairs, U.S. Department of Transportation, before the Subcommittee on Commerce, Consumer, and Monetary Affairs of the Committee on Government Operations, U.S. House of Representatives, on the consumer cost of continued state motor carrier regulation, March 29, 1990, p. 6.

3. Ibid., p. 7.

4. Statement of Thomas J. Donohue, president and chief executive officer of the American Trucking Associations before the Subcommittee on Commerce, Consumer, and Monetary Affairs of the Committee on Government Operations, U.S. House of Representatives, on the consumer cost of continued state motor carrier regulation, March 29, 1990, p. 6.

5. See House Report no. 102-171 (I) for the principal motivations and reasons behind various components of this act.

Below, we discuss in greater detail each type of highway-use tax, explaining their purposes and filing requirements. We also describe the difficulties associated with the administration and enforcement of these restrictions. Finally, we outline the latest programs for promoting uniformity among various jurisdictions, evaluating the successes and failures of these approaches.

Vehicle Registration Fees. All states require that carriers register their vehicles before operating within their jurisdiction and pay a license fee ranging up to $2,200 per vehicle.[6] For years, states required vehicles to provide proof of compliance by displaying a license plate or a "waffle plate" with a state sticker affixed to it. Often little uniformity existed among the states, creating an administrative nightmare for interstate truckers who needed to provide vehicle information and fees to each state their vehicles might travel through.

After years of study, the American Association of Motor Vehicle Administrators drafted a plan in 1973 to unify vehicle registration requirements and license fee collection, known as the International Registration Plan.[7] It was immediately adopted by nine states (Colorado, Kentucky, Minnesota, Missouri, Nebraska, Oregon, Tennessee, Texas, and Utah). In the ensuing twenty years, thirty-eight more states joined the agreement.

The International Registration Plan requires that trucking firms register with a base state, at the same time indicating the other jurisdictions in which the fleet maintains operations.[8] Registration fees for fleet vehicles are determined by the particular fee requirements of the states affected and are calculated according to the mileage the fleet accumulates in each jurisdiction. While the registration requirements and fees are different for many of the states, with the plan only one license plate and one cab card are issued for each vehicle. This greatly reduces the financial burden for firms by elimi-

---

6. Statement of Donohue, p. 6.

7. *Report to Congress*, submitted to Federico Pena, secretary of transportation, the Senate Committee on Commerce, Science and Transportation, the House Committee on Public Works and Transportation, and the House Committee on the Judiciary by the Base State Working Group on Uniform Motor Carrier Programs, December 17, 1993, p. 3.

8. Ibid., p. 4.

159

nating the need to file applications and affix identification to each truck for each participating state.

As part of the 1991 MCA, Congress mandated that all remaining nonmember states conform with the agreement by September 30, 1996, or lose the right to collect vehicle registration fees altogether.[9] As of 1994, only a few jurisdictions still did not belong to the plan; however, compliance by Delaware, New Jersey, and Rhode Island is expected in late 1995 or early 1996.[10] To date, the plan has operated quite effectively, with few disagreements among the states. Since nearly all states were involved voluntarily in the plan before the mandate, administrative problems have been limited.[11]

Closely tied to the concept of vehicle registration, thirty-nine states required interstate carriers to register their Interstate Commerce Commission (ICC) operating authority, provide proof of insurance, and pay annual administration fees.[12] Decals or "bingo stamps" from each applicable jurisdiction had to be displayed on each vehicle within a firm's fleet as evidence of compliance. In addition to the administrative and financial burdens these directives placed on carriers, the bingo stamps proved to be particularly frustrating since they had "different renewal dates; often faded or fell off a truck; when a door or windshield needed to be replaced they had to be repurchased; they complicated the transfer of an old vehicle or the entry into the fleet of a new one; and the required placement of some on the vehicle unsafely impeded a driver's view."[13]

In an effort to alleviate the waste associated with these provisions, the Intermodal Surface Transportation Efficiency Act repealed the bingo stamp program as of 1994.[14] States were still permitted to collect revenues generated by these decals, but they were required to do it through a system established under the ICC's direction.

---

9. Public Law 102-240.

10. *Report to Congress*, p. 13.

11. Thom Rubel, National Governors Association, personal communication, May 10, 1994.

12. "ISTEA-91 Pours on the Changes," *Common Carrier Journal*, April 1992, p. 62.

13. Statement of Donohue, March 29, 1990, p. 10.

14. P.L. 102-240.

Under the Single State Registration System, a carrier pays its fees and provides proof of insurance to a single state that is responsible for reimbursing the other member states.[15] Fees are based on the number of vehicles the carrier operates in each state. States are prohibited from imposing any other fees in connection with the registration of interstate operating authority. Only the thirty-nine states that allowed such fees before the passage of this act are allowed to participate in this agreement, and they cannot charge fees greater than they permitted as of November 15, 1991, or $10 per vehicle.

In sum, the major problems with the administration of first-structure taxes have been addressed and substantially reduced. State cooperation was finally achieved, but not before federal intervention required it. While it is still too early to discern how effective the Single State Registration System will ultimately be, if the International Registration Plan is any indication, the program should be quite successful in eliminating the overlap and duplication produced by varying state demands.

Fuel-Use Fees. Another area where lack of uniformity creates inefficiencies for truckers is fuel-use reporting and taxation. All states require trucks carrying a certain size payload to pay fuel taxes based on the amount of mileage accrued within their state, in part to finance highway maintenance. Fuel taxes represent over 60% of all highway user taxes. To do this, most states require carriers to: (1) complete a state's decal permit application form; (2) display a fuel registration decal on each vehicle; (3) report either monthly or quarterly the amount of fuel consumption and purchases; and (4) file an annual fuel tax return specifying much of the same information.[16] For years, this procedure was required by every state in which the carrier operated. Furthermore, state differences existed in everything from the definition of a taxable vehicle to the timing of the tax collection to

---

15. "ISTEA-91 Pours on the Changes," p. 62.

16. Statement of Anthony Burns, chief executive officer of Ryder System, Inc., before the Subcommittee on Commerce, Consumer, and Monetary Affairs of the Committee on Government Operations, U.S. House of Representatives, on the consumer cost of continued state motor carrier regulation, March 29, 1990, pp. 12–13.

the amount of tax to be paid. Together, these procedures created huge administrative costs for the truckers.

Testifying before a 1990 congressional hearing on the consumer costs of continued state trucking regulation, Anthony Burns, chief executive officer of Ryder System, Inc., claimed:

> Approximately 56,000 of our 140,000 vehicles are liable for interstate fuel taxes. Last year, we obtained, distributed and affixed over 575,000 individual fuel permit decals. In order to accomplish this feat, we have a staff of 7 full time headquarter employees and approximately 100 field-support employees whose primary purpose is to ensure that each Ryder vehicle has the proper fuel tax permits and decals displayed for the states in which those vehicles operate.
>
> Using an estimate of 5 minutes per decal for time spent physically affixing the decals, you can see we spend an additional 54,000 man hours in compliance efforts. We estimate that Ryder's administrative cost to affix the correct fuel tax decals on the right truck at the right time to be $3,320,000 annually. This does not include the cost of the decals or the actual fuel tax liability.[17]

Not only were these procedures expensive, but at times they bordered on the ridiculous. At these same hearings, Robert Moga, owner of Moga-1 Transportation Company, Inc., complained:

> We traveled 36 miles in Kansas during 1989. You see the forms that had to be filled out. They are so complicated that even a professional who does the fuel reporting suggested that we take them to an accountant. At this point, I have no idea what I am going to do with them. I'm certainly not going to pay an accountant $100 or $200 to fill out paperwork for 36 miles. However, if I ignore this, penalties will be assessed and permits will not be given to us. We are between a rock and a hard place. For 36 miles?[18]

---

17. Ibid., p. 13.

18. Statement of Robert Moga, before the Subcommittee on Commerce, Consumer, and Monetary Affairs of the Committee on Government Operations, U.S. House of Representatives, on the consumer cost of continued state motor carrier regulation, March 29, 1990, p. 193.

In the past decade, extraordinary progress has been made with respect to fuel-tax administration. Two base-state fuel-tax agreements have been initiated to alleviate many of the burdens of these overlapping requirements. In 1982, the International Fuel Tax Agreement was formed among Arizona, Iowa, and Washington. After securing the endorsement of the National Governors Association in 1986, twenty-four more states joined by the end of 1993.[19] During this period, the agreement evolved from a tacit understanding among several state regulatory agencies into a private, nonprofit organization that oversees the administration and collection of fuel taxes within the participating states.[20]

The fuel-tax agreement operates similarly to the International Registration Plan. Under the terms of this agreement, carriers select a base state, typically the state within which their operations are headquartered, and register their fleet as a unit, not as individual vehicles.[21] The base jurisdiction issues a fuel-use tax license to the carrier that is honored by all participating states. While the base state may levy decal fees for carriers registering within their jurisdiction, they may not impose such fees on carriers registering in other jurisdictions. Subsequently, a motor carrier's base state collects the fuel-use taxes for all the states in which the carrier operates for a given year, audits the return, and redistributes the revenue to the other jurisdictions based on the proportion of trucking operations within each state. As a result, carriers are required to: (1) display only a single fuel-tax decal, which is identical for all vehicles within the fleet; (2) complete a single tax return; and (3) provide trip records to a single auditor from their base state rather than for each jurisdiction in which they operate.[22]

---

19. As of November 19, 1993, states that held membership within the International Fuel Tax Agreement were Arizona, Arkansas, Colorado, Florida, Idaho, Illinois, Indiana, Iowa, Kansas, Louisiana, Minnesota, Mississippi, Missouri, Montana, Nebraska, Nevada, New Mexico, North Carolina, North Dakota, Oklahoma, Oregon, South Dakota, Tennessee, Utah, Washington, Wisconsin, and Wyoming.

20. *Report to Congress*, pp. 4–5.

21. Carriers are required to register all gas or diesel vehicles with two axles and a gross vehicle weight over 26,000 pounds or three or more axles regardless of weight with a base state.

22. *Report to Congress*, pp. 4–5.

A second agreement, the New England Regional Fuel Tax Agreement, was established in 1985 among Maine, New Hampshire, and Vermont. It arose in response to the particular needs of these New England states. All three states are geographically small, contain numerous access points with few formal ports of entry, and are typically crossed by regional carriers many times in a single period. This agreement uses a base-state system of tax collection, similar to the International Fuel Tax Agreement, although it has several major differences. First, the New England agreement is less formal than the international agreement. Member states administer the agreement, with no formal repository overseeing their activities. Second, the weight thresholds for fuel-tax registration vary in each of the states, ranging from 7,000 to 26,000 pounds. Finally, a trucker is required to pay a decal fee in each state in which the carrier operates. This allows states to compensate for some of the lost fuel-tax revenue through lack of significant mileage accumulated by many carriers.[23]

These agreements, particularly the international agreement, have enjoyed widespread support among trucking firms nationwide. They greatly simplify the process of fuel reporting and taxation by reducing the amount of paperwork and accelerating filing procedures. The American Trucking Associations called the International Fuel Tax Agreement "the best hope of the trucking industry for a way out of the thicket of confusing and conflicting current state fuel tax laws."[24]

One-third of the states, though, continued to resist joining either of these agreements for several reasons. First, fuel-tax decals generate enormous revenues for states. By allowing only those states to impose decal fees on carriers that use them as a base jurisdiction, states lose the annual fees from the purchase of decals by firms not located there. Second, some states are concerned with the auditing procedures in other states, believing that they would not receive all the taxes allotted them. Finally, some states were not willing to cede any of their state sovereignty.[25]

Responding eventually to the appeals of the American Trucking

---

23. Ibid., p. 5.

24. Statement of Donohue, p. 9.

25. "Preliminary Findings of the Base State Working Group Survey of Non-IFTA States," conducted by the National Governors' Association and the National Conference of State Legislatures, November 20, 1992.

TABLE 5-1
PROJECTED ENTRY OF NONMEMBER STATES INTO THE
INTERNATIONAL FUEL TAX AGREEMENT, 1995 AND 1996

Alabama	—	New Jersey	1996
California	1996	New York	—
Connecticut	1994	Ohio	1995
Delaware	1994	Pennsylvania	—
Georgia	1996	Rhode Island	1996
Kentucky	—	South Carolina	1995
Maryland	1996	Texas	1995
Massachusetts	—	Virginia	1996
Michigan	—	West Virginia	1996

NOTE: States with no dates are to be determined.
SOURCE: *Report to Congress,* submitted by the Base State Working Group on Uniform Motor Carrier Programs, Washington, D.C., December 17, 1993, pp. 15–16.

Associations and the recommendations of the National Governors Association, Congress mandated as part of the 1991 MCA that all remaining states join the International Fuel Tax Agreement by September 30, 1996.[26] Any state not in conformity with this legislation will lose the right to collect fuel taxes in the future. An exception was stipulated for those states comprising the New England Regional Fuel Tax Agreement, which were allowed to continue their compact. Consequently, the International Fuel Tax Agreement gained considerable authority, in the process transforming from a voluntary agreement among a small coalition of states to an organization of substantial power to limit the actions of state governments. Table 5–1 provides the projected entry dates for nonmember states into this agreement.

As states conform with the congressional mandate, the agreement faces a number of new challenges. First, administrative difficulties will arise as the remaining states attempt to comply. Many states must purchase or convert computer and management systems to accommodate the new collection and auditing procedures. The Base State Working Group on Motor Carrier Programs was estab-

26. P.L. 102-240.

lished under provisions within the 1991 MCA as a means of identifying and addressing such problems arising under this mandate by
training state officials.[27]

The second major challenge for incoming member states is the
possible loss of significant revenues. Pennsylvania estimates that
procedural changes will cost the state more than $13 million annu-
ally, while New York claims that the new rules will cost it roughly $6
million per year.[28] In addition, many of these states will face extensive replacement costs as they convert their existing administrative
systems to those consistent with agreement guidelines. To address
these costs, the 1991 MCA allocated funding for each state, called
uniformity grants, during the interim period, but their funding has
been inadequate.[29]

Finally, and perhaps most important, is the question of dispute
resolution. The agreement has established a set of procedures for
dealing with differences of interpretation and compliance among
member states.[30] In most cases, though, continued noncompliance
would force the agreement's governing board to request the secretary
of transportation to seek injunctive relief. Currently, questions are
being raised among nonmember states about the authority of the
agreement to impose sanctions, the role of the Department of Transportation, and states' rights. Legal challenges to the legitimacy of a
nongovernmental entity governing state actions will develop.

Weight-Distance Taxes. Third-structure taxes are the least pervasive, but the most controversial, of the highway-user taxes levied
today. In general, these taxes are calculated on the weight of the
vehicle, or the number of miles traveled within the state, or some
combination of the two. Historically, four types of third-structure
taxes have been applied by the states:[31] mileage taxes, axle taxes,

---

27. *Report to Congress*, pp. 9–12.

28. Ibid., p. 7.

29. Ibid., pp. 21–23.

30. Ibid., pp. 27–30.

31. Ronald K. Snell, "Weight Distance Taxes and Other Highway User Taxes: An
Introduction for Legislators and Legislative Staff," Legislative Finance Paper no.
71, prepared for the National Conference of State Legislators, 1989.

ton-mile taxes, and weight-distance taxes.[32] Now, though, only two forms of third-structure taxes are in effect. One state (Kentucky) levies mileage taxes, while five states (Arizona, Idaho, New Mexico, New York, and Oregon) administer weight-distance taxes.[33]

Third-structure taxes are generally applied to compensate for the financial shortcomings of first- and second-structure taxes. In theory, third-structure taxes are considered more equitable than the other forms because they come closer to reflecting the actual costs trucks impose on highways.[34] While all highway-use taxes are intended to be user charges, generally most are not. A 1984 study by the Federal Highway Administration found that combination trucks impose nearly eleven times more highway damage than passenger automobiles.[35] State registration fees and fuel-use taxes, while greater for heavier vehicles, do not reflect this difference. In fact, a 1980 Oregon study revealed that an 80,000-pound truck used only four times more fuel than a passenger car.[36] By designing a rate structure that accounts for both distance and vehicle weight, third-structure taxes can come considerably closer to matching the cost responsibility of different vehicles on the highway.

In practice, third-structure taxes have proved to be expensive to administer, difficult to enforce, and discriminatory. Little consistency exists among states, with different forms, different information, and different filing dates. Moreover, most states (with the exception of

---

32. Mileage taxes are flat taxes applied to specific classes of vehicles based on the number of miles traveled within a jurisdiction. Axle taxes base the levy on distance and the number of axles, which serves as a proxy for weight. Ton-mile taxes are determined by the gross vehicle weight and mileage for each trip taken by the vehicle. Weight-distance taxes typically calculate the registered maximum gross vehicle weight the vehicle can carry by mileage.

33. John Schulz, "National Weight-Distance Tax Study Recommended by GAO in New Report," *Traffic World*, June 27, 1994, p. 41.

34. Snell, "Weight Distance Taxes," p. 7. See Kenneth Small, Clifford Winston, and Carol Evans, *Roadwork: A New Highway Pricing and Investment Policy* (Washington, D.C.: Brookings Institution, 1989), for a detailed analysis that shows weight per axle is the most important cause of higher damage.

35. Federal Highway Administration, *Alternatives to Tax on the Use of Heavy Trucks: Report to Congress*, January 1984, p. III-5.

36. H. Scott Coulter, "The Oregon Weight-Distance Tax," *American Association of State Highway and Transportation Officials*, vol. 63, no. 4 (July 1984), p. 28.

Oregon) enforce these taxes by tracking vehicles through various points of entry within a state. At times, the costs incurred by truckers because of these stops surpass the taxes themselves.[37] States even found that certain types of third-structure taxes are more expensive to administer than other highway-user taxes. The Colorado Highway Legislation Review Committee revelation that collection costs for the state's ton-mile tax were nearly 10 percent of the revenue generated, for example, eventually led to the repeal of this tax.[38]

The inequities of these taxes are worse than the inefficiencies. While states design formulas to compensate for the damage to their roads by tractor-trailers, the calculations of these taxes do not correspond to the amount of road damage produced by a vehicle. For instance, states that use weight-distance taxes base their taxes on the maximum capacity of a vehicle, rather than on the actual size of its payload. Not only is this inconsistent with the objective, but also it ignores the fact that road wear results more from the amount of weight carried by *each axle* rather than from the total weight of the load. For example, a 60,000-pound three-axle truck will cause greater highway damage than an 80,000-pound five-axle vehicle.[39]

Furthermore, states often discriminate against interstate carriers in the collection of these taxes. Trucks involved with vital aspects of a state's economy are frequently given exemptions, leaving the payment of these taxes disproportionately to the interstate fleets. In addition, interstate carriers are required to keep mileage records, whereas intrastate carriers are not, leaving interstate carriers more susceptible to audits by state regulators. Finally, intrastate carriers have a much easier time evading a system where vehicles are tracked through particular points of entry.[40]

Some of the more blatant inequities have been addressed, but many still exist. Federal courts found that the weight-distance taxes formerly in effect in Arkansas, Kentucky, and Pennsylvania violated

---

37. John Reith, "Ton-Mile Taxes Revisited," *American Association of State Highway and Transportation Officials*, vol. 63, no. 3 (July 1984), p. 15.

38. Snell, "Weight-Distance Taxes," p. 12.

39. Mileage taxes can be even worse because they do not reflect even the weight of the vehicle. Statement of Donohue, p. 13.

40. Ibid., pp. 13–14; Snell, "Weight-Distance Taxes," pp. 19–23.

the Constitution's commerce clause by discriminating against inter-state carriers.[41] Legal questions led Nevada to repeal its weight-distance tax. Generally, Congress has devoted little attention to third-structure taxes. In fact, the Intermodal Surface Transportation Efficiency Act, which explicitly addressed state highway-user taxes, did not address these taxes at all.

Outstanding Issues. With the exception of third-structure taxes, the most glaring problems surrounding the administration and implementation of highway-use taxes have been addressed. Several issues, however, warrant attention in the near future. Most important is the implementation of the North American Free Trade Agreement.[42] NAFTA calls for a level playing field for firms operating in the United States, Mexico, and Canada. This means that trucking regulations need to place the same burden on Mexican and Canadian carriers as they do on U.S. firms. NAFTA should not prove to be particularly problematic for Canada, which already has in place a system parallel to the United States for registration and fuel reporting. While at the end of 1993 only Alberta belonged to the International Registration Plan and no Canadian provinces belonged to the International Fuel Tax Agreement, the remaining Canadian jurisdictions are expected to join both in the next few years.

Mexico, though, is a different case. As of 1995, the Mexican government did not collect fuel taxes or registration fees or even require registration for motor carriers. NAFTA, though, permits Mexican truckers to operate within the U.S. border states by December 1995 and anywhere in the United States by 2000. In 1995, border states are likely to provide one-time trip permits (with fees) for Mexican carriers. In the future, however, it is unclear what will be done. Several options are available. First, Mexican truckers could choose a U.S. state as a base state and have their taxes apportioned much like American carriers. Second, the Mexican government could be pressured to institute its own registration and fuel-use procedures and then eventually join the International Registration Plan and the International Fuel Tax Agreement. Representatives from all three

---

41. Snell, "Weight-Distance Taxes," pp. 2–3.

42. Rubel, personal communication.

nations met in July 1994 to discuss these issues.[43] By mid-1995 Mexico continued to disappoint NAFTA members by not committing to stable trucking regulations.

Vehicle Size and Weight Requirements

Vehicle size and weight requirements are a second major form of state operating restrictions. Historically, the federal government has shied away from uniformity of state vehicle size and weight restrictions, allowing states to pursue a wide range of approaches. Over time, though, the emergence of longer, heavier trucks raised the need for increasing federal intervention.

Standard Vehicle Size Restrictions. States began regulating truck size and weights nearly from the time of their first appearance on the nation's roads. Concerned with the damaging effects to their highways from heavy axle weights, Maine and Massachusetts implemented the first laws restricting weights in 1913, just before the first state economic regulation of trucking. Other states quickly followed, so that by 1933 all states regulated the dimensions and weights of trucks, typically imposing axle weight, gross vehicle weight, length, and width restrictions.[44]

Since these regulations were applicable to all trucks, regardless of whether they were used for common, contract, or private carriage, they served as a powerful form of entry regulation. Often the pattern of weight restrictions that materialized in different states reflected the economic interests of relevant interest groups. In his seminal work, George Stigler found that weight restrictions were more onerous in states where railroads were highly competitive with the trucking industry, where trucks played a smaller role in farming, and where the state highway system was less developed.[45]

---

43. Kevin Hall, "U.S. Truckers See Access to Mexico Lag," *Journal of Commerce*, June 27, 1994, p. A-8.

44. Transportation Research Board Special Report 211, *Twin Trailer Trucks: Effects on Highways and Highway Safety* (Washington, D.C.: National Research Council, 1986), pp. 19–20.

45. George Stigler, "The Theory of Economic Regulation," *Bell Journal of Economics and Management Service*, vol. 2 (1971), pp. 3–21.

In response to growing concern in the industry over the lack of uniformity in state size and weight restrictions, the American Association of State Highway Officials issued a blueprint for uniform state regulations in 1946, proposing that weight limits be set at 18,000 pounds for a single axle, 32,000 pounds for a tandem axle, and 73,280 pounds for gross vehicle weight.[46] Federal standards were not set, however, for another decade. The Federal Aid Highway Act of 1956, which financed the construction of interstate highways, imposed the weight limits recommended by the American Association of State Highway Officials and a 96-inch width limit for all vehicles operating on the interstate system.[47] Since some states already permitted vehicles in excess of those values to operate, the law included a grandfather clause that allowed states to enforce either the federal standards or the corresponding maximum weights established by the state before 1956. The result substantially compromised efforts to impose national uniform size and weight regulations.[48]

In the years that followed, considerable variation among the states in permissible truck sizes began to surface. Generally, the Federal Highway Administration allowed states to exercise the grandfather clause and institute a higher limit on vehicle weights if they provided documentation, backed by an attorney general's opinion substantiating the claim, that the state had permitted such weights before 1956. As a result, many states allowed gross vehicle weight in the 76,000–78,000 pound range, with several states permitting vehicles in excess of 80,000 pounds to operate on interstate roads.[49] Moreover, the administration decided to allow preexisting state laws that permitted tolerances on their weight restrictions to be included within the grandfather provision. As a result, twelve states authorized weight tolerances ranging between 2 and 10 percent.[50]

46. U.S. Congress, Office of Technology Assessment, *Moving Ahead: 1991 Surface Transportation Legislation*, OTA-SET-496 (Washington, D.C.: U.S. Government Printing Office, 1991), pp. 36–42.

47. Transportation Research Board, *Twin Trailer Trucks*, pp. 26–27.

48. Charles Medalen, "Grandfather Rights under 23 U.S.C. 127," unpublished manuscript, pp. 1–2.

49. Ibid., p. 2.

50. Transportation Research Board, *Twin Trailer Trucks*, p. 29.

Responding to industry concerns about the economic effects of lowering the federal speed limit to 55 miles per hour, Congress increased vehicle weights permitted on the interstate system as part of the Federal Aid Highway Amendments of 1974. Weight limits were pushed to 20,000 pounds for single axles, 34,000 pounds for tandem axles, and gross vehicle weights of 80,000 pounds, where they stand today. In addition, weight restrictions for trucks traveling on federally financed bridges were adopted as part of the amendments.[51] The legislation, however, permitted states to preserve bridge formulas or axle-spacing tables in effect before 1975. Few states had existing formulas; however, many permitted certain short-wheelbase trucks, such as dump trucks, to operate on bridges up to the maximum limit allowed. These existing conditions were grandfathered in as well, further expanding the state variation.[52]

The federal government failed to adopt standards in either the 1956 or the 1974 Federal Aid Highway Acts. Consequently, a sizable spread in permissible truck-length limits emerged in the states. Most states adopted sizes that reflected the most common configuration in the industry. As the most popular trailer length increased from 24 feet in 1946 to 45 feet in 1973, most states shifted combination vehicle-length limits from 45 to 60 or 65 feet. The eastern states generally implemented these changes more slowly than states in the West, waiting to see if savings in highway maintenance materialized.[53]

While these disparities caused logistical difficulties, these were not especially problematic until the growing popularity of twin trailers in the 1960s. With twin trailers, one tractor pulls two 28-foot trailers over five axles. These allowed greater volume capacity and more flexibility in cargo handling than standard tractor semitrailers. Legalization of twin trailer trucks spread gradually among the western states; however, by 1980 fourteen states still prohibited their use. Since all these states were concentrated along the East Coast, numerous problems for interstate carriers arose as they were unable to move products from coast to coast.[54]

---

51. Office of Technology Assessment, *Moving Ahead*, pp. 42–43.

52. Medalen, "Grandfather Rights."

53. Transportation Research Board, *Twin Trailer Trucks*, pp. 32–36.

54. Ibid., pp. 32–36.

In addition to vehicle lengths, the trucking industry expressed growing concern with the 96-inch vehicle width limit in effect since 1956. Considering that before construction of the interstate highway system most traffic occurred on standard 22-foot, two-lane highways, a 96-inch width seemed reasonable at the time. It also gave railroads a distinct competitive advantage over trucks, however, since 96 inches is exactly the double-pallet size of standard cargo pallets, as well as the inside dimension of a railroad boxcar. The 96-inch limit imposed on trucks was the distance measured *outside* the vehicle. For trucks to be able to load standard pallets side by side within the same vehicle, a 102-inch outside truck width would be required. This proved to be a burdensome obstacle, particularly to agricultural transporters.[55]

The 1982 Surface Transportation Assistance Act addressed these outstanding issues with four principal elements, all intended to reduce the inefficiencies caused by inconsistencies in state size and weight restrictions.[56] First, Congress increased vehicle width limits to 102 inches, to allow agricultural carriers to compete more effectively with the railroads. Second, it required all states to allow the 1974 weights for vehicles operating on the federal highways, overcoming the obstacle to interstate commerce stemming from stricter regulations in particular states.[57] Third, it prohibited states from limiting the length of a semitrailer to less than 48 feet or each trailer of a combination with two trailers to less than 28 feet on the interstate and designated highways, in the process preempting state rules in thirty-five states. Finally, this legislation modified the 1956 law, allowing the states rather than the Federal Highway Administration to decide which vehicles fell under the grandfather clause.

While the 1982 Surface Transportation Assistance Act and the Federal Aid Highway Acts went a long way toward addressing the inconsistencies in state vehicle size and weight restrictions, many disparities continue to exist. Several states, for example, replaced

---

55. Office of Technology Assessment, *Moving Ahead*, p. 43.

56. Transportation Research Board, *Twin Trailer Trucks*, pp. 48–51.

57. While the federal government set weight limits on vehicles operating on the interstate system, several states required gross vehicle weights to be substantially less. Unfortunately, these states were concentrated in the Mississippi Valley, making cross-country transport problematic.

federal weight regulations with their own based on insupportable claims, as a result of the modification to the grandfather clauses. Currently, twelve states allow greater weight than that authorized by the federal government.[58] Eight states, including Connecticut, Georgia, Hawaii, Massachusetts, New Jersey, New Mexico, New York, and Rhode Island, permit single-axle limits higher than the federal standard of 20,000 pounds. Six states, including Alaska, Colorado, Connecticut, Florida, New Mexico, and Wyoming allow limits on tandem axles higher than the federal standard of 34,000 pounds. And two states, New Mexico and Wyoming, allow far higher gross vehicle weights than the federal standard of 80,000 pounds.

Furthermore, by placing only a floor on the length and width restrictions that states are allowed to implement, the federal government has left the door open for increasing differences within the states. While current road dimensions effectively prevent states from instituting greater vehicle widths, the same cannot be said about permissible lengths of semitrailers. Table 5–2 shows that most states now allow semitrailer lengths of more than 53 feet on the interstate and designated highways.

Special Permits and the Proliferation of LCVs. In addition to the vehicles authorized to operate under the weight limits set by the federal government, a separate class of heavier vehicles is allowed to operate on the interstate system: the various longer combination vehicles (LCVs) that require a special permit. LCVs are generally defined as multiunit combination trucks with gross vehicle weights greater than 80,000 pounds. There are essentially three basic configurations of LCVs operating on the interstate system: turnpike doubles, Rocky Mountain doubles, and triple trailers.[59] Determining the legality of these types of vehicles on the interstate system has been one of the principal sources of disagreement between the Federal Highway Administration and the states over the past several decades.

Before 1956, most states that provided permits for overweight vehicles did not distinguish between divisible and nondivisible loads.

---

58. Department of State Laws, *Summary of Size and Weight Limits*, American Trucking Associations, 1994.

59. Office of Technology Assessment, *Moving Ahead*, pp. 36–37.

TABLE 5–2
SEMITRAILER LENGTHS PERMITTED ON INTERSTATE AND DESIGNATED
HIGHWAYS, 1994
(in feet)

Alabama	57	Montana	53
Alaska	48	Nebraska	53
Arizona	57½	Nevada	53
Arkansas	53½	New Hampshire	53
California	53	New Jersey	53
Colorado	57⅓	New Mexico	57½
Connecticut	53	New York	53
Delaware	53	North Carolina	53
Florida	53; 57½ w/pᵃ	North Dakota	53
Georgia	53	Ohio	53
Hawaii	NR	Oklahoma	59½
Idaho	53	Oregon	53
Illinois	53	Pennsylvania	53
Indiana	53	Rhode Island	48½
Iowa	53	South Carolina	53
Kansas	59½	South Dakota	53
Kentucky	53	Tennessee	50
Louisiana	59½	Texas	59
Maine	48; 53 w/p	Utah	48; 53 w/p
Maryland	53	Vermont	53
Massachusetts	48; 53 w/p	Virginia	53
Michigan	53	Washington	48; 53 w/p
Minnesota	53	West Virginia	53
Mississippi	53	Wisconsin	53
Missouri	53	Wyoming	60

a. w/p = with permit.
SOURCE: Department of State Laws, *Summary of Size and Weight Limits*, American Trucking Associations, 1994.

Therefore, when the 1956 Federal Highway Act grandfathered in existing state weight requirements, it was somewhat unclear what state practices were permissible. The Federal Highway Administration took two different interpretations. For nondivisible loads, it allowed states to issue single-trip or short-term permits under federal guidelines, regardless of the existence of previous statutes.[60] For divisible loads, the meaning of the law was less clearcut. Initially, the highway administration interpreted the act to mean if these vehicles were lawfully allowed before 1956, then such vehicles could operate on the interstate system; otherwise, such vehicles would not be authorized to operate on federal highways.[61]

Two state court decisions cast this strict interpretation in doubt, however, substantially liberalizing the definition and meaning of the 1956 grandfather clause. In 1974, the Montana Supreme Court found in *Dick Irvin, Inc. v. Anderson*[62] that even though Montana statutes did not explicitly allow overweight divisible load permits, they did not prohibit such practices either; hence, the grandfather clause authorizes the state to issue such permits today.[63] Seven years later, the South Dakota Supreme Court further clarified this decision by ruling in *South Dakota Trucking Association v. South Dakota Department of Transportation*[64] that since the clause allowed the continued permitting of vehicles "that *could* be lawfully operated" before 1956, it did not require that vehicles actually be operated before that time, only that they could have been operated (emphasis in opinion).[65]

As a result, a number of states began issuing multitrip special permits for divisible loads even though such practices did not exist on the books before 1956. As figure 5–1 illustrates, by 1992 twenty-three states, primarily located west of the Mississippi, allowed some form of LCV operations. The most widely approved LCVs are Rocky Mountain doubles, with twenty-two states allowing their operation. Permits for turnpike doubles are issued in eighteen states, with triple trailers allowed in seventeen states.

Great controversy has always surrounded the operation of LCVs, involving the safety, highway infrastructure, and economic effect of these vehicles. The biggest debate involves LCV safety. Accident

---

60. Ibid., p. 43.

61. Medalen, "Grandfather Rights," p. 3.

62. Dick Irvin, Inc. v. Anderson, 525 P.2d 564 (1974).

63. Ibid., p. 3.

64. South Dakota Trucking Association v. South Dakota Department of Transportation, 305 N.W. 2d 682 (1981).

65. Ibid., pp. 3–4.

FIGURE 5–1

STATES PERMITTING THE OPERATION OF LONGER COMBINATION VEHICLES, 1992

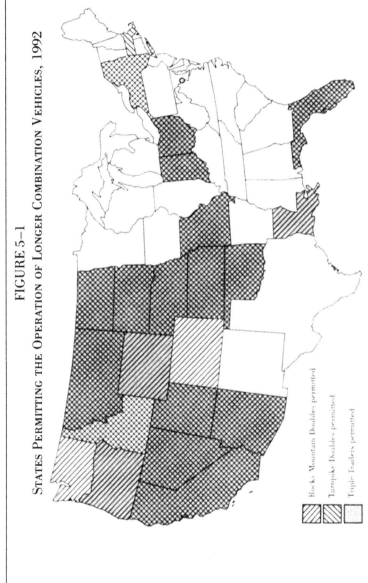

Rocky Mountain Doubles permitted

Turnpike Doubles permitted

Triple Trailers permitted

NOTE: Alaska and Hawaii do not permit the use of longer combination vehicles of any type.
SOURCE: "ISTEA-91 Pours on the Changes," *Commercial Carrier Journal*, April 1992, p. 68.

records from different states show that LCVs have fewer or equal fatal and nonfatal accident rates per vehicle mile than those of standard-sized trailers. In fact, triple trailer combinations exhibit the best accident record of any vehicle configuration currently on the road.[66] Very little quality data currently exist, however, that allow a systematic investigation of the safety of different configurations of these vehicles. Furthermore, LCVs possess certain vehicle characteristics that make them more prone to accident. For instance, longer trailer wheelbases, like those found on Rocky Mountain or turnpike doubles, are more susceptible to off-tracking, which occurs when the back axles shift to the center of the curve during vehicle turns.[67] The reason such factors have failed to result in a worse accident record for LCVs likely stems from the permitting requirements of many states that usually designate travel on the safest highways and the experience that many carriers demand before allowing a driver behind the wheel of an LCV. The railroads have argued that expanding LCV operations would lead to far greater safety problems.

LCVs are not more likely to damage infrastructure than standard tractor semitrailers. Since these vehicles contain more axles over which weight can be distributed and require fewer trips to carry equivalent weight, LCVs cause less road damage per unit moved. A study by the American Trucking Associations estimated that if LCVs were legalized nationwide, $16–55 million would be saved on pavement costs.[68] This is offset, though, by the need for significant segments of the interstate highway system to be redesigned to accommodate these vehicles with wider lanes and stronger bridges. Studies have placed the cost of upgrading bridges alone to allow for nationwide use of LCVs at $6–30 billion.[69]

LCVs allow carriers to move commodities more efficiently than standard-sized trailers. Increased trailer space enables more products to be transported by a single vehicle, reducing costs for driver wages and fuel expenses. A study conducted for the American Trucking Associations claims that if LCVs were introduced nationwide,

---

66. Office of Technology Assessment, *Moving Ahead*, p. 48.

67. Transportation Research Board, *Twin Trailer Trucks*, pp. 270–73.

68. Office of Technology Assessment, *Moving Ahead*, p. 55.

69. Ibid., p. 56.

productivity benefits would be $2–4 billion annually.[70] This estimate, however, needs to be weighed against the infrastructure investment required to strengthen roads and bridges.

During the 1980s, LCVs began to compete effectively with the railroads for long-distance shipments of heavy products, primarily in the western states. In 1991, the railroads began lobbying to prohibit LCVs. In several states, they ran an intensive advertising campaign depicting potential dangers with this form of transport. Responding to these railroad demands, citizen group concerns, and Department of Transportation recommendations, Congress passed a provision within the Intermodal Surface Transportation Efficiency Act that froze the operation of LCVs to the states in which they were legally permitted to operate as of 1991. Concerned with not losing any of the gains they had made in a number of states, truckers accepted the freeze. States that allowed LCVs are prohibited from expanding routes or removing restrictions related to the operation of these vehicles. Moreover, the act mandated that the Federal Highway Administration establish minimum training requirements for LCV operators, including certification of an operator's proficiency with these vehicles.

The possibility of expanding LCV use nationwide remains. The act commissioned two studies to explore different aspects of LCV operations. First, the comptroller general was required to undertake a study by December 1993 comparing the safety and economic performance of LCVs with those of other commercial vehicles as well as to examine various state initiatives to ensure LCV safety. Second, the Federal Highway Administration must conduct road tests of LCV drivers and vehicles by the end of 1995 to determine if any changes to the new LCV provisions need to be made. Pending the outcome of these reports, the current LCV freeze could be substantially modified or even removed.

Trucking Safety Requirements

Trucking safety has long been a concern for both the federal and the state governments. For years, however, their efforts were hampered by a lack of resources for enforcement. While the 1980 MCA sub-

---

70. SYDEC, Inc., *Productivity and Consumer Benefits of Longer Combination Vehicles*, Trucking Research Institute, 1990, pp. 13–14.

stantially reduced the federal government's role in the economic regulation of truckers, recent legislative changes have expanded the scope and breadth of federal safety requirements. Not only have attempts been made to improve highway safety, but also the federal government has stepped up efforts to increase national uniformity by providing incentives for states to adopt federal regulations and coordinate enforcement of safety standards.

Federal Safety Programs. Historically, trucking safety regulations were issued and enforced by the Federal Highway Administration within the Department of Transportation.[71] The administration set equipment standards for vehicles, established qualifications for drivers, and inspected and audited carriers. Before the 1980s, though, the administration lacked sufficient resources to monitor and enforce many of these standards. To bolster inspection efforts, it often entered into cooperative agreements with state agencies. Lack of funding, however, usually hampered such practices. Furthermore, the safety regulations themselves were often poorly defined, inadequately coordinated with state requirements, and typically lagged behind industry innovations. As a result, safety measures often proved to be inadequate and ineffective. During the 1980s, four major pieces of legislation were passed addressing these concerns, providing the federal government with the capability to regulate the safety of trucking operations.

In 1982, as part of the Surface Transportation Assistance Act, Congress introduced the Motor Carrier Safety Assistance Program. Administered by the Federal Highway Administration, this program provides federal funds for inspection and enforcement of motor carrier safety regulations to states that adopt federal standards or compatible regulations. Grants are financed through the Highway Trust Fund on a matching basis, with the federal government contributing 80 percent and the states 20 percent. In addition, the act financed

---

71. There are two principal exceptions. The National Highway Traffic Safety Administration established regulations for the manufacture of new vehicles and the Research and Special Programs Administration issues and enforces regulations for carriers of hazardous materials. Both agencies are also within the Department of Transportation. U.S. Congress, Office of Technology Assessment, *Gearing Up for Safety: Motor Carrier Safety in a Competitive Environment*, OTA-SET-382 (Washington, D.C.: U.S. Government Printing Office, 1988), pp. 58–61.

the development of SAFETYNET, an information system designed to house data on program inspections, audit reviews, and commercial vehicle accidents.[72]

In 1984, Congress passed the Motor Carrier Safety Act. This legislation directed the Department of Transportation to revise the existing body of federal safety regulations, clarifying the applicability of these regulations and bringing them up to date with new technologies. Subsequently, all state laws pertaining to commercial motor vehicle safety were reviewed to ensure consistency with these federal requirements. State regulations deemed "less stringent" than those established by the Department of Transportation were preempted, while those with the "same effect" or "more stringent" were allowed to remain in place as long as they exhibited a certifiable safety benefit and did not hinder interstate commerce. In addition, this act established procedures for determining the safety fitness of carriers and called for annual commercial vehicle inspections.[73]

The 1986 Commercial Motor Vehicle Act addressed concerns over the adequacy of licensing requirements for trucking operators. It prohibited drivers from holding multiple licenses and established a uniform classified license system.[74] The Commercial Driver's License program set minimum standards for state testing and licensing of commercial drivers, requiring drivers to demonstrate that they can operate their vehicles "competently and safely." Results from these tests are linked to a national information clearinghouse, which makes information available to the Department of Transportation and the states.[75]

Finally, Congress approved the Truck and Bus Safety and Regulatory Reform Act in 1988, which removed a major loophole in the applicability of federal regulations. Previously, vehicles operating

---

72. Statement of Paul F. Rothberg, Congressional Research Service, before the Subcommittee of Surface Transportation of the Senate Committee on Commerce, Science, and Transportation, April 18, 1989, pp. 1–3.

73. Office of Technology Assessment, *Gearing Up for Safety*, p. 57.

74. Ibid., pp. 57–58.

75. Statement of Richard P. Landis, associate administrator for motor carriers, Federal Highway Administration, before the Subcommittee on Surface Transportation of the Senate Committee on Commerce, Science, and Transportation, April 18, 1989, pp. 6–7.

wholly within a commercial zone designated by the Department of Transportation were exempt from federal safety standards unless they were transporting substantial quantities of hazardous materials.[76] These laws have resulted in a three-pronged approach to trucking safety on the federal level that allows the Federal Highway Administration to inspect and enforce safety standards.[77] First, all trucking firms undergo a safety review process of their management practices. Each carrier receives a rating based on an audit of both the practices the firm initiates to ensure compliance with federal safety standards and the firm's accident experience. Satisfactory carriers operate according to federal rules and do not have any significant accident experience. To prevent problems in the future, the Federal Highway Administration offers technical assistance so these carriers can continue to operate in compliance and safety. Firms labeled conditional or unsatisfactory demonstrate increasing number of safety violations and accidents. Both groups must undergo a second, more intensive review process, which pinpoints in greater detail inadequate management practices and controls, and allows the administration to determine sanctions in a more systematic, equitable fashion. If an unsatisfactory carrier continually fails to comply with federal standards, demonstrating neither sufficient action nor effort to overcome its deficiencies, the firm can be prevented from doing further business.

The second method to ensure motor carrier safety is the Commercial Driver's License program. The program assesses drivers' qualifications by requiring them to pass a written test as well as a road test in the vehicle configuration they plan to operate. Drivers who fail either portion are disqualified from operating commercial vehicles until they demonstrate the appropriate skills.

Finally, vehicles in operation are routinely inspected by both Federal Highway Administration and state officials for safety violations. The Motor Carrier Safety Assistance Program has substantially increased the quantity and quality of roadside inspections, with more than 1 million inspections per year. Information from all three areas is collected and monitored through a set of clearinghouses that the

---

76. P.L. 100-690, Section 9102.

77. This overview is summarized from a presentation, cited in note 75, by Landis.

administration oversees. In total, these federal mechanisms provide numerous opportunities to identify and correct deficiencies before accidents occur. Even with such provisions, though, a number of safety problems remain. As a result, states have adopted their own safety regulatory standards to complement the federal programs.

State Safety Programs. For years, states implemented and enforced safety restrictions independently from the Federal Highway Administration, creating a number of problems in the process. State regulations were at times inconsistent with one another or contradictory with federal requirements. This created administrative problems for truckers as they attempted to ascertain which rules were applicable in particular jurisdictions as well as to comply with them. In addition, state inspection and enforcement procedures often complicated carrier efforts to transport products in a timely fashion. Certain states did not recognize the inspections from other states, leading some vehicles to be stopped and reinspected multiple times in the same day as they passed through different jurisdictions. Both of these problems were further compounded by the poor funding and inadequate resources that also existed on the federal level, exacerbating inequities in administration and enforcement already present.

Two programs, introduced during the 1980s, allowed states to deal with these vexing issues. With the formulation of the Motor Carrier Safety Assistance Program, inconsistencies in state safety requirements and inadequacies in funding could be addressed. Under this program, two types of grants, development and implementation, are available to the states.[78] Development grants provide money for states to establish or substantially modify a trucking safety enforcement program. Most states have received development grants and progressed to the implementation phase. Implementation grants are awarded to states on a continuing basis to initiate enforcement programs or improve established ones. States become eligible by agreeing to adopt and enforce federal safety regulations or rules that are compatible.

The program has been an unqualified success in organizing and enforcing state and federal safety activities. By 1994, all but two states had participated in some way in the program. Before the pro-

---

78. Office of Technology Assessment, *Gearing Up for Safety*, pp. 64–65.

gram, the Federal Highway Administration performed 36,000 safety inspections each year. After this program was instituted, state officials carried out more than 1.55 million inspections in 1990 alone.[79] Congress extended the program through 1997.

The second program for alleviating coordination difficulties among state safety regulatory authorities is the Commercial Vehicle Safety Alliance. Responding to the colossal growth in the number of trucks relative to state inspection resources, representatives from California, Oregon, Washington, and Idaho designed a program in 1980 to coordinate inspection activity. Membership grew to include every state except Hawaii and South Dakota. Under this agreement, states adopt essentially the same inspection procedures. Moreover, when a vehicle is inspected, a unique inspection decal, valid for three months, is affixed to the windshield and recognized by other participating states. Thus, vehicles that pass inspection in one state can pass through other member states without further inspection, unless an obvious violation is detected.[80]

Current Safety Issues. Federal and state legislative and regulatory efforts to improve the implementation of trucking safety regulations have been highly successful. Gains have been made in clarifying and updating safety requirements, in removing inconsistencies between jurisdictions, in reducing needless duplication and overlap, and in enhancing inspection and oversight. A number of problems still persist, however.

First, the effectiveness of the Commercial Vehicle Safety Alliance is frustrated by its status as a voluntary agreement. While it works reasonably well in coordinating inspection and enforcement among various state agencies, duplicative inspections of interstate vehicles continue to occur, even in participating states. This problem is particularly troublesome among owner-operators who do not have the benefit of belonging to a large fleet with a reputation for safety.[81]

Second, states frequently levy different sanctions and fines for identical safety violations, creating inequities in the penalties ap-

---

79. House Report No. 102-171(I).

80. "A Guide to Interstate and Intrastate Trucking," *Heavy Duty Trucking Magazine*, 1985, pp. 30–35.

81. Office of Technology Assessment, *Gearing Up for Safety*, pp. 72–78.

plied to unsafe carriers. Moreover, some states have chosen to use these fines as a revenue-generating device, rather than simply as a deterrent or for safety-related purposes, in the process creating incentives for state officials to pursue interstate carriers at the expense of intrastate carriers.[82]

Third, and possibly the most glaring problem with the Motor Carrier Safety Assistance Program, is that the Federal Highway Administration does not currently require state officials to reinspect vehicles that have been removed from operation because of safety problems. According to Paul F. Rothberg, "The effectiveness and integrity of the current program frequently relies heavily on an inconsistently enforced and ineffectively audited process that allows industry to self-certify that critical safety defects were corrected properly."[83]

Finally, the Federal Highway Administration still lacks the manpower to complete its duties in a timely and effective manner. For instance, a large number of interstate truckers, many of which are small or are among the 30,000 new entrants since the 1980 MCA, have still not received a safety rating for their internal management systems. In addition, none of the private fleets have been inspected, even though they represent about half of all trucks on the road.[84]

Special Forms of Operating Restrictions

Above and beyond these state-operating restrictions faced by all truckers, certain types of trucking companies confront additional regulations that often increase the cost and difficulty of moving the products they carry. In the remainder of this chapter, we detail two special forms of operating restrictions that raise questions about the relationship among federal, state, and local authority. We begin by discussing issues surrounding transporters of hazardous materials. Then we turn our attention to state environment regulations issued under the Clean Air Act and their impact on the trucking industry.

---

82. Statement of Donohue, president of the American Trucking Associations, before the Subcommittee on Surface Transportation of the Senate Committee on Commerce, Science, and Transportation, April 18, 1989, pp. 20–21.

83. Statement of Rothberg, p. 3.

84. Ibid., pp. 16–17.

Hazardous Materials Transportation. More than 500,000 shipments of hazardous materials occur each day, resulting in the transportation of more than 4 billion tons of hazardous products each year.[85] Hazardous materials—defined as those that pose an unreasonable health or safety risk when transported in commerce—include explosives, poisons, flammable liquids and gases, oxidizers, and etiologic agents. More than half these shipments are carried by truckers across the nation's roads. Government jurisdictions further distinguish between two particular dangerous materials—radioactive substances and hazardous wastes—typically applying more stringent regulations to movement of these materials.[86]

Hazardous materials have always posed unique questions for legislators because of the danger inherent in their movement. It has often proved difficult to strike a balance between necessary precautions to ensure the safety of the public and overbearing regulations that impede the transport of these materials. Historically, the regulation and enforcement of hazardous materials transportation rested in the hands of the federal government. In 1975, Congress passed the Hazardous Materials Transportation Act, which gave the Department of Transportation regulatory and enforcement authority over the transportation of hazardous materials interstate or any transportation that affected interstate commerce. Despite the opportunity to expand its jurisdiction, the department has chosen not to apply federal regulations to intrastate transportation except for certain movements of hazardous wastes, flammable cryogenics, and liquefied petroleum gas.[87] In fact, most truckers operating exclusively intrastate are exempt from many Department of Transportation regulations.

In the last two decades, however, states, as well as local communities, have increasingly monitored these activities, often prompted by a growing awareness of the dangers in this type of transport and the realization that responsibility for emergencies typically falls on state and local agencies. States' involvement has ranged

---

85. U.S. Congress, Office of Technology Assessment, *Transportation of Hazardous Materials: State and Local Activities* (Washington, D.C.: U.S. Government Printing Office, March 1986), pp. 3–4.

86. Lawrence Bierlein, *Hazardous Materials: A Guide for State and Local Officials*, U.S. Department of Transportation, 1982, pp. 4–7.

87. Ibid., pp. 24–25.

from registration and permitting to such operational regulations as highway routing and prenotification. Unfortunately, though, state intervention in hazardous materials transportation has often been misguided, producing costly, confusing, and inconsistent regulations.

With the passage of the Hazardous Materials Transportation Uniform Safety Act of 1990, many of these problematic areas have been addressed. It is still too early to gauge how successful these changes will be; however, some of the more egregious regulations should prove far less problematic in the future.

Registration and permitting. Forty-one states and more than two dozen localities have some form of registration or permitting requirements for the transportation of hazardous materials. Table 5–3 identifies the types of registration requirements that exist for each state.

While the procedures for obtaining a permit vary from state to state, most require carriers to file an application detailing the characteristics of their operation. In some cases, this involves fingerprinting of certain employees, submission of financial records, or demonstration of safety fitness. Moreover, fees generally accompany this application, costing in some cases hundreds of dollars for a single hazardous waste vehicle.[88]

The purpose of these requirements is well intentioned, designed to ensure public and environmental safety, with money often targeted for state hazardous materials programs such as emergency training or cleanup operations. In practice, though, this multiplicity of state and local registration and permitting requirements for transporters of hazardous materials creates problems for these truckers like the vehicle and fuel-tax registration procedures outlined above. Requiring carriers to file separate applications within each jurisdiction frequently leads to excessive paperwork, duplication, and extensive accounting resources, creating administrative and financial burdens on carriers and, ultimately, higher costs for shippers and consumers. Furthermore, some industry representatives argue that the proliferation of registration requirements compromises safety by inducing some carriers to use secondary highways and engage in circuitous

---

88. See National Governors Association and National Conference of State Legislatures, *Alliance Phase One Subgroup Reports*, prepared for the Alliance for Uniform Hazmat Transportation Procedures, 1992, pp. 14–36, for a summary of state registration and permitting requirements.

TABLE 5–3

STATE REGISTRATION AND PERMITTING REQUIREMENTS FOR THE TRANSPORTATION OF HAZARDOUS MATERIALS, 1993

State	Hazardous Materials		Hazardous Waste		Radioactive Materials	
	Registration	Permitting	Registration	Permitting	Registration	Permitting
Alabama				X		
Alaska						
Arizona			X			
Arkansas			X			
California	Cargo tanks	Regular and liquefied petroleum gas tanker		X		
Colorado						
Connecticut		X		X	X	
Delaware				X		
Florida			X			X
Georgia		Pcb/liquefied natural gas				X
Hawaii						
Idaho	X			X		
Illinois			X			
Indiana						
Iowa						

188

State					hazardous liquid waste/ tunnels
Kansas				X	
Kentucky					
Louisiana		Liquefied petroleum gas/ explosives		X	
Maine	Petroleum				
Maryland			Tank trucks	X	
Massachusetts				Lpg/explosv	X
Michigan	Petroleum			X	X
Minnesota	Petroleum			X	
Mississippi				X	X
Missouri				X	
Montana				X	
Nebraska					
Nevada		Reg + driver	X		
New Hampshire				X	
New Jersey			Tanker/lpg	X	X
New Mexico					X
New York			Port authority	X	X
N. Carolina					
N. Dakota					
Ohio	X				

(Table continues)

TABLE 5–3 (continued)

State	Hazardous Materials		Hazardous Waste		Radioactive Materials	
	Registration	Permitting	Registration	Permitting	Registration	Permitting
Oklahoma				X		
Oregon	X		X	X		X
Pennsylvania	X	Turnpike		X		X
Rhode Island				X		X
S. Carolina				X		X
S. Dakota						
Tennessee			X			X
Texas		Liquified natural gas/compressed natural gas				
Utah		Lpg				
Vermont	Limited		X			X
Virginia		Tank truck		X	X	
Washington						X
W. Virginia						
Wisconsin	X			X		
Wyoming	Pesticides				Trip	X

SOURCE: *Report of the Alliance for Uniform HazMat Transportation Procedures*, U.S. Department of Transportation, Alliance for Uniform HazMat Transportation Procedures, November 17, 1993.

routing to avoid certain jurisdictions that maintain these require-ments.[89]

To ameliorate the problem of multiple registration procedures, the 1990 safety act requires the Department of Transportation to establish uniformity requirements by the middle of the 1990s. To assist in this process, the act established a working group, the Alliance for Uniform Hazmat Transportation Procedures, to explore this issue and develop recommendations for the Department of Transportation. In the succeeding four years, the alliance developed a base-state system for the registration of hazardous materials carriers.[90] Within states choosing to participate, truckers would select a base state that would be responsible for collecting registration fees for all participating jurisdictions and distributing them accordingly. To prevent "state shopping" by truckers, a firm's base state should be the state that houses the carrier's principal place of business. If that state is not part of the base-state agreement, then the carrier must choose the state within the program where the greatest proportion of mileage was traveled.[91] A governing board composed of representatives from the participating states would oversee compliance with the base-state program, as well as issue interpretations of the terms of the agreement. While the governing board would have no legal authority to take action against the signatories, its power lies in its ability to recommend punitive actions that might be taken by the secretary of transportation.[92] Furthermore, the governing board would

---

89. Testimony of Clifford J. Harvison, president of National Tank Truck Carriers, in Hearings on Hazardous Materials Transportation, before the Subcommittee on Surface Transportation of the Senate Committee on Commerce, Science, and Transportation, 1987.

90. *Report of the Alliance for Uniform Hazmat Transportation Procedures*, pp. 4-1–4-13.

91. More than two dozen localities also have permitting or registration requirements. To avoid the proliferation of local requirements, the task force recommended that localities be incorporated with the base-state agreement. In other words, base states would collect and allocate information and fees for localities as well. In those cases, where local governments required registration but states did not, the state could designate one jurisdiction to serve as the base state. *Report of the Alliance for Uniform Hazmat Transportation Procedures*, pp. 3-5–3-7.

92. Experience with the International Registration Plan and the International Fuel Tax Agreement has shown that the courts frequently take into account these recommendations when legal action has been taken by interested parties.

develop and monitor a national repository to house information provided by carriers and shippers in compliance with this agreement as well as details of the registration programs of the participating jurisdictions.

Currently, a pilot program is testing the feasibility of this agreement as well as assessing the extent that the base-state program reduces the administrative burden on carriers and affects the safety of hazardous materials transportation within participating jurisdictions.[93] Four states were selected to participate in this pilot effort. West Virginia and Nevada began administering the program July 1, 1994, with Ohio and Minnesota joining the program October 1, 1994. If twenty-two other states pass enabling legislation to participate in this program by September 30, 1996, then the secretary of transportation is likely to codify this system as part of the final Department of Transportation regulations. Otherwise, the department will develop and implement its own program for establishing uniform procedures for the registration of carriers of hazardous materials. It is too early to determine whether the base-state system devised by the alliance will succeed; however, states are likely to conform with the plan to avoid federal preemption.

Operational regulations. In addition to various permitting and registration programs, many states and localities have implemented a number of operational regulations for the transportation of hazardous materials. These range from record-keeping requirements to personnel training to designated routes. Together they are intended to provide information needed for emergency preparedness as well as reduce the risk of accident for these carriers.

The 1975 Hazardous Materials Transportation Act provides that any state or local restriction that is "inconsistent" with regulations issued by the federal government is preempted and therefore invalid. To assess whether an inconsistency exists, the Department of Transportation applies two different standards.[94] First, it evaluates whether

---

93. Thom Rubel, National Governors Association, personal communication, June 10, 1994.

94. Larry Abbott, George Bulanowski, Barry Foster, and James Jordan, *Hazardous Materials Transportation: A Legislator's Guide* (Denver, Colo.: National Conference of State Legislators, 1984), pp. 41–43.

it is possible to comply with both the state and the federal requirements ("the dual compliance test"). Second, it determines if the
state requirement is an obstacle to fulfilling the act's intentions ("the
obstacle test"), which were to improve total safety as well as to
prevent the proliferation of conflicting regulations. While these procedures were designed to avoid litigation, the judgments of the department were only advisory and frequently ended up in the courts.
Judicial interpretations have generally coincided with the department's rulings, but the process was expensive and time-consuming,
with some cases taking years to resolve.[95]

Experience throughout the 1980s demonstrated that the inconsistency concept was an underused and unreliable tool to clarify the
relationship between federal and state authority over the transportation of hazardous materials. State and local regulations proliferated,
often producing costly, confusing, and contradictory requirements.
Not only do these restrictions inhibit carriers' ability to provide service in a timely and efficient fashion, but also at times they jeopardized public safety by diverting hazardous materials traffic to times
and places ill equipped to handle them. Three particularly troublesome forms of operational regulations—time-of-day restrictions,
highway routing, and prenotification—highlight the problems with
the wide variation in state laws.

A number of localities have implemented time-of-day restrictions for the movement of hazardous materials through their jurisdictions. In most cases, traffic is shifted to off-peak times in an effort to
reduce the risk of accident. Such restrictions, though, have a significant impact on the flow of commerce. During the hours not permitted
for travel, carriers must "park and wait," delaying the delivery of
their products. Furthermore, businesses within jurisdictions with
time restrictions must adjust employee schedules to coincide with
permissible delivery times, often resulting in increased costs through

---

95. Between 1978 and 1990, the Department of Transportation issued only thirty-
two inconsistency rulings. In general, nonfederal requirements already covered by
federal regulations, such as vehicle placarding and insurance requirements, were
found inconsistent, while nonfederal requirements falling within the domain of
traffic regulations, such as vehicle inspections and headlight use, were judged
consistent. "Index to Preemption of State and Local Laws and Regulations under
the Hazardous Materials Transportation Act," prepared by the Research and Special
Programs Administration, April 19, 1994.

higher wages.[96] Some jurisdictions are not even aware of the detrimental effects these restrictions can have on the flow of goods. A case cited by the Private Truck Council of America during hearings on hazardous materials transportation makes the point:

> Recently a county in the Washington, D.C. metropolitan area imposed a ban on all movements of federally-regulated hazardous materials on all highways in the county between the hours 7 a.m. and 7 p.m. When informed that this would mean that no service station could receive shipments of gasoline during those hours, the county council members were surprised—they did not mean to include gasoline, only "hazardous materials."[97]

Such consequences might be deemed an acceptable trade-off for improved public safety. There is little systematic evidence, however, that time-of-day restrictions actually improve the safety of transporting hazardous materials. In fact, such restrictions could even increase the potential for accidents. Restricting travel during certain times means that much larger concentrations of hazardous materials are traveling together than under normal circumstances, greatly increasing the risk. Furthermore, the delays caused by these regulations substantially increase the amount of time these products spend in transit.[98]

Highway routing is another important tool used by state and local governments to prevent accidents and ensure the protection of their residents. By designating specified roads for travel, localities hope to decrease the risks associated with the transportation of these products. As of 1987, state agencies in eighteen jurisdictions used their authority to regulate the highway routing of hazardous materials shipments.[99]

---

96. Statement prepared by the American Trucking Associations for Hazardous Materials Transportation Hearings before the House Subcommittee on Surface Transportation of the Committee of Public Works and Transportation, July 30, 1987, pp. 7–8.

97. Ibid.

98. Ibid., pp. 4–6.

99. In addition, local authorities in fourteen states exercise routing control for hazardous shipments on highways within their municipal limits. American Association of State Highway Officials, Subcommittee on Highway Transport, Task Force on Hazardous Materials Routing and Signing, *Draft Report*, 1987.

Historically, the federal government has interfered little in the routing decisions of local communities other than by publishing guidelines to assist jurisdictions in implementing these restrictions.[100] While the federal government encouraged local jurisdictions to solicit input from community officials and industry representatives, routes were frequently established without regard for neighboring jurisdictions or carriers' concerns. As a result, state and local routing restrictions created a number of problems for carriers. For instance, some communities, particularly large cities like New York and Boston, have used routing to divert hazardous materials traffic to neighboring localities. Not only has this practice placed greater demands on the emergency resources of adjacent communities that are often ill equipped to handle them but also it has occasionally sparked retaliatory routing that left truckers in a precarious position. For example,

> when Boston banned hazardous materials, carriers were forced to use alternate routes around the city, including Route 128. Shortly, thereafter, numerous communities around Boston, through which Route 128 passed, restricted hazardous material shipments from their roadways. Carriers found themselves in an impossible situation since transporting hazardous materials through the city of Boston or its surrounding suburban area was virtually impossible when in compliance with these requirements.[101]

Finally, many state and local governments require truckers to notify authorities of their intent to transport certain types of materials through their jurisdictions. Prenotification of the amount, timing, and routes of hazardous material shipments provides communities with information that can be used for emergency response planning for possible accidents, such as escorts and resource coordination, as well as data on the flow of these commodities that can enhance enforcement activities. As figure 5–2 illustrates, currently twenty-

---

100. While the 1975 Hazardous Materials Transportation Act gave the Department of Transportation the authority to regulate the routing of hazardous materials, the department has chosen to exercise this authority only for the transportation of radioactive materials where it has designated specific interstate highways for the movement of these products.

101. Statement by the American Trucking Associations, July 30, 1987, p. 5.

FIGURE 5–2

STATES WITH HAZARDOUS MATERIALS NOTIFICATION REQUIREMENTS, 1986

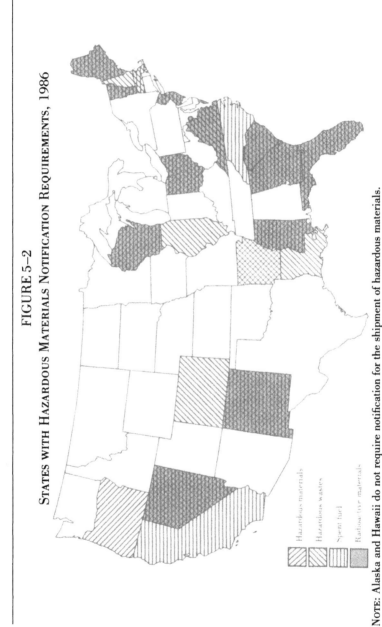

NOTE: Alaska and Hawaii do not require notification for the shipment of hazardous materials.
SOURCE: "Transportation of Hazardous Materials: State and Local Activities," U.S. Congress, Office of Technology Assessment (Washington, D.C.: GPO), 1986, p. 92.

196

one states have enacted notification laws for some form of hazardous materials.

While there is ample justification for such requirements, many jurisdictions fail to use this information properly, adversely affecting the flow of hazardous materials without improving safety. For instance, some jurisdictions require several days' notice, creating costly problems for carriers operating under just-in-time delivery. Not only does this create scheduling problems for carriers, but also it results in increased inventories of certain products to allow for immediate delivery, which in certain cases is more dangerous than the actual transport of the product. Furthermore, several studies for the Department of Transportation have shown that prenotification does not increase enforcement activities or emergency preparedness for a significant number of jurisdictions, meaning that much of the costly paperwork necessary to comply with these regulations is simply wasted.[102]

Through the 1990 Hazardous Materials Transportation Uniform Safety Act, the federal government has taken steps to ameliorate the problems stemming from the multiplicity of state and local operating restrictions.[103] First, Congress revised the preemption standards to reduce the amount of varying and conflicting nonfederal regulations. The "dual compliance" and "obstacle" tests were given statutory status, meaning that preemption determinations are now legally binding subject to judicial review. This legislation also preempted any state or local regulation that was not "substantively the same" as federal law for the following subjects:

(i) designation, description and classification of hazardous materials; (ii) packing, repacking, handling, labeling, marking and placarding hazardous materials; (iii) preparation, execution, and use of shipping documents pertaining to hazardous materials and requirements respecting the number, content, and placement of such documents; (iv) the written notification, recording and reporting of the unintentional release in transportation of hazardous materials; and (v) the design, manufacturing, fabrication, marking, maintenance, reconditioning, repairing, or testing of a

---

102. Abbott et al., *Hazardous Materials Transportation*, pp. 31–32.

103. P.L. 101-615.

package or container which is represented, marked, certified, or sold as qualified for use in the transportation of
hazardous materials.[104]

Furthermore, the act specifically addressed the problem of highway routing. Congress chose to keep responsibility for highway route
designations within the domain of the states, rather than preempting
them. Existing routes were grandfathered in as part of this provision
as long as states reported them by a set date and they fulfilled the
"dual compliance" and "obstacle" tests. In the fall of 1994, the
Department of Transportation issued a series of standards and factors
that states must follow when overseeing the designation of new highway routes within their jurisdiction. According to the Notice of Proposed Rulemaking, states establishing a new route must comply with
these regulations as well as advertise, take comments, and under
certain circumstances hold public hearings on the proposed route.
Once the regulations are established, affected parties can challenge
the procedures or facts surrounding these regulations before the Federal Highway Administration or in court. Only if it can be determined
that states did not conform to federal standards or take local citizens'
demands into consideration will the highway route designation be
preempted.

Environmental Standards. Air quality standards set by the Environment Protection Agency (EPA) under the auspices of the Clean
Air Act are another issue that is becoming increasingly problematic
for segments of the trucking industry. For decades, ground-level
ozone and carbon monoxide levels across the country have been
rising. Ground-level ozone, typically associated with smog, results
when sunlight reacts with hydrocarbons and nitrogen oxides. Carbon
monoxide, however, is a poisonous gas formed primarily from the
incomplete combustion of fuel.[105] Dense concentrations of these pollutants produce severe health problems among the population, such
as lung and eye damage, and destroy billions of dollars in crops each
year. While these gases are emitted from many different sources,

---

104. P.L. 101-615, Section 4.

105. U.S. Environmental Protection Agency, "Fact Sheet: Federal Implementation
Plans in California," February 15, 1994.

mobile sources produce almost half the ground-level ozone and nearly all the carbon monoxide.[106]

In the late 1960s, the Clean Air Act was passed to reduce concentrations of certain pollutants nationwide. Subsequent amendments to this act tightened these standards and extended them to an increasing number of sources. Historically, clean air legislation only marginally touched large trucks, generally targeting other sources of harmful emissions. In 1990, however, Congress made sweeping changes to the act, focusing more on reducing pollution from commercial vehicles than in the past. Not only will this legislation affect the operating costs of trucking companies, but also in some cases it may severely alter the logistics of motor transport.

1990 Clean Air Act Amendments. The 1990 Clean Air Act Amendments had two major sets of provisions affecting the operation of heavy-duty vehicles or vehicles with a registered loaded weight over 8,500 pounds. Title I of this act established acceptable concentrations of various pollutants nationwide. In addition, the EPA designated certain nonattainment areas for different pollutants based on the severity of the problem. These nonattainment areas were required to take specific actions, such as transportation planning and traffic control, to rectify the problem by specified dates. While these measures did not necessarily focus on trucks, some may ultimately have severe effects on industry operations.

Title II of the 1990 act contained specific provisions to reduce emissions from mobile sources.[107] In particular, the act instituted five major changes for heavy-duty vehicles, all of which are likely to have a substantial economic impact on the industry. First, these amendments lowered the sulfur content of diesel fuel for all trucks in all states except Alaska or Hawaii. Fuel used in 1991–1993 model year vehicles could not have a sulfur content exceeding .10 percent by weight. This figure dropped to 0.5 percent by weight in late 1993.

---

106. Federal Highway Administration, *Transportation Programs and Provisions of the Clean Air Act Amendments of 1990*, 1992.

107. For a discussion of the effects of the 1990 Clean Air Act Amendments, see Stephen J. Thompson, "Trucking and the Clean Air Act Amendments of 1990: Some Economic Implications," Congressional Research Service Report for Congress, February 1, 1991; and Federal Highway Administration, *Transportation Programs and Provisions of the Clean Air Act Amendments of 1990*, 1992.

Unlike other provisions, there is little question about the technological feasibility of reaching these standards, since California has had them in place for several years. Lowering the sulfur content, however, is expected to increase diesel fuel prices up to seven cents per gallon. [108]

Second, the 1990 amendments authorized EPA to introduce new federal standards to regulate engine rebuilding practices by the mid-1990s. Since it is still unknown what actions EPA will take, it is too early to gauge the economic consequences of such measures. Considering that diesel truck engines for tractors pulling standard-sized semitrailers are typically rebuilt two to three times over their lifetime, though, the potential economic effects on trucking companies could be substantial. [109]

Third, this act requires EPA to revise existing standards for vehicle exhaust emissions on heavy-duty diesel trucks. Specifically, EPA must prescribe limits for hydrocarbons, nitrogen oxides, carbon monoxide, and particulate matter for each model year through the rest of the decade. Congress designated a specific limit only on nitrogen oxide emissions, requiring that they not exceed 4 grams per brake horsepower starting in model year 1998. When setting these new standards, EPA must take into account cost, safety, and technological feasibility. Furthermore, once limits are set, they must remain in effect for at least three model years. These standards are likely to increase the price for new trucks significantly. Reductions in nitrogen oxide emissions alone could increase the cost per engine by as much as $1,000. [110]

Fourth, the 1990 amendments require fleets with ten or more trucks operating in nonattainment areas to adopt "clean fuel vehicles."[111] Beginning in model year 1998, half of all newly acquired

---

108. Allen Schaeffer, "Clean Air for the 1990s and Beyond: Understanding the Issues and Implications for the Trucking Industry," prepared for the American Trucking Associations, 1991.

109. Thompson, "Trucking and the Clean Air Act," p. 7.

110. Ibid., p. 8.

111. These are defined as vehicles using fuels whose combined nitrogen oxide and hydrocarbon emissions do not exceed 3.15 grams per brake horsepower/hour. This emission limit is half of what is currently permitted under federal law. The 1990 Clean Air Act Amendment contained a provision that permitted EPA to reduce emission concentrations by only 30 percent, if the agency determined that a 50

trucks with registered loaded weights between 8,500 pounds and 26,000 pounds must qualify as a clean-fuel vehicle. Only alternative fuels (for example, natural gas, propane, or electric) are expected to qualify; however, diesel was maintained on the list of clean fuels because of the possibility that future research may uncover a formula that can reach the emissions standards. Industry representatives, though, indicate that many of the allowable fuels, propane and electric in particular, are currently unable to generate enough power to propel most sizes of trucks.[112] It is too early to assess whether such a reduction is technologically feasible by the end of the decade, but in either case implementation of this measure will be costly to the industry.

Finally, the amendments allowed states with more than one nonattainment area to enforce more stringent emission limits on new trucks as long as these standards could meet those already established in California. Such a provision was undertaken for two primary reasons.[113] First, Congress sought to prevent the proliferation of differing state requirements that would have imposed an unnecessary burden on the industry. Furthermore, Congress hoped to create a broader market for such vehicles, thereby reducing the competitive disadvantage for trucking companies based in California. Even with such provisions, though, costs for vehicles with more restrictive emission limits are still likely to be considerably higher than those needing to meet only federal standards.

In total, the revisions within the 1990 amendments are likely to have a profound effect on the trucking industry. Not only will purchasing costs for new vehicles rise, but also operating expenses for existing vehicles will increase with new regulations on fuel content and engine rebuilding. While consumer prices will surely climb in response to these costs, the trade-off is substantial improvements in air quality in years to come.

The California Implementation Plans. Similar to the 1990 Clean Air Act, the Clean Air Act Amendments of 1977 set nationwide

---

percent reduction was not feasible and informed Congress of this decision by December 31, 1993. Thompson, "Trucking and the Clean Air Act," p. 10.

112. Earl Eisenhart and Tim Morgan, National Private Truckers Council, personal communication, May 20, 1994.

113. Thompson, "Trucking and the Clean Air Act," pp. 7–8.

standards for ozone and carbon monoxide levels. The 1977 amend-ments required all areas to devise plans to reach these goals by 1987. Such massive changes were necessary in Sacramento, Ventura, and the greater Los Angeles area in California that state agencies ap-proved implementation plans that fell far short of federal expecta-tions. Meanwhile, EPA recognized these shortcomings but did not order revisions to the plans, instead choosing to assist state agencies in improving them. Several public interest groups (for example, the Coalition for Clean Air, the Environmental Council of Sacramento, and the Sierra Club) challenged EPA's decision to approve these inadequate plans. The courts ruled in favor of the interest groups and ordered EPA to institute alternative plans that would enable compliance with federal standards.[114]

In early 1994, EPA released its proposed clean air plans to enable the areas surrounding Los Angeles, Ventura, and Sacramento to attain federal air quality standards within the next decade. If possible, though, the federal government would like to avoid dictat-ing to state and local jurisdictions how air quality goals should be reached. State agencies were required to submit their own attainment plans by November 1994. Hearings were held in early 1995, leading to a two-year postponement of implementation of either state or fed-eral implementation plans.[115]

The Federal Implementation Plan introduced by the EPA seeks to reduce emissions from virtually every possible source, stationary or mobile.[116] In particular, the plan includes a series of proposals targeted at heavy-duty trucks in excess of 14,000 pounds gross vehi-cle weight. In an effort to convert vehicles to alternatively fueled or redesigned diesel engines, the plan mandates that new or rebuilt heavy-duty truck engines must meet more stringent nitrogen oxide and hydrocarbon emission standards in California, similar to those for passenger cars, starting in model year 1999. Manufacturers whose engines do not comply with these levels will be required to recall the engines. These recall responsibilities will be determined by testing

---

114. Environmental Protection Agency, "Fact Sheet: Federal Implementation Plans in California," February 15, 1994.

115. Ibid.

116. We gathered information about the Federal Implementation Plan for California from the Federal Register, January and February 1994.

the performance of "typical" truck engines, rather than simply ones operating properly as in the past. Moreover, stricter evaporative hydrocarbon requirements would also be applied to prevent a shift from diesel to gasoline fuel, which would reduce the level of nitrogen oxide emissions but at the expense of higher hydrocarbon levels.

To ensure that trucking companies eventually retire inadequate vehicles and adopt the improved technology, the proposed implementation plans would require companies to meet a fleet average emission rate. Beginning in the year 2000, companies whose fleets exceed federal emission standards would have to pay a fee based on excess emissions.

Furthermore, EPA recommends placing restrictions on interstate carriers to avoid either compromising their efforts for cleaner air or putting California trucking companies at a competitive disadvantage. The California Air Resources Board reports that nearly 20 percent of all mileage accumulated by heavy-duty trucks in California is by vehicles registered outside the state. Therefore, the proposed rules require interstate trucks either to comply with California's stricter air quality standards or to be limited to two stops in the state, with only one stop permitted in the Los Angeles, Ventura, or Sacramento Federal Implementation Plan areas. Any pickup or delivery would be considered a stop under these regulations.

The implementation plans generated considerable opposition from the trucking industry. Many believe that the proposed regulations require technology not yet available, are not enforceable, and are prohibitively expensive. The California Trucking Association estimated that this plan would produce emission fees totaling $600 million, vehicle replacement costs totaling $4.2 billion, and engine rebuilding costs of $7,800 per truck.[117] The interstate restrictions, in particular, attracted substantial opposition. California trucking companies believe, counter to EPA claims, that they will still be at a competitive disadvantage with the rest of the nation.[118] Many question whether these restrictions are even legal. David Titus, director of public relations for the California Trucking Association, contends that "[they] would be instantly thrown out on interference on inter-

117. Bill Mongelluzzo, "S. California Transport Sector Unites to Resist Proposed Clean-Air Rules," *Journal of Commerce*, July 6, 1994, p. B-8.

118. Ibid., B-2.

state commerce grounds."[119] The two-year postponement will allow further research, but the postponement will not push back the effective dates of these regulations.

Conclusions

While economic regulations typically receive greater attention, state operating restrictions on trucking firms are more pervasive. The level of detail necessary to understand these different state restrictions illustrates, in a small way, the problems that trucking firms have faced. From fuel-reporting requirements to height limitations to prenotification of hazardous shipments, these rules cover nearly every aspect of motor-carrier operations. In this chapter, we addressed the three primary forms of state operating restrictions (registration and operating taxes, vehicle size and weight limits, and safety requirements) as well as two other types of special regulations (hazardous material requirements and environmental standards) that affect a sizable subset of the truck population.

Historically, states have demonstrated a predisposition toward drafting and implementing their own independent operating restrictions, generally failing to adopt those established by surrounding jurisdictions. State vehicle registration procedures, for example, often requested different information, imposed different filing dates, and required different indicia to be displayed. Moreover, in establishing these rules, states, at times, have shown a blatant disregard for interstate commerce. States in the Mississippi Valley adopted weight limitations considerably less than those in the rest of the nation, effectively preventing shipments of a certain size from being transported along particular cross-country routes. In some cases, states took rule making one step further, attempting to construct operating restrictions that shifted the entire movement of some products either outside their states or to the most thinly populated areas.

The variance in state operating restrictions produced by such uncoordinated decision making created an administrative nightmare for the trucking industry. Billions of dollars were wasted annually in excessive paperwork, accounting fees, and vehicle outfitting, as

---

119. Bill Mongelluzzo, "EPA's LA Proposals 'Draconian,'" *Journal of Commerce*, February 17, 1994, p. 1.

companies attempted to comprehend and comply with differing state laws and directives. Moreover, many of these regulations jeopardized just-in-time delivery systems. Time-of-day restrictions, highway routing, and access requirements all added expensive delays to carrier operations. Not only did the inefficiencies produced by inconsistent state requirements escalate carriers' operating costs, and ultimately consumer prices, but they adversely affected the nation's ability to compete internationally with foreign manufacturers who did not face such constraints.

In recent years, a number of base-state agreements have been initiated to create more uniformity among states. Most began as voluntary compacts; however, the refusal by some states to join, combined with the growing need for nationwide uniformity, has led the federal government to mandate that all states take part in certain ones. Rather than satisfying the requirements for every state, under these accords trucking companies need apply only to a single state, which is then responsible for redistributing the relevant information and fees to the other states the company operates within. The International Registration Plan and the International Fuel Tax Agreement were set up to ease the burden of inconsistent registration and fuel-use reporting requirements, while the Commercial Vehicle Safety Alliance was designed to accommodate state enforcement of safety regulations. To date, all of these new institutional arrangements have encountered considerable success without noticeably altering the revenues generated for each state.

While these reciprocal agreements have substantially reduced the inefficiencies stemming from inconsistencies in state operating restrictions, a significant number of questions still remain unresolved. For instance, what can be done to ease the administrative burden of weight-distance taxes? Is there a way to achieve more uniformity in vehicle size and weight restrictions? Can the enforcement of safety requirements be further improved within the trucking industry? Will preemption of state economic regulation push the states to tighten insurance and safety regulations, and raise fees? In the final chapter, we offer some recommendations to deal with these outstanding issues, as well as those still remaining in interstate and intrastate economic regulations.

6

Conclusions

Truckin' . . . *what a long, strange trip it's been.*
—R. HUNTER, J. GARCIA, P. LESH, AND B. WEIR, 1970

Various modes of freight transportation have faced similar regulatory issues over the past 100 years. State and federal governments first promoted the development of these industries and then began to regulate them, tentatively at first, but with more restrictive regulations developing over time. These regulatory regimes were effective to varying degrees, but none was satisfactory, as they protected regulated firms or classes of shippers rather than consumers generally.

Under regulation, airline service did not evolve as a dynamic industry, and regulation contributed to the diminution of the railroads from an integral position in the American economy to a relatively minor one. Trucking regulation helped many truckers and the industry grew rapidly, but such regulation certainly harmed shippers and the broader American economy. As a result, in the late 1970s deregulation emerged as the common cure to the differing problems of the freight transportation industry. Careful studies of various deregulation initiatives have shown them to be great successes, exceeding even the most optimistic expectations.

Recent congressional activity has further deregulated the trucking industry, nearly completely. Now, the remaining regulatory barriers that fail to accomplish important policy goals need to be removed to complete the deregulatory agenda. What has evolved, and will develop further, is a competitive, multimodal freight transportation sector that is responsive to the changing needs of shippers. Overnight package delivery, just-in-time inventory, containerization, and hub-and-spoke networks have all been impressive technological or organizational adaptations to the new competitive environment.

But the focus of this book is federalism and regulation. Federal

206

deregulation was usually coupled with preemption of state regulatory authority. In national, and increasingly international, transportation markets, it made sense to eliminate or reduce the other vertical layers of regulation along with the federal entry and rate controls.

As we identified in chapter 5, the major remaining regulations are at the state level in the most important sector of freight transportation—trucking. Trucking represents nearly 80 percent of freight transportation revenues in the United States, a proportion that has been growing for several decades. Approximately half this trucking activity takes place within the states and has therefore been potentially subject to state regulation. Until 1995, state economic regulation of trucking was the last bastion of 1930s-style entry and rate controls that had long been discredited across the entire spectrum of transportation, both in freight and in passenger areas.

In 1994 the impetus in Congress to preempt state regulation of intrastate trucking came from air package carriers, as a result of several years of political pressure applied by this growing industry. In many ways, it is fitting that the effective end of state-level economic regulation of trucking came through the activity of carriers in another transportation mode, airlines. Those changes completed a large part of the deregulatory agenda and the cycle of promotion-regulation-deregulation-preemption in all transportation industries. Still, the recent preemption does not signal the end of all federal and state regulation of freight transportation. Other issues need to be resolved to make those industries truly competitive and efficient.

In this chapter, we first summarize the important findings of this book. Then we address several continuing policy issues and suggest ways to resolve them. These suggestions flow from the analysis we presented in the previous chapters. We also present best estimates of the savings that the American economy should gain from these recent and proposed changes in transportation regulation. Finally, we analyze the implications of these deregulatory cases for the three major political economic theories of regulation that we discussed in chapter 1.

Summary

The composition of the freight transportation sector has evolved substantially over American history. Initially, water barges were dominant, and state and federal governments struggled with the appropriate mechanisms both to promote and to control this industry. Barges were followed rapidly by the ascent of the railroads, which dominated freight and passenger carriage for several decades. Internal combustion engines allowed the development of perhaps the most transforming technology of the twentieth century, the automobile for passenger transportation. Such engines also allowed the development of motor trucking, which eclipsed the role of the railroads in freight transportation nearly as rapidly as railroads had previously eclipsed water barges.

Although barges and railroads declined, they continue to be part of the multimodal freight transportation environment. While trucking is preeminent now in freight transportation, the other sectors are performing much better and are much more competitive than they were before deregulation.

The theory of regulatory federalism as applied to freight transportation illustrates that a two-tiered system of regulation can have advantages, depending on how much regulation in one state affects interested parties in another state. Even though a system of federal regulation of interstate commerce and state regulation of intrastate commerce has clear advantages, a single regulatory, or deregulatory, policy for the nation as a whole also has advantages, particularly as freight carriers now move goods more often across state lines and increasingly across international boundaries.

The actual historical development of transportation regulation featured a prominent role for the states. In nearly every sector, states began to regulate before the federal government. Inevitably, and fairly quickly, state regulation led to legal questions about control over and the boundaries between interstate and intrastate commerce. Congress and the courts generally expanded the scope of federal jurisdiction in these cases. When state interests fought particularly hard, however, as they did in the development of the Motor Carrier Act of 1935 *and* in the development of the Motor Carrier Act of 1980, they were able to retain substantial control over intrastate transportation.

The historical evidence also shows that approaches to regulation in one mode have greatly influenced those in other transportation sectors. The airlines were regulated after the railroads and soon after interstate truckers, in the late 1930s. But they were deregulated *before* those other sectors, in the mid-1970s. That experience, moving from a concern about "destructive competition" in the New Deal era to a recognition that regulation had been captured and did not allow dynamic development of the industry, laid the groundwork for the bolder deregulation of railroads and trucking than might otherwise have occurred. Similarly, the early successes of airline deregulation made the politics of deregulation in the other sectors easier and more feasible.

Deregulation, and other changes in the industry, have revitalized the nearly moribund railroad sector. Railroads are now important in freight transportation again, and the sector is likely to expand in the future as intermodalism increases. Railroads have some obvious advantages over trucks for long freight hauls, and a $400 billion freight transportation industry has room for a healthy railroad sector.

Our detailed examination of the ICC's regulation of interstate trucking and of the movement toward deregulation shows the utility of scholarly analysis. Deregulation of interstate trucking has proved successful by every measure. While proponents of regulation have cited concerns about supposed negative impacts of deregulation, these concerns are remarkably similar to those expressed for airline and railroad deregulation and do not stand up to critical examination. Just as academic studies helped to provide a stimulus and justification for deregulation, scholars have carefully chronicled the effects of deregulation.

While interstate trucking is in much better shape than twenty years ago, more could be done to improve the industry. The 1994 congressional approval of federal preemption of intrastate trucking regulation was a big step in the right direction. As our survey evidence illustrated, state trucking regulators in forty-one states did not appear to have any intention to deregulate completely before being forced to do so by Congress. To those who had not followed this industry closely, it might seem surprising that, until recently, so many states still regulated intrastate trucking strictly. Despite the federal success and the success of deregulation in the states that tried it, about half the states continued to use the relatively strict regulatory model of the 1930s until the time of federal preemption. Evidence suggests that this resistance to change was largely a function of the strength of the truckers protected by those regulations and of organized labor, as well as of the interests of state regulators in

209

maintaining their positions. The political power of this coalition in the states was impressive, given attempts in many large states by fairly well-organized and well-funded shipper groups that had pressured legislators to reduce regulations. And the academic evidence that guided federal deregulation was not influential enough on the state level to neutralize the power of those entrenched interests. In the appendix to chapter 4, we summarized twenty studies performed from 1979 through 1991 that clearly illustrated the substantial harm to state economies caused by rate and entry regulation.

Congress tried and failed to preempt state regulation several times after 1980. From about 1985, the momentum of state deregulation under states' own efforts had clearly stalled. As a result, after 1985 preemption efforts were increased, including several congressional bills, ICC redefinitions of intrastate commerce to turn it into (deregulated) interstate commerce, and, finally, the recent successful attempt to preempt state trucking regulation based on federal airline law.

While more attention has been paid to state economic regulation, other state regulations, or operating restrictions, over the trucking industry are also extremely important. These include operating taxes, vehicle size limits, and safety regulations. While taxes and safety regulations are quite reasonable uses of state police power that should not normally be preempted by the federal government, those regulations have been imposed in a highly inefficient and often inequitable manner. Lack of coordination among the states led to very high administrative compliance costs for truckers. In the past ten years, substantial gains have been made in coordination, either through explicit federal preemption or through coordination efforts by the National Governors Association and other groups. These have solved many compliance problems, but several issues remain.

In addition, two newer environmental issues have arisen to create coordination problems for the trucking industry and for the freight transportation industry more generally: hazardous materials transportation and the implications for truckers of the 1990 Clean Air Act Amendments. To some extent, these can be addressed through the flexible federalism mechanism of state planning and enforcement of federal goals, but some form of preemption or coordination may be required to handle those emerging issues in a balanced manner.

210

Continuing Policy Issues

The preceding summary isolated several continuing policy issues in the trucking industry. Here, we discuss those issues further and suggest ways in which policy makers may usefully address them. In formulating our specific suggestions, we have been guided by several general objectives. First, policy changes should increase competition and efficiency in the transportation industry. Second, it is important to find ways to reduce transportation operating costs and increase productivity without sacrificing safety. Third, to reduce transaction costs, policy makers should promote uniformity in the administration and enforcement of transportation regulations. Fourth, where possible, it is best to find alternatives that allow states to maintain as much sovereignty as possible, without interfering with interstate commerce. Our discussion of continuing issues is consistent with these objectives.

Implementation of State Trucking Deregulation. After January 1, 1995, preemption of state regulation became the law of the land. Some states resisted by challenging the preemption in the courts, individually or collectively. The National Conference of State Legislatures (NCSL) advised the states that preemption violates the U.S. Constitution and oversteps federal authority to regulate commerce. NCSL expected implementation problems with taxing authority, consumer protection, trucker compliance with remaining regulations, workers' compensation laws, and court jurisdiction for contract disputes.[1] Based on the legal outcomes of challenges to the Staggers Act preemption and other similar congressional legislation, however, it was very unlikely that these state challenges would succeed. Indeed, by mid-1995 most of these challenges had been defeated in or turned back by the courts.

How quickly states will make the transition to a deregulated environment is less clear, as mandating policy change and actually having it implemented are two different things. Some states, such as Illinois, moved quickly to abolish their trucking regulatory agency. Others, such as New Mexico, claim they will disregard the preemp-

---

1. Rip Watson, "Trade Association Mounts Offensive against Intrastate Trucking Deregulation," *Journal of Commerce*, November 3, 1994, p. 3B.

tion and continue to regulate. Robert Pitcher, director of state laws for the ATA, said: "I suspect most states will fall somewhere between these two."[2] In some states, major staffing decisions are involved; in Texas, for example, sixty employees handled intrastate economic regulation of trucking. Of particular importance in the transition are fees for regulatory agencies, tax implications of now worthless state operating certificates, and state safety enforcement. Pitcher believes it may take up to two years for all states to deal fully with these issues.

In a recent scandal related to trucking regulation in Tennessee, the Republican-controlled state Senate and the Republican governor agreed to phase out the Public Service Commission over one year, starting in May 1995.[3] The case had interstate dimensions as members of the PSC were found to have accepted money from Tennessee-based trucking firms in return for selectively enforcing regulations against out-of-state truckers. Thus, some states are changing quickly.

States still retain the authority to insure truckers' intrastate activities, so a multistate group of regulators is developing a uniform insurance filing procedure for firms that want to operate in their state. Truckers believe that the proposed rules are intrusive and expensive, directly contrary to the intent of recent federal policy changes, and that those rules will act to control entry, using noneconomic regulation to achieve entry limitations that are no longer explicitly allowed. States claim that many new entrants will raise safety and reliability problems, requiring tightened insurance regulation.[4] Since there is considerable variation in the current language of the state laws, the multistate group has not yet agreed on appropriate language for a uniform state statute.

Thus, while economic regulation has been preempted, clearly some court challenges remain, and states are likely to use their remaining insurance and police powers to try to retain fees and to

---

2. Bill Mongelluzzo, "Truckers Brace for Chaotic Year As States Tackle Deregulation," *Journal of Commerce*, October 18, 1994, p. 1A.

3. The PSC had always been a thorn in the side of the Republican party in Tennessee as the state voters never elected a Republican to the agency in its 98-year history.

4. Rip Watson, "Industry Rips State Proposals to Register Motor Carriers," *Journal of Commerce*, November 2, 1994, p. 2B.

maintain oversight nearly as tightly as in the past. Obviously, given the considerable evidence presented in this book, we believe that the states should maintain only minimal regulations, relaxing even these when the market shows that shippers are served well by intrastate trucking competition. Some early evidence suggested that intrastate deregulation was helping to spark a large reduction in trucking rates in mid-1995, especially in the western states.[5]

Eliminating the Activities of the ICC. In the severe fiscal climate of 1995, there is no doubt that the ICC will be eliminated. The only issues under debate in mid-1995 were how quickly it would be put out of business and how many of its functions would remain and to which agencies they would be transferred.

We believe Congress should eliminate the ICC and transfer a few of its remaining important functions and staff associated with those functions to the Department of Transportation,[6] following the recommendations of the Department of Transportation rather than the ICC. Congress should not eliminate certain elements of the ICC, however, without first passing legislation that would address issues that remain on the books as law but without an agency to handle them. Without this intermediate step, unanticipated consequences could arise.

In particular, we support the elimination of all antitrust immunity for trucking firms and conferences, the elimination of all trucking regulation except Department of Transportation licensing and undercharge resolutions, and the transfer of all truck licensing and insurance monitoring to the Department of Transportation. We believe that nearly all special rules related to the railroad industry should be eliminated and that these competitive and merger issues be handled as antitrust problems are handled in other industries. Recognizing that some shippers do not have competitive choices, we believe that railroad maximum-rate regulation and abandonment oversight should

---

5. Chris Isidore, "Rate War Is On, and Truckers Feel the Pain," *Journal of Commerce*, June 14, 1995, p. 1A.

6. For a detailed argument favoring this transfer by a former ICC commissioner, see Gregory Walden, "Whither the ICC? To the Department of Transportation—It's Ready and Able, Even If It's Unwilling," Papers and proceedings of the Association of Transportation Practitioners, 65th Annual Meeting, Asheville, N.C., pp. 23–37.

be transferred to the Department of Transportation but should continue to be administered in a relaxed manner. Regulation of household goods carriers should be transferred to the Federal Trade Commission, as a consumer protection issue. Finally, the ICC should truly be eliminated and not retained as a separate body within the Department of Transportation. The more than century-old ICC should see its remarkable history come to a close.

Reducing Administrative Complexity through Base-State Systems. The base-state concept, as implemented in the International Registration Plan and the International Fuel Tax Agreement, has been a great improvement over the previous administrative morass in which each firm had to comply with fifty-one different sets of state and federal regulations. The base-state approach should be extended and coordinated so that several different issues could be handled through a single coordinating agency rather than through the multiple organizations that now exist.

First, Congress should give the Department of Transportation authority and funding to commission a study to evaluate the operating procedures of the International Registration Plan, the International Fuel Tax Agreement, and the other major base-state systems and to detail any difficulties and possible solutions to overcome them. Assuming the study reveals no major obstacles, Congress should create a single base-state system for all state registration requirements and highway-use taxes. With this program in place, trucking firms can file first-, second-, and third-structure taxes, as well as fulfill their registration procedures for hazardous materials transportation, with a single state. Congress should also create a small division within the Department of Transportation to oversee and enforce the provisions of this agreement. Perhaps some of the transferred ICC staff could fill these job slots when their ICC-related tasks are completed.

Related to NAFTA, Congress and the Department of Transportation should encourage Canada and Mexico, and any other subsequent signatories, to establish their own highway-use restrictions that can be adopted into this agreement. If this arrangement cannot be worked out politically, the Department of Transportation should mandate that carriers from these nations select a base state through which they may fulfill existing operating requirements in the United States.

214

Congress should also encourage the Department of Transportation to create a second base-state system for the inspection and enforcement of all state safety restrictions. Thus, inspections and sanctions applied in one state will be recognized by the others. This same system can be used to monitor compliance with the hazardous materials transportation regulations.

We do not suggest combining all these functions into a *single* base-state system because safety is such a sensitive issue and we do not want to create any possible conflict of interest between safety and tax provisions. While progress has been impressive in recent years, some states still use overzealous safety enforcement as a revenue-generating technique. By maintaining two different organizations, both to be monitored by the Department of Transportation, the public will be assured that safety will not be compromised within their state or across the nation's highways.

Developing and Funding a Nationwide Network for the Use of LCVs. As chapter 5 revealed, a series of grandfather clauses within the several Federal Aid Highway Acts have allowed inconsistent state vehicle size and weight requirements to remain. Congress should repeal these grandfathered exemptions to eliminate the remaining inconsistencies. Subject to the findings of the two long combination vehicle (LCV) studies commissioned by Congress under the Intermodal Surface Transportation Efficiency Act of 1991, the Department of Transportation should determine the feasibility of extending the number of states that currently permit LCVs on their highways. To continue to obtain the economic benefits of longer vehicles, while ensuring safety, the Department of Transportation should institute a nationwide LCV operating license. Currently, although many trucking firms are very careful, some carriers do not take any steps to ensure that drivers of LCVs possess more skill than operators of conventional tractor semitrailers. Careful monitoring of LCV safety is critical to achieving these efficiencies.

Congress should authorize the Department of Transportation to work with the states to develop a nationwide network of interstate roads for LCV use, authorizing climate, time of day, speed, surface, driver qualification, and safety standards. To ensure that LCVs stay only on these authorized routes, Congress should authorize matching grants to be administered by the Department of Transportation to

215

fund highway access stations for local standard-length trucks to receive and drop off freight for LCVs to transport by interstate highway.

As chapter 5 noted, academic studies have shown clearly that weight-distance taxes come closer than others to approximating the road-damage costs of large vehicles. Although their administration by a small number of states has been problematic, according to a recent GAO study, "if a weight-distance user fee were national, this problem would not arise."[7] To fund the road and bridge improvements that will be necessary to allow LCVs to travel on a nationwide scale, Congress should implement a nationwide weight-distance tax. It could be administered effectively through the base-state system discussed above. To overcome what is likely to be strong opposition, policy makers should make clear that these taxes can gradually replace other current user charges that are not well matched to highway damage and can lead to efficiencies for all parties.[8]

Finally, Congress should authorize the Department of Transportation to develop a permanent database for LCVs that includes the types of vehicles, operating restrictions, road conditions, and accidents to allow future studies and adjustments to any elements of this program, as implemented.

Addressing Emerging Environmental Issues. While the new pilot programs for hazardous materials transportation described in chapter 5 show promise, many carrier groups are skeptical that voluntary coordination will succeed. If it does not succeed, the Department of Transportation will need to develop a stronger set of federal guidelines that force the states to comply. And in this case it is not just states but individual localities that are influencing national transportation policy and traffic flows. The Department of Transportation might encourage state and even regional planning of hazardous material transportation routes, so that individual community concerns do not determine national policy. The Department of Transportation should continue to work to develop routing plans in partnership with

---

7. John Schulz, "National Weight-Distance Tax Study Recommended by GAO in New Report," *Traffic World*, June 27, 1994, p. 41.

8. Kenneth Small, Clifford Winston, and Carol Evans, *Roadwork: A New Highway Pricing and Investment Policy* (Washington, D.C.: Brookings Institution, 1991).

the various interested states and, if necessary, use its power to pre-empt unreasonable state restrictions.

The Environmental Protection Agency must consider the effect on freight transportation of the proposed Federal Implementation Plan for the 1990 Clean Air Act Amendments in areas of California, as well as for other nonattainment jurisdictions around the country. While not strictly a trucking issue, these restrictions bear on regulatory federalism and will affect the transportation sector disproportionately. The environmental restrictions proposed in California in 1994 were too extreme. As the implementation of these restrictions has been postponed for two years, policy makers should consider them in the context of the need to move products into and within the state at a reasonable cost. Hearings held in 1994 showed that this is a big issue for transportation firms and their consumers, which ultimately include most members of the American public.

Potential Gains from Policy Changes. Evidence shows that the approaches we suggest, combined with the congressional initiatives of 1994 and 1995 to preempt state-level economic regulation of the trucking industry and to eliminate the ICC, should yield substantial gains to the American economy. Congress could truly "deliver the goods" by following these suggestions for addressing continuing policy issues.

Several of these issues are likely to be on the congressional agenda in the near future. An article on the political influence of trucking firms concluded:

> Among the issues the trucking lobby expects to address in the 104th Congress [1995–1996] are safety concerns over increasing truck size and combinations, the National Highway System and related project funding, labor issues revolving around striker replacement, merging the now-independent ICC with the Department of Transportation, and federal implementation of the Clean Air Act.[9]

We list below the potential gains from both recent congressional actions and from policy changes that would accord with our suggestions:

---

9. William Roberts, "Truck PACs Target Funds to Powerful in Congress," *Journal of Commerce*, November 2, 1994, p. 8A.

- from properly implemented elimination of state economic regulation (1995): $3–8 billion
- from repeal of filed-rate doctrine (1994): $100 million
- from eliminating ICC: $30 million
- from eliminating antitrust exemption: $1–2 billion
- from implementing new base-state approach: $1 billion
- from expanding LCV use nationwide: $2–4 billion

These are very conservative estimates. The savings from preempting state economic regulations, for example, which were analyzed in some detail in chapter 4, do not include the logistics savings that Delaney believes could exceed $15 billion per year. Similarly, the estimate for the elimination of filed rates, which includes the effort that carriers must put into this activity, does not include the legal and administrative costs of settling the multibillion dollar undercharge cases that are avoided without filed rates. We have included the low-end estimate from chapter 5 for savings from our base-state policy suggestions, as the estimate of $1–3 billion was made before the requirement that all states join the International Fuel Tax Agreement, the International Registration Plan, and the Single State Registration System.

Thus, the potential *direct* savings from completing all these aspects of the deregulatory agenda could range from over $7 billion to more than $15 billion per year. The costs of implementing these policies are very low because they largely involve ending, rather than establishing, programs. Preemption of state economic regulation in other industries did not generate any large or unexpected material or psychic costs. Similarly, although some who specialize in filing rates may need to find more productive work, the economy as a whole will benefit, and many new jobs will be created through the innovations that deregulation can facilitate.

Substantial gains should largely be distributed, ultimately, to all American consumers, since so many products in so many competitive industries are carried by trucks. In addition, as in other transportation industries under deregulation, other unanticipated gains will likely emerge from opening up all aspects of freight transportation to competition, as well as from addressing safety and highway maintenance issues more efficiently.

Finally, we move from these highly specific policy recommendations in transportation regulation to more general lessons and theoretical implications of deregulation and federalism in this field.

Implications for Theories of Regulation

In the first chapter, we outlined three major theories of regulatory change that have been advanced by political economists—the economic theory, institutionalism, and the politics of ideas—that have largely been developed using evidence from federal regulation. Throughout the book, we have tried to examine how these theories apply to the deregulation of the trucking industry. With our focus on state-level regulation, it is important to address these questions: Do these theories apply at the state level? Must they be modified? If so, how? We will consider each of the three theories in turn.

The extreme version of the economic theory is that regulated interests capture the regulatory process to gain private benefits. More sophisticated versions of this theory, or multi-interest group capture, involve the efforts of several groups to gain private benefits at the same time. As we have seen, there is considerable evidence in trucking to support this theory. Quantitative and qualitative studies show the power of trucking firms and unionized trucking labor to extract benefits from regulation at both levels of government. After this power was greatly reduced at the federal level in 1980, it still continued in a number of states until 1995. We also found considerable evidence of other interested parties, particularly organized shipping groups, railroad interests, and agricultural interests, influencing trucking regulation, although not as much as the trucking groups that held even higher stakes in regulation.

At the state level, the power of the trucking interests was even more pronounced. The interest group environment was usually less balanced than in Washington, D.C., allowing trucking interests to gain more protective regulation for a longer period of time. Less media attention at the state level also seemed to keep this issue off the agenda and allowed a more extreme form of capture in the state capitals.

When trucking deregulation did happen, a variant of the economic theory called the "deregulatory snowball" also seems to have come into play, as a dynamic process.[10] The federal deregulation in 1980 led to profound changes in the industry that altered the political balance of power as surely as they altered the economic balance. New firms, such as Federal Express, grew rapidly and had different concerns about how regulation affected them. As we illustrated in chapter 4, in the 1990s the unity of the trucking firms unraveled, as UPS joined Fed Ex in the battle against state regulation. Firms like Yellow Freight realized that state regulation had become more a handicap than an advantage at that point and helped tip the equilibrium within the largest industry group, the ATA, against state regulation. At that point in 1994, federal preemption of state regulation was not as difficult a choice for federal politicians as it had been when the dominant interest groups were more solidly opposed. Similarly, changes stemming from the deregulation of 1980 greatly reduced the power of the Teamsters Union, and by 1995 they were no longer the potent force that was able to block federal preemption of the states.

Strong interest groups in favor of a policy change, at either the federal or the state levels of government, are required to put regulatory issues on the political agenda. But typically interest groups battle on both sides of these regulatory issues, not always evenly balanced, but not usually completely one-sided, either. When the balance *is* one-sided, the policy outputs from federal or state legislative or bureaucratic action are not surprising: they usually support the dominant group. When the interest group environment is more balanced, which may be true more often at the federal level of government, choices favored by key institutional actors become more important.

Thus, supporters of institutional theories believe that Congress, the president, the courts, or even the agencies themselves are the most critical actors. Institutions mediate the interest group input they receive and shape policy to conform to their own preferences. It is not difficult to find evidence for institutional influence over trucking deregulation. At the federal level in the late 1970s, new presidential appointments to the ICC led the agency to start to deregulate. In 1980, Congress, in opposition to most versions of the economic theory, went against the dominant interest groups, and put these ICC

---

10. Thomas Hammond and Jack Knott, "The Deregulatory Snowball," *Journal of Politics*, vol. 50 (1988), pp. 3–30.

decisions and even more extreme deregulatory changes into statute. The recent push to eliminate the rest of trucking regulation and the ICC itself has come largely from Congress, bolstered by the idea of cutting back government spending.

For state-level deregulation, we also find influence from some of these federal institutional actors. After 1986, the ICC attempted to preempt the states through the expansion of their own powers, by redefining intrastate commerce as interstate. The court decisions in the Federal Express cases, particularly the Ninth Circuit Court decision, provided the initial impetus that led to the successful preemption of the states in 1994. The courts changed the equilibrium position of key interests, and by starting a deregulatory snowball, they changed the perspective on this issue in Congress. While President Clinton's administrative support of these regulatory changes was important, particularly by not supporting the Teamsters' position, most of this public support came after the policy changes were moving forward. Thus, in contrast to much of the transportation deregulation of the late 1970s,[11] it would be hard to argue that the main push for the 1994 deregulation came from the presidential administration.

Although we have provided some anecdotal evidence of the importance of state institutional actors in our case studies, there is not yet any quantitative evidence that they influenced state deregulation. We did show that state public utility commissions and departments of transportation have regulated differently, but these distinctions did not achieve high levels of statistical support. Many state PUCs have fought to maintain their ability to regulate the trucking industry in their state. The case studies show that governors have often played important roles in deregulating trucking. And after 1980, state legislatures considered many bills related to trucking deregulation and enacted some of them.

While differences in institutions and institutional actors are no doubt important, all of them are influenced to some extent by similar intellectual ideas about regulation and deregulation at the same time. When regulation was the idea in good currency in the 1920s and 1930s, state politicians expanded intrastate trucking regulation, and

---

11. See Martha Derthick and Paul Quirk, *The Politics of Deregulation* (Washington, D.C.: Brookings Institution, 1985); and Lawrence Rothenberg, *Regulation, Organizations, and Politics* (Ann Arbor: University of Michigan Press, 1994).

federal politicians extended ICC regulation to the trucking industry and established airline regulation. By the 1970s, however, such regulation was seen as more damaging than beneficial, and deregulation was the idea whose time had come, across all transportation sectors. Derthick and Quirk argue that the "politics of ideas" best explains the deregulation of the late 1970s, including federal-level trucking deregulation, as economists showed a connection between such economic regulation and harm to the macroeconomy. In 1994, the idea of cutting back federal expenditures clearly influenced congressional efforts to eliminate the ICC and its role over trucking regulation.

Policy makers, at least federal ones, learn from experience across different sectors of the economy. They do not always apply the same lessons at exactly the same time, but a few years in the late 1970s and early 1980s were a remarkable time for transportation deregulation, when many barriers fell. Federal policy makers typically coupled such deregulation with preemption; when they did not, as in state trucking deregulation, their goals were frustrated for more than a decade. A second burst of deregulatory activity took place in 1994, as the application of state trucking regulation to air cargo carriers was challenged by the courts and as the political need to cut the federal budget, like the anti-inflation policies used to justify deregulation in the 1970s, combined to lead to more extensive trucking deregulation *and* preemption.

At the state level, it is clear that the idea of deregulation did not march, Sherman-like, through the states after 1980. In chapter 4, we illustrated how some states gradually relaxed regulation, either by legislative or by administrative action. But even this action largely stagnated after 1986, as the larger idea of deregulation received perhaps its first strong negative media coverage from the severe savings and loan industry problems. We did not find evidence of any new idea emerging to justify the federal preemption of the states in 1994.

The trucking case shows clearly that successful policy experiments are not always imitated by all, or even most, of the states. The combination of airtight empirical evidence of the success of federal and some state trucking deregulation *and* the incentives states have to be attractive for economic development was insufficient to overcome powerful interests in many states. Clear evidence existed that some states had lost jobs as a direct result of their trucking regulations, suggesting that these economic incentives may not be as powerful as many analysts have assumed in pushing states in efficient policy directions.

Despite a number of such examples in recent years, policy experiments in a federalist system do not always percolate from the bottom up. In all these cases of deregulation, the federal government was the policy leader, preempting the states in airline, railroad, and intercity bus regulation. By this preemption, federal policy makers must have recognized that the states would not necessarily deregulate themselves in these areas. And the trucking case, in which they did not initially preempt, proved them right.

A case could be made that eventually the system did achieve greater efficiency through the 1994 deregulation and preemption, but that is a different case from one in which states move rapidly in efficient directions by themselves. This cautionary note should temper the arguments of those who believe that market-like competition between the states will *always* push them toward efficient policy choices. State political institutions may still be open to capture by powerful interest groups, and politics in many states may be insufficiently pluralistic to allow competition to drive them inexorably toward efficient policies.

When federal preemption of state trucking regulation was opposed by powerful interests who gained from intrastate regulation, such as trucking firms and organized labor, Congress could not summon the collective will to implement it, even when evidence showed it to be the appropriate policy. Preemption seemed to require at least three critical elements: (1) a reduction in the opposition's strength, as happened with the marginalization of the Teamsters' role in trucking regulation; (2) a gradual building of political support within key institutions, which required compromises among critical actors; and (3) clear evidence that preemption was appropriate policy in economic terms. Note that the first of these elements is a part of the economic theory, the second relates to institutional theories, and the third deals with the politics of ideas. To the surprise of many analysts, these elements all came together in the preemption of 1994.[12]

Some important questions for theories of regulatory federalism re-

12. According to Ed Emmett, president of the National Industrial Transportation League, "It's an amazing thing that all this has come up in the summer of 1994 and nobody really saw it coming to this extent.

main unanswered but may be addressed by looking at other regulated industries in addition to transportation. Why are state regulatory bodies seemingly easier to capture than federal ones, even in large states like Texas? How do state institutions matter in the deregulatory process? How will changing state institutions, such as more professional legislatures, affect their approaches to regulation? With a reduction in federal regulatory roles, how will states adapt? When the same ideas about regulation are in circulation, how do they influence different state interest group configurations and state institutions?

However these questions are ultimately answered, it is clear that regulatory policy in a federalist system is complex. Interest groups look for favorable policies on both levels of government, and an appropriate balance of federal and state policy is difficult to achieve. Further, changing circumstances will alter the relationship between the two levels of regulation, calling for changing policies. More freight moved interstate, for example, as the national economy became more linked. Federal deregulation changed the configuration of economic and political interests in the industry at all levels. With the current policies of deregulation and preemption, it appears that an equilibrium has been reached that is satisfactory to most parties. It is appropriate, we believe, that reliance on the market as a regulator will be the main American policy toward freight transportation in the next century.

Index

creation of and exemptions for trucking, 33–34, 53
with deregulation, 70–71
for maritime shipping, 53
post-1980, 72–73
post-1980 role, 100
rate-setting role, 62–64
under Reed-Bulwinkle, 35
under Transportation Act (1940), 34–35

Rates
filed-rate doctrine, 83–86
ICC oversight of common and contract carriers, 62–65
in index of state regulatory strictness, 103–7
intrastate regulation of, 97–99
Negotiated Rates Act (1993), 85–86
post-1980 reductions, 74
post-1980 state-level regulation, 97–99
railroad, 48–49
undercharges, 83–87, 100

Rate setting
under Motor Carrier Act (1980), 70
operating ratios in, 110–11
post-1980 trucking industry, 71–72
by regional rate bureaus, 62
See also Interstate Commerce Commission (ICC); Rate bureaus, or rate conferences

Reagan administration, 70, 132–33
Reed-Bulwinkle Act (1948), 33, 35, 62, 100
Regional Rail Reorganization Act (1973), 42
Regulation
arguments for state- as opposed to national-level, 8–10
attempts to harmonize federal and state, 34
economic theory of, 13–14, 219
effect of government, 6–7
with emergence of interstate routes, 11–12
See also Railroad regulation; Trucking regulation
Regulation, federal-level
beginnings, 25–27, 31–35
government control, 11–12

Regulation, state-level
evolution of, 10–11, 28–36
index of state regulatory strictness, 104–8
Regulatory federalism
practice, 11–13
theory, 8–11
theory applied to freight transportation, 208
Regulatory policy
economic theory of, 13
effect in Michigan of interest group actions, 119–21
effect in Texas of interest groups, 117–19
influence in California of interest groups, 121–23
influence in Indiana of interest groups, 123–24
potential gains from changes in, 217–18
role of interest groups in shaping, 112–24
Reith, John, 168n37
Richmond, Samuel, 38n77
Roberts, William, 217n9
Robson, John, 40
Robyn, Dorothy, 7n8, 33n52, 68n30, 69n31, 129n73
Rogers, Hampton, 118
Romer, Thomas, 14n16
Roosevelt administration, 31–32
Rose, Nancy, 46, 68n26, 76
Rosenthal, Howard, 14n16
Rothberg, Paul F., 185
Rothenberg, Lawrence, 32, 56, 58n2, 60n6, 62, 66, 67n33, 69n35, 70, 111, 130nn80, 130, 131n81, 221n11
Route structures
for hazardous material transport, 194–98
post-1980 rationalization, 74

Safety issues
of airline industry, 46
coordinating federal- and state-level standards, 183–84
current, 184–85
hazardous materials transport, 186–98
of railroads, 51–52
with trucking deregulation, 80–81

About the Authors

PAUL TESKE is associate professor of political science at the State University of New York at Stony Brook and an affiliated research fellow at the Columbia University Institute for Tele-Information. Mr. Teske received his B.A. from the University of North Carolina at Chapel Hill and his M.P.A. and Ph.D. degrees from Princeton University's Woodrow Wilson School of Public and International Affairs. He is the author of a book on state telecommunications regulation, the editor of a book on telecommunications regulatory federalism, and the coauthor of a book on the role of political entrepreneurs in local government. He has written numerous articles on regulation and on state and local policy in professional journals, and he has prepared regulatory studies for the U.S. Congress Office of Technology Assessment, the Aspen Institute, and the New York State Telephone Association.

SAMUEL BEST is assistant professor of political science at the University of Notre Dame. Mr. Best received his B.A. from the University of North Carolina at Chapel Hill and his M.A. and Ph.D. degrees from the State University of New York at Stony Brook. Mr. Best has been the coauthor of professional journal articles on state trucking regulation, on jurisdictional competition, and on the strategies politicians use to avoid blame for failed policies. He is currently writing a book on the meaning and influence of a "national policy mood" on elections and policy outcomes.

MICHAEL MINTROM is assistant professor of political science at Michigan State University. Mr. Mintrom received B.A. and M.A. degrees from the University of Canterbury in New Zealand, and M.A. and Ph.D. degrees from the State University of New York at Stony Brook.

235

Mr. Mintrom has written several professional journal articles on state policy issues, including regulation and educational finance. He is currently writing a book on the role of state policy entrepreneurs as advocates of school choice programs.

*This book was edited by Cheryl Weissman and Dana Lane of the
publications staff of the American Enterprise Institute.
The text was set in Bodoni Book.
The figures were drawn by Hordur Karlsson.
The index was prepared by Shirley Kessel.
Coghill Composition Company of Richmond, Virginia,
set the type, and Data Reproductions Corporation
of Rochester Hills, Michigan, printed and bound the book,
using permanent acid-free paper.*

AEI Press is the publisher for the American Enterprise Institute for Public Policy Research, 1150 17th Street, N.W., Washington, D.C. 20036; *Christopher C. DeMuth,* publisher; *Dana Lane,* director; *Ann Petty,* editor; *Leigh Tripoli,* editor; *Cheryl Weissman,* editor; *Lisa Roman,* editorial assistant (rights and permission).

www.ingramcontent.com/pod-product-compliance
Lightning Source LLC
Jackson TN
JSHW011934131224
75386JS00041B/1369